LIVING ABROAD IN
INDIA

MARGOT BIGG

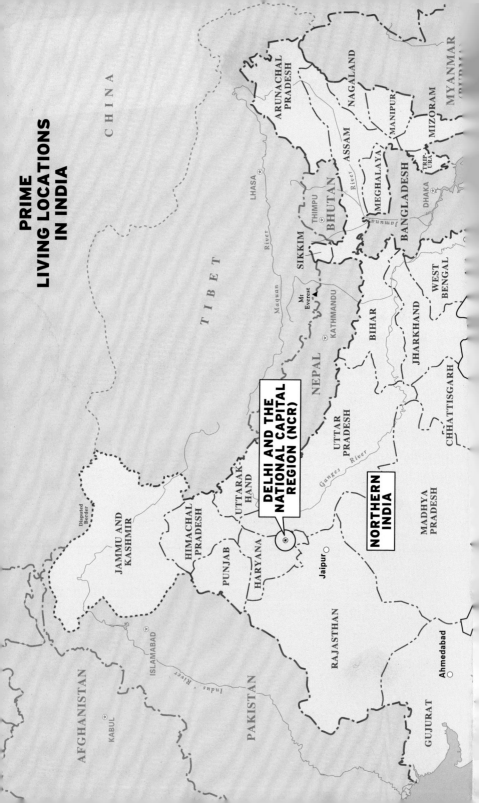

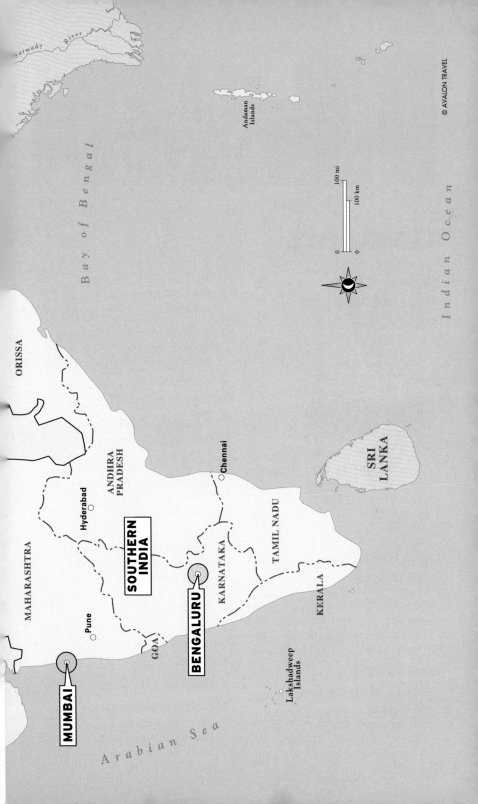

Contents

At Home in India 6

WELCOME TO INDIA 9

▶ **Introduction** 10
The Lay of the Land. 12
Social Climate 17

▶ **History, Government,
and Economy** 21
History. 22
Government. 35
The Economy. 37

▶ **People and Culture** 41
Ethnicity and Class 42
Customs and Etiquette 43
Family Life 48
Gender Roles. 49
Religion 53
The Arts. 57
Sports and Games 60

▶ **Planning Your
Fact-Finding Trip** 62
Preparing to Leave 63
Arriving 66
Sample Itineraries 68
Practicalities 78

DAILY LIFE 87

▶ **Making the Move** 88
Immigration and Visas. 89
Moving with Children. 96
Moving with Pets 99
What to Take 101

▶ **Housing Considerations** 103
Finding a Home 104
Settling In 107

▶ **Language and Education** . . .118
Learning the Languages 119
Education. 123

▶ **Health** 131
Hospitals and Clinics 132
Insurance. 134
Pharmacies and Prescriptions . .136
Diseases and Preventive
Measures 137
Environmental Factors 140
Safety .143
Crime. .144
People with Disabilities 146

▶ **Employment** 147
The Job Hunt. 148
Self-Employment. 151
Business Culture 152
Labor Laws 156
Volunteering 158

▶ **Finance** 159
Cost of Living. 160
Banking 163
Taxes 168
Investing 170

▶ **Communications** 171
Telephone Services 172
Internet Access 176
Postal Services 178
Media. .180

▶ **Travel and Transportation** 183
   Map 184
   By Air 185
   By Train 186
   By Bus .189
   By Car .190
   Other Modes of
      Transportation 194

PRIME LIVING LOCATIONS 199
   Map 200

▶ **Overview** 201
   Delhi and the National
      Capital Region (NCR) 202
   Mumbai 203
   Bengaluru 204
   Northern India 205
   Southern India 207

▶ **Delhi and the National Capital Region (NCR)** 209
   Map 208
   The Lay of the Land 210
   Where to Live 213
   Daily Life 220
   Getting Around 225

▶ **Mumbai** 227
   Map 228
   The Lay of the Land 229
   Where to Live 231
   Daily Life 236
   Getting Around 241

▶ **Bengaluru** 243
   Map 244
   The Lay of the Land 245

   Where to Live 248
   Daily Life 252
   Getting Around 256

▶ **Northern India** 257
   Map 258
   The Lay of the Land 259
   Ahmedabad 261
   Jaipur 266
   Kolkata .268

▶ **Southern India** 273
   Map 274
   The Lay of the Land 275
   Chennai 276
   Goa 282
   Hyderabad and Secunderabad . .286
   Pune 290

RESOURCES 293
   Embassies and Consulates 294
   Planning Your Fact-
      Finding Trip 295
   Making the Move 295
   Housing Considerations 297
   Language and Education 297
   Health .298
   Employment 299
   Finance 299
   Communications 299
   Travel and Transportation 300
   Prime Living Locations 301
   Public Holidays 306
   Glossary 307
   Hindi Phrasebook 307
   Suggested Reading 311
   Suggested Films 312

Index 313

At Home in India

They say anything is possible in India, and most people who spend any significant amount of time here would agree. Although life in India isn't always easy, it's certainly not boring – *anything* could happen next. For the past decade or so, India has been undergoing a dramatic cultural revolution, and the country is filled with people who are putting new ideas into action. There are a lot of opportunities in the world's largest democracy, so it's no surprise that India is becoming a more popular place to call home than ever before.

The first thing that comes to many people's minds when they think about India is the heat, the crowds, and the poverty. Yes, most of India has summer temperatures that can make even the most gung-ho sun worshiper dream of cold rainy days. And there's no doubt that in the world's second-most populous country, you're more likely to find yourself maneuvering through a crowd than you are to be walking an empty street. True, heartbreaking poverty is out in the open for everyone to see – India is a developing country, after all, and a few days here will quickly make you realize how fortunate you are to have food, shelter, and clothes on your back.

It may sound cliché, but India really is a land of extremes. There's no denying that in many ways, especially when it comes to the reliability of basic infrastructure, India lags far behind the developed world. In other ways, life in India can be very comfortable, at least in the big cities. There are air-conditioned cafés serving French wine and Italian espresso, art galleries, gargantuan shopping malls, and movie theaters so modern that your average Californian cinema would look rustic in comparison. You can hire a full-time cook for a few hundred dollars per month, or simply deck

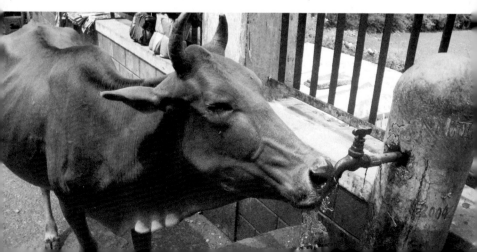

out your kitchen with the same appliances you would find back home. And if you feel like a change of scenery, you can quickly hop on a plane or a train and be in a completely different landscape within a few hours and without breaking the bank.

When I moved to India in January 2007, I was worried that I wouldn't be able to handle living here long-term. Perhaps the heat, the poverty, the traffic, and the pollution would be too much to handle. I promised myself I would stick it out for six months. Some four years later, I'm still living in India, and although I will always remain an outsider, in many ways I feel more at home here than anywhere else I've ever lived. Life hasn't always been a cakewalk: I've had to learn to deal with some of the challenging realities of daily life here, including power cuts, water shortages, and a whole lot of dust. I've also had to make some changes in my lifestyle, ranging from dressing more conservatively than I normally would on a hot summer's day to making sure the water I drink has been properly filtered. However, I haven't had to sacrifice my cultural identity or sense of self in order to adapt to my new home. Foreigners are definitely expected to respect local customs, but they will never be asked to change who they are in order to conform. Moreover, Indian society operates on the premise of unity in diversity, and because of its pluralism, there's space to be who you are and practice what you believe. And that alone might just be why so many people from around the world have chosen to make this awe-inspiring country their home.

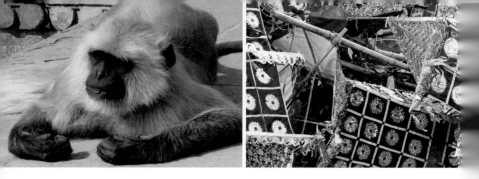

▶ WHAT I LOVE ABOUT INDIA

- On an average day, you are likely to cross paths with a variety of fauna, including dogs, monkeys, cows, and sometimes even elephants.

- Dance, music, art, literature — India has it all. India's traditional arts are complex, ancient, and mesmerizing.

- No matter where you are in India, a different culture, language, and landscape is never more than a few hours' drive away.

- India's time zone is abbreviated to IST, or Indian Standard Time; however, IST has become short for "Indian Stretchable Time" because the attitude toward time management is much more flexible than in the West.

- Although supermarkets are increasingly commonplace, you can still buy fresh milk and yogurt from the neighborhood dairy stands and fresh fruits and vegetables from the roaming produce carts.

- People are quick to welcome you into their homes, feed you, and make sure that you are safe and happy in their country.

- With summer comes India's mango season, where you can sample dozens of varieties of the country's favorite fruit.

- Masala chai, a concoction of tea, spices, milk, and a lot of sugar, is comforting, delicious, and available on every street corner.

- When it rains, water is collected in large cisterns to be used later. This widespread practice is not only cost-effective, it's ecofriendly.

- The traditional dress of women across India, the sari is beautiful, elegant, and figure-flattering.

- There's a *wallah,* or tradesperson, for everything. From having a sign hand-painted to blowing up balloons, you're pretty much guaranteed there is someone who specializes in the service in question.

WELCOME TO INDIA

INTRODUCTION

Nothing can truly prepare you for India, because India is not like anywhere else in the world. Oftentimes you feel like you are on another planet, or at least in a parallel universe, where order is replaced with what seems like chaos, where extreme wealth and shocking poverty exist side-by-side in some sort of idiosyncratic harmony. India is at the same time home to the world's oldest continuous civilization and a hub of technological advancement, which makes it appear as though the country has one foot in the past and the other stretching into the future. For these reasons, India is often described as a land of contrasts, but this only scratches the surface of the Indian experience.

Indian society is pluralistic, as it has to be, given that the country is home to hundreds of cultures, languages, and types of terrain, stretching from the chilly peaks of the Himalayas to the balmy southern tropics. Religion is an integral part of daily life here, and while relations between members of the many religious communities are often painted as strained by the media, there is a pervasive sense of tolerance that allows people of different faiths to coexist

© MARGOT BIGG

harmoniously most of the time. India's rich diversity makes it a fascinating place to live, for no matter where you go, you are likely to have amazing new experiences and encounter extraordinary people.

Although India's many cultures and traditions mean that it would be simplistic to make sweeping statements about the country, there are a couple of things that visitors to this land are likely to observe no matter where they are. The first is the warmness of the people: Most Indians value family and community very highly, and they have been raised to treat guests like gods. This means that whether you are invited for tea in a mud hut in rural Rajasthan or to a grand banquet in the buzzing metropolis of Mumbai, you will likely be treated with unimaginable hospitality and leave with a new set of lifelong friends.

Then there are the crowds and the ensuing noise. While some areas of rural India are quite isolated, most expatriates set up their new homes in one of India's crowded cities. Newcomers to India often get the sense that they are never really alone—India is, after all, the second-most populous country in the world, and decades of urbanization mean that India's cities often feel like they are bursting at the seams. If you live in a city, you will also quickly notice that India is modernizing at an incredible pace, with new high-rise office towers and luxury shopping malls springing up to accommodate a sharp upturn in business and mass consumption. A couple of decades of economic liberalization has led to a burgeoning middle class in a country that used to be strictly divided between the rich and the poor, and the landscapes of many of India's cities are beginning to take on an increasingly international look and feel.

Although India's infrastructural improvements are making it a much more comfortable place to live than ever before, it's still among the world's more difficult places to move to, and living in India is not for everyone. The seemingly endless bureaucracy, disorder, and low sanitation standards are enough to put many people off moving to the country. Even the most laid-back of people will likely find their patience regularly tested by infrastructural problems (such as blackouts and water shortages), the thick red tape that surrounds the most simple of tasks, and general communication difficulties that can arise when dealing with people with a very different outlook on the world. If you are the type of person who values punctuality and order, you might find India a bit too relaxed and chaotic for your liking. However, if you are willing to deal with the crowds, heat, and a lot of cultural differences, you will be rewarded with an exciting new life in a country where the opportunities to learn and explore are endless. Whether you love it or hate it, India will open your eyes to the richness of the world and to humanity as a whole.

The Lay of the Land

India's landscape is as diverse as its population, and the country is home to snow-clad mountains, sparse deserts, tropical beaches, and dusty plains. The Himalayas cut through the northernmost states, receding into foothills and finally flattening out by the time they reach the densely populated Indo-Gangetic Plain, which stretches all the way into India's Northeast states. South of the plain lies the vast mass of the Thar Desert. The desert fades away as it meets with the plateaus of India's Central Highlands, including the Deccan Plateau, which extend all the way to the south of the country. Much of India is surrounded by its humid coastland, and thin strips of plain run up its western and eastern coasts. Then there are the Andaman and Nicobar Islands to the east, which are actually closer to Thailand and share little in common with mainland India and the islands of Lakshadweep near Kerala.

Northern India is home to many of India's best known cities and historic capitals, and this is the region that has most come to represent India overseas. This area is home to India's capital, New Delhi, as well as the well-known former capital of Kolkata. Northern India is defined differently for different purposes, but is most often associated with the territory north of the Indian Peninsula, and it is where Indo-Aryan languages (such as Hindi and Punjabi) are spoken and the climate is temperate. The Northeast is sometimes grouped with the North, although this area is culturally and geographically distinct from the rest of the country; its incorporation into India is relatively recent, dating to the British Raj era.

© MARIYA ZHELEVA

Kerala's tranquil backwaters

WELCOME TO INDIA

© MARGOT BIGG

the stark Himalayan kingdom of Ladakh

South of the Vindhya Mountain Range is Southern India. Although the southernmost Dravidian states of Karnataka, Kerala, Tamil Nadu, and Andhra Pradesh are always included in classifications of Southern India, the coastal states of Maharashtra and Goa are also often grouped with Southern India, usually due to cultural and historical similarities. The climate here is tropical, and the lush green landscapes that stretch across this region are only occasionally interrupted with sprawling cities, such as the IT hub of Bengaluru and the financial capital of Mumbai.

STATES AND UNION TERRITORIES

India is divided into 28 states, each with its own elected government, and seven union territories that are controlled directly by the federal government, comparable to the structure of the U.S. government. In 2008, two of these union territories, Delhi and Puduchery, were granted partial statehood and now have their own elected legislative assemblies. The other five union territories are administered directly by the federal government under an appointed lieutenant governor.

Prior to India's independence, the country was divided into provinces that were ruled directly by the British and locally autonomous, indirectly ruled princely states. After independence, these states and provinces were organized into states and union territories, and then reorganized again in 1956 to reflect the cultural and linguistic groups living in each area. Over the years, some of these states, such as Uttar Pradesh and Bihar, were divided into smaller autonomous states, usually to ensure the most accurate representation of local inhabitants in the federal government. At the time of writing, residents of the area of Telangana in Andhra Pradesh are ardently campaigning for independent statehood.

URBAN AND RURAL INDIA

India is the world's second-most populous country after China and is home to about 1.17 billion people, around half of whom are under the age of 25. Three-quarters of India's population live in rural areas, and the disparity between rural and urban India is alarmingly wide. Access to basic infrastructure in rural areas is low, and while electricity and telecommunications infrastructure is improving in much of rural India, access to potable water, decent education, and health services in these areas is mediocre at best, especially when compared to the urban centers with their world-class facilities. Most people in rural areas are engaged in agricultural work, although many move to larger cities in search of a better life, often to find themselves with no choice but to take up menial day-labor jobs. Unless you are a development worker, you are much more likely to find yourself moving to one of India's urban centers.

CLIMATE

India's large and diverse landmass means that the weather here is as diverse as the people and the landscape. The four seasons here are winter (mid-Dec.–mid-Mar.), summer (mid-Mar.–mid-June), monsoon (late June–Sept.), and the sticky postmonsoon time (mid-Sept.–mid-Dec.). Northern India has more

© MARIYA ZHELEVA

Coconuts are an essential part of the South Indian diet.

distinct (and extreme) seasons than the tropical south, with winter temperatures dropping to near freezing and summers peaking well past 100°F. The South, conversely, shifts from hot and humid in the winter months to very hot and humid in the summer months that lead up to the monsoon.

The most notable feature of India's climate is the annual monsoon. Contrary to popular belief, there are actually two monsoons in India: the southwest monsoon and the northeast monsoon. The southwestern monsoon starts in June, moving up from the Indian Ocean and pushing rain across the subcontinent and to the east. The northeast monsoon runs during the postmonsoon season, and sometimes carries on well into winter, dumping rains along peninsular Southern India. Monsoon in India is welcomed joyfully, and people of all ages can often be spotted running out into the streets to soak up the first drops of rainfall. While these rains provide the landscape with the hydration it needs to remain fertile, global warming has led to drastic changes in the monsoon's patterns over the past few years, resulting in many devastating floods.

FLORA AND FAUNA

India's vegetation is incredibly varied, and over 47,000 types of plants have been identified by the government's Botanical Survey. The temperate Himalayan region, quite similar to the Pacific Northwest in the United States, abounds with wildflowers, evergreens such as firs, birch, junipers, and Indians' beloved Deodar Pine. The eastern regions are full of mangroves, grasslands, and bamboo forests. The much-farmed northern plains are covered with wheat, mustard, and sugar cane, and the southern regions are major producers of pepper, coconut, rubber, and cashews. India's national fruit, the mango, grows throughout most of the country, although the sweetest and juiciest are grown in the humid state of Maharashtra, which doubles as India's major wine-producing region.

The diversity of India's bioregions means that the country is home to an incredible diversity of creatures,

© MARIYA ZHELEVA

India's diversity extends to its flora and fauna.

SAVE THE TIGERS

India's national animal, the royal Bengal tiger, is on the verge of extinction, and only an estimated 1,411 of the beasts are alive in the wild today. Visitors to India's tiger reserves rarely spot the animals, and conservationists fear that populations will continue to decline. However, not long ago, huge tiger populations were considered a threat to farm animals, and hunting parties were common – pay a visit to any royal hunting lodge in Rajasthan and you will likely see a trophy tiger head mounted on the wall.

Reuters reported in 1951 that the Indian government believed that 500-1,000 tigers could be killed in India annually "without affecting the general tiger population." In the 1950s tiger hunting holidays were promoted as a way to increase U.S. tourism to India and provide income to members of royal families whose livelihood began to diminish when their princedoms were incorporated into independent India. These initiatives also helped keep tiger numbers stable, but after decades of poaching and modern encroachments on the big cats' traditional environment, tiger numbers are dwindling.

India's government passed the Wildlife Protection Act of 1972, which included a slew of new regulations and a ban on hunting. The passing of this act led to the establishment of Project Tiger, a tiger protection agency designed to increase sanctuary land and promote public awareness about wildlife conservation. While efforts to protect the tiger have been ongoing for decades, it wasn't until late 2009 that the World Wide Fund for Nature (WWF) launched a major publicity campaign featuring images of an adorable baby tiger, and tiger protection was put back in the spotlight. Tiger conservation is currently a hot topic in India, although poaching is still reported. One can only hope that these efforts prove fruitful and that tiger populations can once again flourish in India.

including lions, tigers, elephants, and rhinoceroses, along with hyenas, primates, leopards, and scores of different types of bovines. The avifauna here is equally impressive, with large populations of storks and herons, birds of prey and parrots, not to mention the national bird, the peacock. Animals in India often roam freely on the streets, and in urban centers you can expect to encounter mongooses, monkeys, and plenty of errant cows.

© MARIYA ZHELEVA

an elephant and his mahout

Social Climate

With the exception of some interreligious conflicts, Indian society is relatively stable, and you are unlikely to find yourself in a tumultuous situation unless you seek one out. Certain regions, such as parts of Kashmir near the Pakistan border, are more prone to violent outbursts, and it is best to check the U.S. State Department's travel advisories before planning a visit. Political protests are common and can sometimes turn violent. Unfortunately, police brutality is commonplace, although as a foreigner you are unlikely to experience this unless you strike first. Corruption is also a more or less accepted, though certainly not condoned, facet of Indian society, and while corruption exists all over the world, it manifests itself at lower levels here. For example, it's not uncommon for a police officer to turn a blind eye to drunk driving if he's slipped a few hundred rupees.

Political parties are very active in India, and they sometimes wield their political powers by declaring widespread general strikes, known as *bandhs* (closures). During these strikes, community members are expected to close their shops and stay inside. One of the most active, and feared, groups in India is the Naxalites, a far-left group of Maoists with a stronghold in the eastern parts of the country. Violence between the Indian government and the Naxalites has been going on since the onset of the insurgency in the 1960s, although as a foreigner you are not likely to find yourself in the line of fire. Terrorism is not unheard of in India, and it is important always to be vigilant of your

NON-RESIDENT INDIANS

The term Non-Resident Indian (NRI) refers to Indians who have migrated overseas and people of Indian heritage who were born outside of India. India's constitution does not permit dual citizenship, but if you or your spouse have family roots in India and want to move there, you may qualify for one of the following special schemes.

Person of Indian Origin (PIO) Card: This document allows you to live and work in India without a visa until the card expires (usually 15 years), although you must register with the police if you intend to stay in the country for more than six months. PIO cardholders have most of the rights and responsibilities of Indian nationals, although they are not allowed to vote or invest in agricultural land.

Overseas Citizenship of India (OCI): This is the closest India currently has to a form of dual citizenship, although OCI holders are not granted an Indian passport. Like PIOs, OCIs are not entitled to acquire agricultural land or vote. The most notable differences between the two schemes is that OCIs are granted lifelong visas and are not required to register their stay in India with the police.

surroundings and report any suspicious activities or abandoned packages. Recently, foreigners have been targeted by terrorist strikes, notably in the 2008 attacks on Mumbai and the 2010 bombings of Pune's German Bakery. Despite these upheavals, India is a fairly safe country, and violent crime is lower than in many Western countries. There's also a strong sense of community, and you will find that most people will be eager to help you, even if you don't need assistance.

Most Indians are very proud of their country and retain a strong sense of national identity that in some situations supersedes local identities. This is best summed up with the favorite adage of Indian politicians and intelligentsia: Unity in Diversity. Most Indians will happily go out of their way to make you feel welcome and comfortable. They'll also likely be curious about you and may barrage you with questions. Sometimes people do this to gain a rapport with you so that they can later con you out of money, although this generally only happens at major tourist attractions. The majority of Indian people are genuinely curious and friendly, so while you should always be vigilant, just as you would back home, it's best not to be overly suspicious of Indians' inherent warmth and hospitality.

FOREIGNERS IN INDIA

India has a long history with foreigners, and the region has traded with and been invaded by outsiders for millennia. After India achieved independence from Britain, most colonial residents left, and the expat population was limited to teachers, diplomats, missionaries, and scholars. Indian philosophy was repopularized in the West in the 1960s, and plenty of flower children came here, a few of whom stayed on and married Indians. However, it wasn't until the 1990s that India began to see a steady stream of expats, most of whom were high-level managers in the IT or outsourcing industries. These days, expats of all ages and experience levels come to India, many opting to work for lower local salaries in return for the experience, and resident foreigners are no longer an anomaly in India's metropolitan areas. India's recent boom in commercial air travel, coupled with a dire lack of experienced air pilots from India, has led many Indian airlines to recruit seasoned pilots from abroad. India's system of higher education is also quite good, and it is home to some of the world's most reputable technology and business management institutes, which attract students from across the globe. Over the last few years, plenty of entrepreneurs from abroad have begun cashing in on India's booming economy, and many have started up businesses and joint ventures with great success.

One of the first things foreign visitors to India notice is how much people

FAMOUS EXPATS IN INDIA

- **Jim Corbett:** The India-born Irishman is among India's most loved expats of days past. He gained fame in the early 20th century as a hunter, successfully slaying man-eating tigers and leopards that were responsible for hundreds of deaths. Later in life, he became a conservationist and was passionate about the protection of large cats. He helped establish India's largest national park, which was renamed Jim Corbett National Park after his death.

- **Sonia Gandhi:** Perhaps India's best known living expatriate, Italian-born Gandhi is the president of the Indian Congress Party and the widow of former prime minister Rajiv Gandhi. She stayed out of the limelight throughout her marriage but became more active in politics after her husband's assassination in 1991.

- **Rudyard Kipling:** The British author was born in Mumbai when the city was still under the control of the British Raj. His early life in India was the inspiration behind many of his well-known works for children, including *The Jungle Book, Kim,* and *Just So Stories.* Although Kipling is acclaimed for his literary talent, he has also been accused of propagating imperialism.

- **Mother Teresa:** Born in Albania, she is known for her work with the sick and impoverished of Kolkata, for which she gained celebrity status internationally. Although her work was acclaimed worldwide, some people in India are suspicious that there may have been ulterior motives behind her charity.

stare at them. It's important to remember that these stares, which can often be quite intimidating, are usually not meant to be hostile and usually come from less-educated Indians who simply don't know that staring can make some people uncomfortable. India is also a very color-conscious society, and male visitors of African descent are sometimes treated with suspicion. In the same way, foreign women are frequently stereotyped as promiscuous, and some Indian men, especially those whose exposure to other countries has been limited to films (of all varieties), are surprised to learn that most foreign women are not open to unabashed sexual advances. However, most people in big cities are more or less used to seeing foreign faces. You'll likely spend most of your time interacting with highly educated Indians, many of whom have lived or studied overseas, and most of the people you encounter will receive you with a warmth and hospitality surpassing what you might find in your home country.

HISTORY, GOVERNMENT, AND ECONOMY

India is home to one of the world's oldest civilizations and yet is one of the world's youngest democracies. Although India still struggles with poverty and has a lot of social and economic issues to iron out, it's a fast-growing country with a booming economy and seemingly endless opportunities for growth. This abundance of potential is no secret to the world's movers and shakers, and major players in the international market have been seeking cooperation with India since it was made more accessible to foreign investment in the 1990s. However, while India's role in the globalized era is relatively new, it has been something of a promised land for ambitious entrepreneurs and tradespeople throughout history. Millennia of contact with outsiders, through trade or invasions, have shaped India into the pluralistic and multicultural place that it is today.

Even if you're not a history buff, it's helpful to know a bit about where India has come from in order to better understand where it is today. Whether you're

© MARGOT BIGG

wandering the streets of Old Delhi or having a formal dinner with an important colleague, you'll find even a small bit of historical knowledge will come in quite handy. Politics are also a hot topic in India, and voter mobilization is at a level that U.S. campaigners only dream about. While your mother probably taught you to never discuss politics or religion, both are openly talked-about topics in India, so it's best to know a little bit about what's going on—just don't let on too much of your opinions unless you are prepared to engage in a heated discussion. Indians are also proud of their powerful economy, and you may find a bit of knowledge goes a long way, especially if you or your company plans to invest in India.

History

Although the Indian subcontinent is home to some of the world's oldest civilizations, the Republic of India as we now know it has only existed since 1947. Over the millennia, different regions of India have experienced different influences and cultural phenomena. While it's difficult to approach the country's history using present-day geographical boundaries, it's important to know about historical details that have shaped India into what it is today. This section will help you gain a better understanding into the Indian subcontinent's past, but it is by no means exhaustive.

EARLY CIVILIZATIONS

Although some estimate that India has been inhabited for up to half a million years, the earliest traceable settlements were the Rock Shelters of Bhimbetka, which existed some 9,000 years ago in what is now Madhya Pradesh. Archaeologists in Mehrgarh (in present-day Pakistan) have also found traces of Neolithic cultures, although the first heavily documented civilization emerged during the Bronze Age in the 3rd or 4th millennium B.C.

Indus Valley Civilization

One of the world's oldest examples of urban civilization, the Indus Valley Civilization flourished around the Indus River Basin approximately 2800–1900 B.C. The civilization stretched across the northwestern part of the Indian subcontinent all the way into present-day Iran, peaking with the Harappan civilization. The mature Harappan phase started in around 2600 B.C. and was characterized by well-planned cities, the use of irrigation and canals, and the planet's first artificial sanitation facilities, which included advanced sewer systems. The people of this era were mostly traders and artisans who lived in communities with others who practiced the same craft.

The Harappans were skilled in mathematics and are credited with inventing some of the first-known systems of weights and measurements. By 1800 B.C. their civilization began to decline, possibly due to climate change that reduced the monsoon and thereby made crop harvests less bountiful. Another popular theory is that a tectonic shift took place at some point before the Harappans began to disappear, causing the rivers that fed the civilization to shift to a new course. Some legacies of the Indus Valley Civilization live to this day, and archaeologists believe that the practices of Indus Valley subcultures, such as cremating the dead, originated during this era.

Vedic Civilization and the Mahajanapadas

The Vedic period started around 1500 B.C. During this time the Vedic texts, the earliest texts of Hinduism, were composed by the Indo-Aryan people who immigrated east into South Asia after the Indus Valley Civilization. The Indo-Aryans were originally pastoral, surviving largely on cattle rearing, although they later turned to agriculture. Although there is a lot of disagreement about how these people lived, archaeologists trace their earliest influences to the period in which the Rigveda, a collection of hymns sacred in Hinduism to this day, was composed. The people of this era were believed to have been ruled by kings, and society was organized around four social classes, known as *varna,* with each group having a specific role and a hierarchical position in society. The *varnas* are considered to be a precursor of India's more recent caste system.

Religious worship and ritual during this time are also considered by some as precursors to what later developed into Hinduism, and to this day, some people still refer to Hinduism as Vedic Religion. The late Vedic period began around 600 B.C., when the Vedic people turned to agriculture and more politically rigid polities, known as Mahajanapadas, were formed. The 16 Mahajanapadas were similar to kingdoms, and they marked the time when nomadic peoples turned from a nomadic to a settled lifestyle. It was also during this time that another set of sacred texts, the Upanishads, were composed, and certain tenets of Hinduism, such as vegetarianism and ahimsa (nonviolence), are said to have emerged.

THE MAURYA EMPIRE

One of the Mahajanapadas, the Magadha Empire, encompassed much of the parts of India now known as Bihar, Jharkhand, and West Bengal. It later expanded to include other areas of the subcontinent, peaking with the foundation of the Maurya Empire in 322 B.C. under Chandragupta Maurya. With the help of his advisor, Chanakya, Chandragupta usurped the Magadha throne, expanding his reign across India to create the world's largest empire at the time, encompassing almost all of the subcontinent. His grandson, Ashoka the Great, later came to power, violently conquering the southern kingdom of Kalinga before turning to Buddhism and spreading teachings of peace and nonviolence throughout India. To this day, Ashoka remains one of the most beloved characters in India's history.

The Maurya empire is noted for its complex, semicentralized form of governance, subdivided into four provinces. It was during this time that India saw its first common currency, which was possible due to the political and military unification that the Empire provided. Trade increased, as did agricultural output, and India thrived. The Maurya Empire began to decline after Ashoka's death, and India was once again divided into many smaller empires, giving rise to what are known as the Middle Kingdoms.

MIDDLE KINGDOMS

The Early Middle Kingdoms spread across the subcontinent and were ruled by Persian, Greek, and local dynasties. Throughout much of the early part of this era, India was fragmented into many smaller polities. There was also significant contact with outside forces, most notably the Romans. Significant rulers included the Satavahanas, who ruled much of the south and central regions of India and staunchly defended their territory against invasion from Central Asia. They were the first to introduce coins depicting images of their rulers, and they were also responsible for propagating Hinduism in parts of Southeast Asia. The Indian connection with other parts of Asia continued with the dynasty of King Kharavela, whose colonists settled as far south as the Maldives and in Burma to the east. Kharavela also spread the religion of Jainism throughout India.

The Gupta Empire

Heralded by many as the start of India's golden age, the period in which much of the subcontinent was ruled by the Gupta Empire was a great time of artistic, scientific, and philosophical advancement. Examples of achievements during this era include the development of the decimal system and the concept of zero, as well as the composition of some of India's best known texts, including the Ramayana, the Mahabharata, and the Kama Sutra. Chess is also believed to have been invented during Gupta rule. During this period astronomers also argued that the world was round, and they subsequently developed intricate systems of astronomical measurement and used advanced astrological systems that are believed to have originated during the Maurya Empire. The Guptas reigned over most of Northern India thanks to an advanced military, but the empire eventually fell due to heavy invasion by the Huna people, who entered from the northwest. After the fall of the empire, the northern regions split into three dynasties: the Gurjara Pratihara, the Pala, and the Rashtrakuta, followed by the Rajputs, who gained control of much of what is now known as Rajasthan, retaining their rule (at least officially) until India's independence from the British many centuries later.

The Chola Dynasty

While the Guptas reunited the north, much of the south was reigned by different dynasties, the most influential of which were the Tamil Cholas, whose rule is associated with Southern India's golden age. At one point, the Cholas' reach extended as far as Southeast Asia. Southern India was unified under the Cholas' monarchial government, with smaller governance at the village level. These were good times for the people of the south: There was very little political disturbance, populations were highly literate, and the arts flourished. The Cholas were also successful traders and used the wealth they amassed to build many great temples, some of which can still be visited today.

ISLAMIC SULTANATES

Although Muslim communities already existed in some parts of India, it wasn't until the late 12th–early 13th century that sultanates were firmly established in the country. One of the most significant was the Delhi Sultanate, which started at the end of the 12th century when Muhammad of Ghor conquered a stretch of the Indo-Gangetic plain and declared himself Sultan of Delhi. This led to the Mamluk Dynasty (1206–1290), the first of the sultanate's five dynasties. It was ousted in a coup by the Turkic-Afghan Khilji Dynasty, which promoted Persian language in the court, a significant part of the development of the Urdu language. The next dynasty to rule the Delhi Sultanate was the Tughlaq, which came to power in 1320 and continued to expand the sultanate southward, making a few odd choices along the way (among them, shifting the seat of the sultanate and Delhi's entire population to Daulatabad in Maharashtra, only to return two years later after realizing that there wasn't enough water there to sustain a capital).

The Bahmani Sultanate in Southern India was also established during this era when the governor of the area revolted against Delhi. The Bahmani

Sultanate later fragmented into the five Deccan Sultanates that ruled much of the south, except the areas run by the Hindu Vijayanagara Empire, and remained until their territories were taken over by the Mughals. In 1398, Timur, the founder of the Timurid dynasty that encompassed much of Central Asia and northern South Asia, ransacked Delhi and ordered the massacre of the city's Hindu population. The next rulers were the Sayyid, who claimed to be descendants of the Prophet Muhammad. The dynasty was founded by Khizr Khan, whom Timur had appointed as the governor of Multan in Punjab. The final dynasty of the Delhi Sultanate was that of the Lodis, who were eventually defeated at the first Battle of Panipat in 1526 by Barbur, a descendant of Timur.

THE MUGHAL EMPIRE

In 1526, after defeating the Lodis and then Maharana Sangram Singh of Mewar, Barbur began setting the foundation for his empire, although he only lived for a few years as ruler. After his death in 1531, he was succeeded by his son Humayan, who lost the empire to the short-lived Suri Dynasty, regaining it in 1555 only to die within a couple of months. When Humayan died, his 13-year-old son, Akbar the Great, took the throne and later expanded the Mughal Empire across much of present-day Northern India. Although Akbar was hostile toward Hindus during the earlier part of his reign, he later forged marriage alliances with Hindu princesses and appointed Hindus to high-

© MARGOT BIGG

Akbar's Tomb

THE TAJ MAHAL

India's most famous monument, the 17th-century Taj Mahal is heralded as one of the greatest works of Mughal architecture as well as the ultimate expression of love. The mausoleum complex in Agra, Uttar Pradesh, was built by Mughal emperor Shah Jahan in honor of his favorite wife, Mumtaz Mahal, after her death. The perfectly symmetrical onion-domed building, made of shimmering white marble inlaid with semiprecious stones, was constructed by thousands of artisans over a period of about 16 years.

Legend has it that Shah Jahan wanted to build and be buried in an identical structure in black marble across the Yanuma River from his late wife's tomb, but that his plan came to a halt when his son Aurangzeb placed him under house arrest in Agra Fort. However, the stories of the emperor's last wishes have never been verified, and when Shah Jahan died his body was interred in the Taj Mahal next to his beloved Mumtaz.

© MARGOT BIGG

ranking political and military positions. Akbar was also a fond patron of the fine arts, which flourished under his rule. Akbar's son Jahangir ascended the throne after his father's death. He was as known for his fondness of justice as he was for his fondness of alcohol, and he isn't considered a particularly strong leader. His alcoholic tendencies were said to have caused his death in 1627, at which point his son Shah Jahan took over.

Although Shah Jahan was responsible for creating many significant road links and for drastically increasing revenues while on the throne, he is best remembered for his many contributions to architecture, including Delhi's Red

Fort and Jama Masjid as well as Lahore's Shalimar Gardens, not to mention the beloved Taj Mahal. In 1657, Shah Jahan fell ill, and his son Aurangzeb began his conquest of the throne, executing his brothers and placing his father under house arrest in Agra, where the old emperor remained until his death in 1666. Aurangzeb was reputed to have been a strict and intolerant ruler, and there is some indication that he both banned music and destroyed Hindu temples (although these claims are frequently disputed by historians). Aurangzeb spent much of his reign engaged in military struggle, mostly costly attempts at expanding the empire, and he faced many rebellions. After his death came a succession of emperors whose powers slowly decreased, most markedly when the British East India Company (BEIC) moved in. At the turn of the 19th century, Shah Alam II gave up much of his territory in the east to the BEIC, and the Mughal Empire came to a definitive end in 1858 following the Indian Rebellion.

COLONIAL INDIA

In 1498, Portuguese trader Vasco de Gama came to India and set up a trade agreement that resulted in the establishment of the first Portuguese trading post, in Kerala, and soon led to additional trading centers along the west coast. The Portuguese maintained a presence in India, refusing to give up their territories to the newly formed Republic of India until 1961, when the Indian military invaded Portugal's remaining territories. The Portuguese military presence in Goa and the Gujarati ports of Daman and Diu was weak, and the territories were soon encompassed by India. Portugal's influence in these areas remains to this day, however, especially in Goa, where there is a large Roman Catholic community. Over the centuries, Goans have absorbed elements of Portuguese culture into their culinary traditions and the local language, Konkani. Some older people in Goa still speak Portuguese.

Other European countries also set up operations in India, including the Dutch, the French, and to a smaller extent, the Danish. Of these, the French influence is perhaps the most noticeable in modern-day India, and the popular tourist town of Puduchery (formerly Pondicherry) is often likened to New Orleans due to its colonial-style buildings adorned with wrought iron gates. However, while Europe's colonial influence lives on in the architecture and food of former colonial areas, it was the British who left the most noticeable mark on the subcontinent.

British India

Britain's influence over India began with the establishment of the East India

Company in 1612, which was set up to facilitate the trade of everything from cotton to opium. In 1617 the company was granted permission to trade in the region by Jahangir, and by 1717 it was allowed to continue its activities duty-free. In 1757 the Nawab of Bengal opposed the fact that the British were trading without paying duties, which led to the Battle of Plassey, where the Nawab was defeated by the company's mercenary forces. In 1764, after the Battle of Buxar, the East India Company gained administrative power over much of eastern India, and in 1772 it formerly began Company rule in India, setting up its capital in Calcutta (now Kolkata). Its influence continued to widen through the end of the century and into the 1800s as the company annexed different parts of India and defeated the Maratha and Sikh Empires. In the 1857 Indian Rebellion, often referred to as the Sepoy Mutiny, sepoys (soldiers), discontent with British economic, military, and cultural policies and upset that bullet cartridges greased with cow and pig fat were being supplied to the military, rebelled against the company. Many historians also believe that one of the goals of the uprising was to restore the power of the Mughal Empire. The East India Company withstood the rebellion, exiled the last emperor, Bahadur Shah Zafar II, to Burma, and transferred its power to the British Crown. For the next 90 years, India would be ruled directly as a British colony under what is known as the British Raj. The only areas that were spared were the few remaining French and Portuguese colonies and the 565 princely states that the British ruled indirectly.

Like the East India Company administrators, the Raj used divide-and-rule techniques to keep India's citizenry under control. It was a method used throughout the empire that pitted members of different religious and social groups against one another to prevent a unified movement against imperial rule. The Raj would later bring Indians into its political processes, appointing local advisors and eventually creating Indian legislative councils in 1909. Soon thereafter, World War I broke out, and more than 1 million soldiers were sent from India to fight around the world. After the war the League of Nations (predecessor to the United Nations) was formed, and India was represented separately from Britain. By this point, the independence movement had already begun to form, although such a movement had been brewing since the 1857 rebellion.

THE INDEPENDENCE MOVEMENT AND PARTITION

Although many leaders and intellectuals contributed to the independence movement, the first person to gain widespread attention for his efforts was Bal Gangadhar Tilak. A political activist and journalist, Tilak was a major advocate of the Swadeshi Movement, a boycott of British products that later influenced much of Gandhi's techniques. After World War I, India's autonomy increased through self-governance with the Government of India Act of 1919, although the British retained control over financial administrative duties. During the war a Gujarati lawyer, Mohandas Karamchand Gandhi (later Mahatma Gandhi), returned to his native India after a career in South Africa. Gandhi advocated nonviolent civil disobedience as a way forward, not always a favored alternative to the militant uprisings suggested by many of his contemporaries. His original vision was not that of an independent nation but rather of an economically cohesive territory of commerce, as promoted by the Indian National Congress Party at the time.

After the war the Congress Party realigned its goals towards Indian independence, and in 1929 the party resolved to work toward complete autonomy, declaring January 26, 1930, their independence day (still celebrated as Republic Day across India, as this was the date, in 1950, that the republic's constitution came into effect). Gandhi continued his activism after setting up an ashram in Gujarat, advocating for the rights of the lower castes and encouraging the boycott of British-produced goods such as British-made cotton fabric (opting instead to wear khadi, the hand-spun Indian alternative). However, his most remembered act of civil disobedience was when he marched hundreds of miles from his ashram to the coast of Gujarat to harvest sea salt from the water, peacefully but symbolically opposing salt taxes levied by the British. In the days that followed, people along India's coast began to make nontaxable salt, boycott British goods, and refuse to pay taxes. Although some argue that the protests did relatively little to persuade the British, they certainly helped develop a sense of unity among participants, creating stronger forces to counter the British, who had long used the lack of unity in India to their advantage.

In 1935 the Government of India Act, which contained provisions for

A statue of Mahatma Gandhi at his ashram in Ahmedabad.

© MARGOT BIGG

the establishment of an Indian Federation that would include princely states and increase Indian representation in the form of provincial governments, was passed. In 1937 the first elected provincial governments were formed, and Congress became the dominant party in the new governments. In 1939, however, India's Viceroy Victor Hope declared that India would participate in World War II without first consulting the provincial rulers. The Indian public was divided on whether to go to war, and some saw the war and Hope's unilateral decision as a prime opportunity to help advance the long struggle for independence. Subhas Chandra Bose, who headed the Azad Hind Government in Exile, allied with the Axis powers during the war and organized the Indian National Army to fight to overthrow British rule. While their efforts failed, many believe that the army's establishment, and the subsequent realization that Indian troops could not be relied on by Britain to fight her wars, was key to India's eventual independence. Another major movement, Gandhi's Quit India Movement, called for immediate independence, threatening the Raj government with widespread civil disobedience. Again, the movement was considered unsuccessful at the time, although historians argue that it did play a large role in freeing India from British rule. In 1946 the Royal Indian Navy staged a mutiny, later joined by the army and some police forces, which some argue was the final straw that, along with the economic weakness resulting from World War II, led Britain's Governor-General, Louis Mountbatten, to grant India its independence in 1947. Gandhi was assassinated two years later.

Partition

The idea of separate Hindu and Muslim states, which later lead to the establishment of the Dominion of Pakistan (later split into Pakistan and Bangladesh) and the Republic of India, is usually attributed to early-20th-century political thought in the region. In 1906 the All India Muslim League (AIML) was formed to protect the rights of Muslims in a Hindu-majority political climate. Poet Allamah Iqbal was among the first to voice support for an independent Muslim state, although it was Muhammad Ali Jinnah, the AIML leader who later became the "father of Pakistan," who is most credited with promoting the two-nation theory that would eventually lead to the partition. The theory was based on the concept that Hindus and Muslims, by virtue of their differing cultural and belief systems, intrinsically formed different nations. This would later lead to the decision that Muslims should be granted an autonomous state in order to protect their rights under the Westphalian sovereignty concept of nation-statehood.

In July 1947, a mere five weeks before India and Pakistan became independent and separate nations, an English lawyer named Cyril Radcliffe set foot on the subcontinent for the first time in his life. His task was to chair two boundary commissions—one for Bengal and one for Punjab—that would effectively divide the Indian territory into separate Muslim and non-Muslim states. The idea was to distribute land and resources fairly among Muslims and non-Muslims while keeping displacement to a minimum and avoiding separating farmers from their plots. Partition still led to the displacement and death of millions of people, and refugees from Pakistan-controlled areas of Punjab and Bengal would continue to migrate to India for years to come. The Princely States were allowed to become independent or choose which country to join; these included Jammu and Kashmir, whose maharaja opted for independence. However, a revolution in western Kashmir led the maharaja to ask for India's aid, which India agreed to only if Kashmir would become part of India. Pakistan, however, claimed Kashmir as its own, and the result was the first Indo-Pakistani war. To this day the region remains in dispute and is still a major point of contention in India-Pakistan relations.

POSTINDEPENDENCE INDIA

The republic's constitution was drafted in 1949 and came into effect in 1950. Two years later, the first elections were held, and Congress leader Jawaharlal Nehru became India's first elected prime minister. Under his leadership, industries were nationalized, women's and minority rights were drastically improved, education was heavily invested in, and India's socioeconomic model began to develop. Under Nehru the first Indian Institute of Technology (IIT) was established to aid in India's postwar and postindependence technological advancement. Nehru also formed the Non-Aligned Movement, keeping India out of the Cold War without alienating the Western powers or the Eastern Bloc. He had his own foreign policy issues to deal with, including delicate relations with Pakistan, the reclamation of Goa from the Portuguese, and the Sino-Indian War over territorial disputes in the Himalayan region. When Nehru died, Lal Bahadur Shastri took over, but he died two years later under mysterious circumstances while on a state visit to Tashkent in the USSR, where he signed a peace agreement between India and Pakistan just after the second war between the two young states.

The next prime minister was Indira Gandhi (no relation to Mahatma), Nehru's daughter. During her time in office she devalued the rupee and went to war with Pakistan, which resulted in the establishment of Bangladesh as a separate country. Amid strikes and protests over allegations that Congress had committed electoral fraud, she declared a state of emergency, which gave her power to rule by decree. In 1977, after two years of the state of emergency, she lost an election, but she regained her position in 1980. Gandhi launched Operation Blue Star against Sikh separatists in 1984, sending the military into Amritsar's Harmandir Sahib, popularly known as the Golden Temple, the holiest place of pilgrimage for Sikhs. The operation, though successful, was highly controversial, and in 1984 she was murdered by her own Sikh bodyguards.

INDIA'S POLITICAL PARTIES

India is home to hundreds of political parties that operate at both state and national levels. The two most powerful parties are the Indian National Congress, which helped spearhead the independence movement, and the right-wing Bhartiya Janata Party (BJP). Although these two are at the forefront of the national political scene, there are many other smaller parties, some of which represent specific social groups or states, that consistently win seats in the Lok Sabha. These include the Communist Party of India (Marxist), the most popular party in West Bengal and Kerala, as well as regional parties such as Uttar Pradesh's Samajwadi Party and the far-right Maharashtrian party, Shiv Sena, that is notorious nationwide for its reactionary form of Hindu nationalism.

Both state and national elections are big business in India, incurring hundreds of millions of rupees in expenditure every year for an electorate that exceeds 670 million people. Voter turnout in India is higher than in the United States, and interestingly, the majority of voters come from the less-educated and illiterate rural social groups. Campaigners are clued in to this, and in the months leading up to elections, candidates travel throughout rural hubs, rallying the support of the masses by focusing on the issues that concern them most.

© MARIYA ZHELEVA

Painted signs and walls are often used by India's political parties.

The fallout was the 1984 anti-Sikh atrocities in which many Sikhs were massacred by others angered by the assassination, especially in Delhi.

After Indira's death, her son Rajiv Gandhi came to power. He tried to curb the thick bureaucracy for establishing new businesses—known as the License Raj—and increased infrastructure investment in science and technology. He was succeeded in 1989 by V. P. Singh, who resigned after less than a year, and then by Chandra Shekhar Singh, who also resigned in scandal. In 1991 P. V. Narasimha Rao became prime minister, and during his time in office he effectively liberalized the nearly bankrupt Indian economy through privatization and deregulation reforms, ridding India of the License Raj system and opening the economy to foreign investment. Rao's reforms shaped the social landscape in India, and some say that the strong growth of a middle class with large disposable income is a result of Rao's reforms. Rao also improved diplomatic ties with many other countries and increased military and nuclear activity.

After Rao's term, for two weeks governance fell into the hands of the hands of Atal Bihari Vajpayee, founder of the conservative Bharatiya Janata Party (BJP), then to the United Front coalition of parties, and then the Janata Dal party before Vajpayee came back into power. His second time in office, which lasted more than two terms, was marked by the Kargil War, India's fourth war with Pakistan. Congress regained power in 2004, when Manmohan Singh became prime minister, and he retains the post today. Singh, who was minister of finance during Rao's tenure as prime minister, has been active in continuing financial reform in India. He is also heavily involved in foreign policy, including the India–Pakistan peace process, although he is sometimes criticized as being too soft on domestic issues, particularly terrorism.

Today's India is boosted by a burgeoning and highly educated middle class, especially in the fields of IT and engineering, thanks to decades of political action: Nehru's investment in education and the IITs, Rajiv Gandhi's prioritization of science and technology, Rao's and Singh's liberalization policies, and the efforts to increase international cooperation that were central to the policies of all of India's governments except Indira Gandhi's.

India has changed drastically since the economic reforms of the early 1990s. Coupled with the rapid rise in Internet and telecommunications penetration worldwide, India's metropolises have internationalized to a great extent, making them an increasingly popular destination for foreign business. However, while the Republic of India is in many ways a success story, it still has a long way to go, especially in terms of eradicating terrorism, poverty, and corruption.

Government

India is the world's largest democracy, with a system of government that has a lot in common with the United Kingdom and the United States. India's government is based on the Westminster system, a bicameral parliamentary legislature. India's directly elected lower house is known as the Lok Sabha (People's House) and is similar to the UK House of Commons and the U.S. House of Representatives. The Lok Sabha is formed for a period of five years, after which it is dissolved, making way for a new term. The Lok Sabha has the authority to pass motions of no confidence, which can lead to the forced resignation of the prime minister and his Council of Ministers. However, the president retains the right to dissolve the Lok Sabha if such a motion is passed. The Lok Sabha is also responsible for bills related to taxation and government spending, and all new budgetary concerns are presented there first before moving to the upper house, known as the Rajya Sabha (Council of States). The Rajya Sabha and the Lok Sabha share authority over nonbudgetary issues. The Rajya Sabha comprises up to 250 members, 12 of whom are directly appointed by the President of India. The remaining members are elected by the legislatures of the states and Union Territories, and the house cannot be dissolved.

In India the head of state and the head of government are separate, in the form of the president and the prime minister, respectively. The President of India is elected by parliament and the state legislatures, with the value of

Indian parliament building in Delhi

votes based on the population represented by each elector, similar to the U.S. Electoral College. However, members of parliament (MPs) and members of legislative assemblies (MLAs) generally vote for members of their party, so the President of India usually tends to be a member of the current majority party. The president has a number of duties normally conferred on the head of state in the Westminster system; he or she heads the Indian Armed Forces and appoints the prime minister. The prime minister heads the executive branch of government and is considered the leader of the majority party in parliament. He or she also appoints and heads the Council of Ministers, which acts as an advisory board and is responsible for different facets of government, similar to the U.S. Cabinet. As in the United States, India has a judicial branch of government, which includes a federal-level supreme court. While there are many similarities between the structure of government in the United States and in India, the most striking similarity is that both are governed at the federal and state levels. India's federal government, however, plays a larger role in policy-making than the U.S. federal government.

STATES AND UNION TERRITORIES

India is divided into 28 states and seven Union Territories that are governed by local legislatures and a chief minister as well as a state governor appointed by the President of India to look after affairs of federal significance within the state. While India's states have their own elected governments, the Union Territories are directly controlled by India's federal government through a federally appointed governor. The exceptions are Delhi and Puduchery, which have their own legislatures and councils of ministers (albeit with limited powers).

THE PANCHAYATI RAJ SYSTEM

Another level of governance, known as the Panchayati Raj, is the most decentralized aspect of government in India. The idea is to allow for minor issues to be dealt with in a deliberative fashion relative to the local people, and it is helpful for maintaining participatory democracy in such a large and culturally diverse country. In this system, village-level governments, known as *gram panchayats,* deal with issues pertaining directly to the village, such as education, basic infrastructure (road repair and sanitation systems), village events, and agricultural development. Each *panchayat* is administered by a chairperson known as a *sarpanch,* who heads biannual sessions similar to town-hall meetings with his or her constituents. Groups of *gram panchayats* in a given area form blocks known as *panchayati samitis* that deal with some aspects of agriculture as well as education, waterworks, and health care, among other issues. In turn, groups of blocks convene at the district level, or *zilla parishads,* which deal with similar issues as the *grams* and *samitis* along with entrepreneurship and cottage industry programs as well as protecting the rights of and creating opportunities for tribal and low-caste people.

The Economy

Prior to economic liberalization in 1991, India's economy grew at a snail's pace due to strict protectionism and the highly bureaucratic License Raj system. The economy has grown significantly since liberalization and boasts the second-highest growth rate of the world's major economies. As India has a large rural population, its open-market economy is largely driven by agriculture, which employs more than half of the country's labor force of 467 million. There are also strong industrial and service industries, and the latter accounts for more than half of economic output.

Much of the services industry in India is based around IT and technology, and multinational corporations have cashed in on India's large population of educated English speakers, outsourcing back-office work to urban hubs such as Bengaluru and Gurgaon. Although India's economy slowed down slightly after the 2008 global financial crisis, it did not suffer as noticeably as many other countries, partly because its economy is largely fueled by domestic demand and also because it has consistently maintained more conservative banking policies than many countries in the West. However, the financial crisis, coupled with incentives for U.S. companies to reduce outsourcing instated by the Obama administration, spurred many multinationals to close down their Indian operations. India's federal deficit is currently around 6.8 percent and is projected to reach 10.3 percent, although the government has developed a fiscal stimulus plan that includes increasing privatization of state-owned entities in

© MARIYA ZHELEVA

Small shops are more common in India than large supermarkets.

BUSINESS PROCESS OUTSOURCING (BPO)

BPO refers to the outsourcing of business operations to remote locations or offices, and it is usually done to save money. India is at the heart of this industry, and the majority of the world's offshore outsourcing operations are here. India offers multinational companies an inexpensive workforce that is proficient in both technology and the English language. In recent years, however, companies have begun to shift their operations away from India. Many American companies have chosen to move offshore operations to Latin American countries, to take advantage of the Spanish language skills available there, as well as to the Philippines. Like India, the Philippines has a large English-speaking population. Some employers consider the Filipino accent and work ethic closer to that of the United States, which they feel makes it more suitable than India for call-center work. However, India's large number of highly educated English-speaking techies continues to draw in companies from around the world.

order to reduce the deficit. Despite the reforms of the last few decades and the extensive attention the government pays to stimulating the economy, India still has a long way to go.

THE DIVIDE BETWEEN RICH AND POOR

One of the first things you are likely to notice once you move to India is that the rich are very rich and the poor are very poor. If you take a drive down the main thoroughfares in any of India's big cities, you will come across quite a

Rural laborers help build India's cities.

DEALING WITH POVERTY

No matter how hard you try, you will encounter a lot of poverty during your stay in India. You will be approached by beggars, some of whom will be only toddlers, barely old enough to speak but still able to extend a hand in search of alms. Others may be limbless or too deformed to walk. While India definitely has many people in need, a large proportion of beggars are actually working for criminal networks, and sadly, some of the disfigured people you see have actually been disfigured by the gangs that enslave them in order to increase their earnings. Oftentimes women carry babies who are not their own and have been sold into begging by needy families. By giving them money, you may be contributing to their exploitation.

Whether or not you give is entirely up to you, and remember that if you do give to one person, you may attract a flock of others looking for money. As a rule of thumb, I never give to children or to the able-bodied, although an elderly woman (who may have been kicked out of her home once she became a widow) may get my sympathies. Some people suggest giving money to charitable organizations, although you should verify an organization's reputation before donating, as many of them are corrupt. Alternatively, carry some fruit or nuts with you and pass these out when people ask. If they refuse, they are probably only interested in collecting money.

few chauffeur-driven Mercedes (which, due to heavy import duties, cost nearly double what they do in the West). Their passengers will likely be clad head-to-toe in Italian designer wear and will be on their way to a chic restaurant where they will enjoy highly taxed French wine and Japanese cuisine before getting back in their cars to return to their palatial homes staffed by more servants than they know what to do with and filled with fine art brought home from overseas shopping sprees. On the side of the road you will likely encounter construction, because in India the strong demand for new offices, homes, and businesses means that there's always something being built. The builders are likely to be a mix of men and women, day laborers who have come from the countryside in search of jobs. The women will be dressed in colorful saris, far too fancy for doing construction work, but remember, they may only own two or three sets of clothing, and jeans and T-shirts will certainly not be part of their traditional wardrobe. While the men dig holes and nail boards together, the women carry large stacks of bricks on their heads, their necks strong from a lifetime of transporting water in their natal villages. Off to the side, their small children will play joyfully atop bags of cement and piles of dirt, oblivious to the germs they are being exposed to, while their parents build shopping malls and luxury apartments that they will never be allowed to set foot in.

Although the middle class has grown substantially since the 1990s, they do not make up the majority of the population. It's estimated that around 25 percent of the population in India lives below the poverty line. There have been many government-led initiatives to reduce poverty, including the National Rural Employment Guarantee Act, which ensures at least 100 days of rural employment per year to every adult in the country. The scheme has met with controversy, however, and local *panchayats* have been accused of embezzling funds. India still has far to go in narrowing the gap between rich and poor, and the fact that the country's workforce is so inexpensive actually helps fuel the economy. So although salaries are higher than what they used to be, many doubt that a more equal distribution of wealth in India would be a good thing for the country's economy.

PEOPLE AND CULTURE

Trying to define Indian culture as one size fits all is impossible. India is arguably the most diverse country in the world, and everything from language to religious practices changes every few miles. Even within the same city, the many variables of caste, social class, religion, and traditional profession mean that it's difficult to find two Indians from different families who follow the exact same cultural practices. While there is a growing sense of what it means to be Indian and an accompanying sense of national pride, many people identify with their families, upbringings, and regions first before claiming any national identity. Moreover, wherever you are in the world, culture and identity are not fixed concepts, and you can spend a lifetime trying to figure out what it means to be Indian without ever even scratching the surface.

Before moving to India, try to find out as much as you can about the local culture where you are moving. If you are moving to Mumbai or Pune, read up on Marathi customs; if Chennai is your next home, you will want to know more about the Tamil people. While Indian cultural rules and traditions can be bewilderingly complex, just try your hardest to learn what you can and don't worry if you commit a few faux pas. Moreover, while it's essential that you read up on local customs, try not to have too many expectations, as culture is better understood through experience than through reading alone.

Ethnicity and Class

ETHNIC GROUPS

The majority of Indians fall into two major ethnic groups: the Indo-Aryans in the north and the Dravidians in the south. These two classifications are based on the origins of the languages they speak. The Indo-Aryan groups traditionally speak languages from the Indo-European linguistic family such as Hindi and Bengali. These languages, along with languages such as English and Spanish, originated in what's known as the Indo-European protolanguage. Dravidian languages, such as Tamil and Malayalam, seem to be unrelated, and some scholars link them to the disputed Altaic language, from which languages such as Korean and Japanese are thought to have emerged.

While most Indian cultures fall under either the Indo-Aryan or Dravidian umbrella, there's also a sizable number of people whose features, languages, and customs are more closely related to East Asia. This includes the large Tibetan and Nepalese populations as well as the people indigenous to India's culturally distinct Northeast. People from this region speak languages that fall into the Austro-Asiatic linguistic grouping that is believed to be related to languages such as Vietnamese and Khmer. Many of the indigenous ethnic groups from Northeast regions and tribal people from pockets across India are considered "scheduled castes" or "scheduled tribes" by the Indian government, and there are special quotas in areas like civil service positions and university admissions for these *adivasi* people, an Indian version of affirmative action.

CLASS AND CASTE

India is a very class-conscious country, and you will notice huge disparity between the educated, often moneyed upper crust and the disadvantaged poor. While education and social background have become the key indicators of social status in urban environments, the caste system still plays a huge role in most of the country. Traditionally, the highest caste is the Brahmins, the priests, who are responsible for rituals and temple maintenance. Many follow strictly vegetarian diets and are considered the purest of the lot. Next in line are the Kshatriyas, the warriors and rulers, or military class. Then there are the Vaishyas, traditional merchants and artisans. At the bottom of the rank you have Shudras, who traditionally worked as laborers. Dalits, once known as untouchables, are considered so low that they are without a caste and are stuck with jobs such as collecting garbage or cleaning latrines. Many temples forbid these people, as well as foreigners and dogs, from entering.

The caste system is not as straightforward as it's often made out to be, and people often use the word *caste* to refer to their family's subcaste, which is based on their geographical origins and historic occupations. For example, if you ask someone his caste, he may say he is a Rajpoot, which doesn't immediately register as one of the major castes. Rajpoots are traditionally the ruling and warrior caste of the state of Rajasthan and are Kshatriyas. Similarly, Kashmiri Pundits are Hindus from Kashmir and are all Brahmins, although many of them are nonvegetarians. When you get out into rural areas, people will be more likely to identify with the major caste they belong to and follow the practices associated with their group. In the educated urban environment, this is much less straightforward, and you may find that caste comes up only when it comes to decisions about marriage.

Customs and Etiquette

Indians are generally warm people, and you will probably receive lots of invitations to visit people's homes and meet their families and friends. This warmth, coupled with genuine curiosity, can sometimes lead to confusion for Western visitors. Some Indian people, especially those who haven't interacted with many foreigners, can come across as very inquisitive, and questions about age, marital status, and income can be a bit shocking for people who are used to more discretion in conversation. These factors can shake up your sense of privacy at first, but if you remember to be patient, you will be able to use these cultural differences to understand and develop bonds with the residents of your host country.

THE HONORED GUEST

If you find yourself as the guest in an Indian home, which you likely will quite soon after moving here, be prepared for lavish hospitality beyond anything you've likely experienced back home. In India, guests are considered a blessing and are treated like gods. This means you will be offered anything you want. I was once at the home of a young woman who was doing some tailoring

BODY LANGUAGE

One of the first things that visitors to India notice is the famous head wobble, which is best described as a nod that goes side-to-side rather then forward and backward. This gesture is more pronounced in Southern India than in the north, and it generally can be interpreted as "I understand." Variations of this include a side tilt of the head, which usually affirms "yes" or "OK."

Another common gesture in the north is the wrist twist, where someone extends his or her forearm up and out before quickly flicking the wrist in a counterclockwise motion (if right-handed). This expresses questioning or bewilderment, and can be interpreted as "What is this?"

Finally, there's the pinky wave, which is a way to indicate that you're in need of a urinal without having to say as much.

work for me. I complimented her on the pendant she was wearing, a pretty but inexpensive image of a Shirdi Sai Baba, a popular Indian saint. Within seconds, my friend had removed it from her neck and placed it on mine, insisting, despite my protests, that I keep it. While this may not have been the case had she been wearing diamonds, it was certainly a striking example of the unabashed and selfless generosity that one finds in India.

You won't be expected to bring gifts, although a box of Indian sweets is always appreciated. If you are going to an upscale dinner party, a bottle of wine makes a good offering, but first make sure your hosts are drinkers. When you enter an Indian home, be sure to check whether you should take off your shoes, as this is the custom in the majority of homes. You may be offered a pair of flip-flops (referred to as slippers or floaters) to wear inside.

The first thing your host will do is offer you something to drink. In middle- and upper-class homes, water will be bottled or filtered, and some might find it offensive if you inquire about the cleanliness of your libation. When in doubt, ask for a cup of tea—the water used will be boiled to a safe temperature. If your host offers something that you really don't want, be it tea, coffee, or food, the most polite way of refusing is to say, "I already had some food/tea before coming," rather than directly saying no.

DINING ETIQUETTE

Dining customs and eating habits vary from state to state, so try to find out a bit about the local dining habits before you go. In the Punjab, for example, food is often eaten with flat bread known as roti, whereas Southern Indian cuisine is more often served with rice. Some people serve both rice and roti;

normally the roti is eaten first. In many households, rice is eaten with the hand, and this takes some time for the uninitiated to master. If you fear that you might get more rice down your shirt than in your mouth, you can always ask for a spoon. If you are eating with your hands, remember to use only the right hand to bring food to your mouth (even if you are left-handed). The left hand is associated with toilet duties and should not be used at meals or for handing things to people.

Many Westerners find Indian food a bit too spicy for their liking. Your Indian hosts may be aware of this and make their meals extra bland just for you. If you do find your food too fiery, resist the urge to reach for the water, as it will just make matters worse. Instead, try sucking on a bit of plain bread or rice, or cool your tongue with a spoonful of curd or yogurt, often served with Indian meals. No matter how much you've eaten, your hosts will keep filling your plate until they are sure you are full. It's polite to finish what you've been offered, but if you feel like you can't eat another bite, let your hosts know. They will likely insist that you have just a little more, but this is just their way of making sure you are not secretly still hungry. You may have to politely refuse a few times in order to get your point across.

Indians usually wash their hands after meals, especially if they have eaten without cutlery. Many also rinse out their mouths, even at restaurants. While this may be quite off-putting at first, especially if you have to use a sink after someone else, bear in mind that the practice is really no different than brushing your teeth after a meal. You may also notice that belching after a meal is common outside the upper-middle and upper classes, although burping is not an expression of having eaten a good meal the way it is in some other cultures. Many Indian people, especially women, do find belching offensive, so avoid picking up this habit.

CLOTHING
Women
The Indian dress sense is generally much more conservative than in the West, especially for women, and it generally takes foreigners a bit of time to strike the right balance. Women new to India often make the mistake of either wearing only traditionally Indian clothes, often in styles and patterns not suitable for their age group, or of dressing for summer in the same way they would back in the West, which can be too revealing for India. However, things are changing. Just a decade ago it was uncommon to see women in blue jeans. These days, Levi's showrooms dot every market, and most fashionable women own

THE INDIAN WEDDING

If you live in India for any significant amount of time, you are likely to be invited to an Indian wedding, especially if you work with Indians or have many Indian friends. In fact, you may even receive invitations to the weddings or receptions of your colleagues' relatives – many families take a "the more the merrier" attitude toward preparing their invitation list.

The season for Hindu weddings starts just after Diwali, the last major holiday of the Indian festival season. Wedding dates are usually determined by an astrologer, who picks the most auspicious day for the ceremony based on the couple's horoscopes. The most auspicious dates tend to fall during the season's winter months. Every year there are certain auspicious dates when many weddings take place.

© MARIYA ZHELEVA

wedding adornment

If you are invited to an Indian wedding, it's appropriate for women to wear a sari and men to wear a suit and tie or a traditional *sherwani* (long jacket). Female guests also paint their hands with intricate henna designs to celebrate the occasion. Gifts are appreciated, and while many guests give money, you are welcome to pick out a gift of your choice. Wedding registries are beginning to catch on in India, although this custom is not as common as in the West.

Most Indian weddings are lavish affairs that can last for many days and involve dozens of small rituals.

The focus for many guests is more on dressing up in fineries, sampling foods from lavish buffets, and socializing. You may notice that very few guests stop to actually observe the wedding ceremony, instead opting to carry on with general revelry. Many families with children of marriageable age also use weddings as an occasion to meet other families and engage in a little bit of matchmaking. If you are foreign and not of Indian descent, you're probably more likely to find people approaching you to discuss business or socialize rather than to find out about your availability or that of your adult children.

at least a few pairs. When I first came to India in 2005 I would have been very uncomfortable wearing a medium-length skirt outside my hotel. These days, I don a sleeveless sundress that barely reaches my knees to go shopping at my local market, and I still look more modest than many of the other women around. Of course, this would be different if I were living in a village, where traditional dress is encouraged, so if you have a posting in a smaller place or if you will be working with the local population, go the traditional route. In cities such as Mumbai and Bengaluru, tank tops are acceptable casual wear for women. In Delhi and the north, you can wear sleeveless tops, although it's better that they not be too form-fitting. Have a look at what other women in your age group are wearing for a better idea. Outside the big cities, cover your legs and avoid sleeveless tops with plunging necklines.

India's traditional dress varies significantly depending on where in the country you are, although one item of clothing that is worn almost everywhere in India is the timeless sari. Saris are long pieces of cloth, usually around six yards, that women wear with a petticoat and a small blouse. Saris are draped differently in different regions, and getting them on correctly is no easy task, so it's best to get the aid of another woman to tie yours. Saris range from simple casual styles to heavily embellished and expensive designs, the latter of which are reserved for weddings and social events.

Punjabi suits (*salwar kameez*) are popular across the country, especially in the Punjab region from which they originated. These three-piece suits are made up of a tunic, often called a *kurta,* which is worn over baggy drawstring trousers known as a *salwar.* The finishing touch is a long scarf, called a *dupatta,* which is meant to cover a woman's chest but is often viewed as more of

© WONG CHEE YEN /DREAMSTIME.COM

Indian couple at seaside

an accessory to tie the whole look together. The *churidar kameez* is a variation of this look; the *salwar* is traded for the *churidar,* which, unlike the *salwar,* is almost as tight as a pair of leggings.

Men

Men in India sometimes wear the traditional *kurta pajama,* a tunic paired with straight loose-fitting trousers, usually in white cotton, although this style is usually associated with politicians and elderly men. The *dhoti,* a lower-body wrap for men, is also occasionally worn, although rarely in big cities. In the south, many men wear the sarong-like *lungi,* a tubular lower-body garment that can be sported either long and loose or tucked between the legs. Traditional Indian wear is much less commonly worn by men than by women, and even at weddings you will find the majority of men in a Western suit and tie while almost all the female guests are wearing saris.

Men will find that casual wear is less accepted in India than in the United States, and while jeans are fine outside the office, shorts are only worn when playing sports or hanging out in upscale shopping areas where anything goes. Even so, the casual sportswear look is not very common for men over age 35, so if you are middle aged or older, you may feel more comfortable in slacks and a collared shirt. Do not wear shorts or sleeveless tops to places of worship. Men should not, under any circumstances, walk around shirtless in Northern India, although in Southern India baring your chest is more acceptable (and even required for entrance to some temples).

Family Life

The family is the core unit of Indian society, and joint households, often consisting of generations of siblings, cousins, parents, and children, are not uncommon. Many Indian family businesses operate in such a tight-knit way that it becomes almost impossible to separate relatives, and many people wouldn't feel comfortable any other way. In many ways, the Indian family acts as a sort of social safety net, especially for the elderly. In recent years, however, especially in urban India, there has been a marked shift away from extended family living, and nuclear family homes are increasingly becoming the norm. Nevertheless, adult children generally live with their parents until marriage, and oftentimes a woman will move into her husband's parents' home after marrying. While Indian marriages are traditionally arranged, "love marriages" are becoming more and more commonplace, especially in big cities.

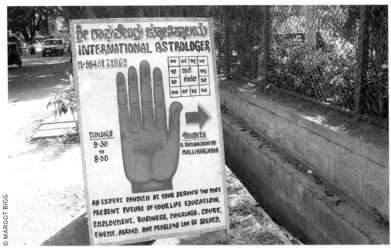

© MARGOT BIGG

Indian astrology, or *Jyotish*, plays an important role in making life decisions.

The adage that blood runs thicker than water rings very true in India. Parents are to be treated like gods and children as sacred. Siblinghood is also very important, and cousins, however distant, are referred to as "cousin-brothers" and "cousin-sisters." There's even a Northern Indian holiday, Raksha Bandhan, that celebrates the bond between brothers and sisters.

Polite forms of address in India also allude to familial ties. Children and young adults address people of their parents' age and older as "auntie" and "uncle" or the equivalent in the local language. A young boy might be called *beta* (son) and a girl *beti*. If you live in a Hindi-speaking area, one of the first things you learn will likely be the word *bhaiya* (brother), which can be used to address everyone from shopkeepers to taxi drivers. The female equivalent of this word is *didi,* which literally means elder sister but can be safely used for any female who is not significantly older than you.

Gender Roles

Most Indian cultures are patriarchal, and if you are a parent, you will likely notice right away that little boys are often given preferential treatment over little girls. Many Indians consider their sons a gift from god, as sons are expected to carry on the family line in future generations. A daughter, on the other hand, is expected to leave the family someday and shift her allegiances to the family of the man she marries. Little girls are also expected to be quieter and shier than their brothers. Boys are expected to be outgoing and fearless. One expat mother recounted a time when her six-year-old son hid behind her when introduced to a group of Indian adults. When she explained that he was shy, her interlocutors looked confused. "But he's a boy; how can he by shy?" one of them asked. These gender roles extend into adulthood, where it sometimes translates to more assertive men and more passive or coy women. However, these behavioral expectations are changing quickly, and they are often reserved only for public interactions. If you visit an Indian home, you will soon realize that it's the senior women in the household who call the shots.

THE ROLE OF WOMEN

There are many expectations of the Indian woman of today: mother, sister, wife, provider. India's women have traditionally worked outside of the home, and India had a female prime minister when most people in the West would have balked at having anyone but a man head their country. The stereotype that most women in India are oppressed by their husbands is dramatically far from reality. While it must be said that women in certain social groups are marginalized by the men in their lives, it's important to remember that Indian culture honors women in a way that few other cultures do. In Hinduism, the very energy that drives the world is considered female; every god has a female consort; and goddesses are the beloved bestowers of fortune and happiness. Many customs that may look oppressive to outsiders, such as allowing sons more freedoms than daughters, are actually meant to protect women and are thus manifestations of Indians' inherent respect for women. Moreover, it's important to remember that in cultures that have dealt with centuries of invasions, certain measures have been developed to keep women, and by extension children, safe from the dangers of the world.

With that said, it should be pointed out that there is still a strong preference for sons among many people, and that female feticide and infanticide remain a big problem. The parents of brides are expected

ladies only

© MARGOT BIGG

to provide steep dowries and pay for lavish weddings for their daughters, and many simply can't bear the burden. Moreover, Hindu sons are traditionally expected to light the funeral pyres of their fathers and are thus considered necessary for the ritual transition between life and death. Tests to determine sex prenatally are actually illegal in India, as many women will opt for late-term abortions rather than go through the shame of having a daughter. Others wait until their daughter is born and then abandon or kill her. Sadly, this is not just a rural phenomenon, and many urban and educated women follow a sons-only policy, despite the emotional devastation they experience by doing so. Remember that this is a very sensitive topic in India, and is best left out of conversation.

MALE-FEMALE INTERACTION

Once upon a time, men and women in India had very little social interaction outside of their family circle. Things have changed dramatically over the years, and these days, male-female platonic friendships are completely normal, especially among the upper classes. However, certain subjects, notably sexuality, remain taboo, so it's best not to ask your opposite-gender Indian friends for intimate dating advice or to discuss your personal life at length. While the middle and upper classes have taken to traditionally Western forms of greeting, such as quick hugs or pecks on the cheek, oftentimes people hug and kiss only with their own gender. When in doubt, a wave or a handshake is fine. Contrary to what you may hear from outdated sources on Indian business etiquette, urban men and women do shake hands in business situations, and Indians in general love shaking hands, although not with the bone-crunching strength favored by many Western men, so go gently. You may notice that some people may shake hands with a pen or a cell phone in their hand, and this should not be interpreted as a lack of respect; it's certainly not intended to be.

GAYS AND LESBIANS

As is the case in most conservative countries, homosexuality is generally heavily frowned upon, and many gays and lesbians find themselves unable to be open about their sexuality. Until recently, same-sex relationships were illegal under Section 377 of the Indian Penal Code, which dated back to British rule. Parts of the law that made homosexual relations between consenting adults illegal were declared unconstitutional in July 2009 by the Delhi High Court, so homosexuality is no longer a crime.

Delhi and Mumbai also have Gay Pride Day rallies every year, although this is still a new concept in India—the first Gay Pride Day event in the capital

Delhi's first Gay Pride rally in 2008

© MARGOT BIGG

wasn't held until 2008. The major cities in India have social and legal support networks for gays, lesbians, and transgendered people. Many of these are listed at www.indiandost.com/gay_group.php. There are also a few magazines aimed at gays and lesbians in India, including *Bombay Dost* and *Jiah*.

HIJRAS

South Asia's "third gender," transgendered *hijras* play an important role in Indian culture. Most *hijras* are born physically male, although some have hermaphroditic characteristics. Many superstitious Indians fear them, for they are said to have powers to bring good luck or cause misfortune. *Hijras* often experience extreme discrimination in India and have limited opportunities for income. They traditionally live in clans and earn their income through begging, dancing at weddings, blessing newborn babies, and, in some cases, through prostitution. You may be approached for a donation by a begging *hijra,* and some may use tactics to embarrass you—usually by exposing their genitalia or uttering obscenities—if you don't pay up, especially if you are male. If you give birth to a child in India, expect a visit from a group of *hijras,* who have their ways of finding out when a baby has been born. This naturally makes some new mothers uneasy, especially if the *hijras* visit while she is home alone. While the choice to give money is entirely up to you, remember to be sensitive to the fact that the social climate in India is such that *hijras* have very few options to earn an income. Moreover, it never hurts to have someone's blessings.

Religion

Although India is legally a secular country, religion is an integral and inseparable part of most people's daily lives and a key element of people's identities. Although the vast majority of Indians—around 80 percent—identify as Hindu, there are plenty of other religious groups in the country. While religion-related conflicts do flare up from time to time, most Indians are highly tolerant of the religious beliefs of others, which is key to India's harmony.

HINDUISM

Some would argue that Hinduism, or Sanatana Dharma, as it is sometimes called, is not a religion so much as a way of life, for the Hindu belief system permeates every aspect of a devout Hindu's life. For many Hindus, god is everywhere, so separating the sacred from the profane is simply not logical. Hinduism is not an organized religion in the way of, say, Roman Catholicism. There's no central governing body, elevated religious leader, or single religious text; Hinduism encompasses a number of different paths and traditions that all trace their origins to the Vedic traditions.

Although Hindus worship thousands of different gods, most view the deities as different aspects of the same higher power, known as Bhagwan, or God. The best known deities in Hinduism are the trinity of Brahma (the creator), Vishnu (the preserver), and Shiva (the destroyer). These gods often manifest in other forms; for example, Vishnu is often worshipped in the form of Krishna,

© MARGOT BIGG

Hindus often maintain small shrines at their workplaces.

a playful prince and one of the most popular characters in Indian religious texts. Another beloved deity is Ganesha, the roly-poly elephant-headed son of Shiva and his consort, Parvati; Ganesha is considered the remover of obstacles. There are also many goddesses in the Hindu pantheon, some of whom are considered consorts of certain gods. Among the best known are Lakshmi, the goddess of wealth, and Saraswati, the goddess of learning and music.

Like most adherents of major religions, Hindus believe that the soul is eternal. Reincarnation is key to Hinduism, and most believe that people are born again and again until finally reaching the state of *moksha* (liberation) from the cycle of rebirth and its inherent suffering. The laws of karma are also observed in Hinduism, although the understanding of karma is not quite the same as the "do unto others" idea found in Judeo-Christian cultures. Instead, the term is sometimes used to refer to fate or actions. Hindus believe that karma stays with the soul throughout incarnations, so you may not reap the rewards or consequences of your actions until your next lifetime.

ISLAM

Islam is the second-largest faith in India, and as of the 2001 census, 13.4 percent of the Indian population consider themselves Muslims. Islam first came to India's Malabar Coast in Kerala with Arab traders in the 7th century, although it really began to penetrate the subcontinent at the end of 12th century through the Delhi Sultanate. Much of the spread of Islam in India happened through the orders of mystic Sufis, notable the Chishti Order. One of

Muslim men praying

the world's best known forms of devotional music, Qawwali, also emerged in the region, and many other forms of Indian art have Islamic roots. Although most Indian Muslims are Sunni, the country is also home to one of the largest populations of Shia Muslims in the world. Many of the traditions followed by India's Muslim population are unique to the region, and South Asian Muslims have their own version of a caste system.

CHRISTIANITY

Christians make up 2.3 percent of India's population, making Christianity the third-largest religion in India. Historians believe that Christianity first came to the subcontinent as early as 52 B.C. when Thomas, one of the original apostles, began proselytizing in what is now Kerala. However, Christianity in India really began to spread through the colonists, first the Portuguese in the coastal areas and later the French and British. The Northeast regions of India, where animism and other indigenous practices used to dominate, also became primarily Christian during the 19th and 20th centuries. Many Indian Christians are easily identified by their Portuguese or English names, although these days it is common to find Indian Christians with Indian-sounding first names and Biblical last names; Mathew and James are both common examples of Christian Indian family names.

SIKHISM

India's fourth-largest religion, Sikhism, was founded in Punjab in the 15th century by Guru Nanak Dev, the first in a lineage of 10 gurus, or teachers, of the philosophy. Most Sikh people in India live in the Punjab region or in Delhi. Sikhs are monotheists, and their term for God is Waheguru. The Sikh holy scripture, a collection of hymns and meditations on God known as the Guru Granth Sahib, is considered to be the final teacher in the lineage. Sikh temples are known as *gurdwaras* and are free from idols, as Sikh practice centers around meditation rather than worship. *Gurdwaras* also have community kitchens, known as *langars,* that serve vegetarian food to anyone who wants to join in. In a *langar,* men, women, and people of every background eat together communally, as the Sikh faith maintains that all people are equal regardless of gender or social background. Foreigners are always welcome to come to pay their respects at *gurdwaras,* which is not the case at some of India's many Hindu temples. Men and women alike should remember to cover their heads before entering a *gurdwara*'s premises. Many Sikh men keep their hair unshorn and tied in a turban, one of the five Sikh articles of faith introduced by Gobind Singh, the last guru.

BUDDHISM

Although Buddhism is often associated with Southeast Asia, the religion emerged in Magadha in the state now known as Bihar. The founder of Buddhism, Siddhartha Gautama, was born in what is now Nepal and spent the first three decades of his life as a prince. According to legend, his protective father sheltered the young Buddha from seeing suffering, aging, and sickness until one day when the prince saw an old man and learned that aging and death were the ultimate fate of all people. Soon after, he gave up his worldly lifestyle and turned to asceticism, traveling around the area and preaching his path to enlightenment. While Buddhism did have a significant impact in India during Siddhartha's life, it was during the reign of Ashoka that the beliefs really began to spread across the subcontinent. Buddhism later declined in India, although a small revival has been happening during the past century, and many Dalits, the "untouchables" of the Hindu caste system, have turned to Buddhism to escape the bonds of their social status. Many of India's Buddhists are Tibetans who have migrated to escape persecution by the Chinese. The town of Dharamsala, in the Himalayan state of Himachal Pradesh, is home to the Tibetan Government in Exile and the 14th Dalai Lama.

JAINISM

Jainism emerged a very long time ago, but nobody really knows when. The 23rd Tirthankar (realized sage), Parshva, lived in the 9th century B.C., but it is uncertain when the previous Tirthankars lived. Many Indians consider Jainism a branch of Hinduism, but it has many unique elements that make it distinct from the Vedic traditions. Like Hindus and Buddhists, Jains believe in karma and reincarnation. They are expected to maintain the "three gems" of Jainism—right view, right conduct, and right knowledge—in order to be liberated from the cycle of mortality. Jains have strict beliefs around nonviolence and are against cruelty to any living being, and thus are expected to be vegetarian. Many also abstain from eating root vegetables due to the bacteria and small insects that their uprooting can harm, and some even avoid eating at night, when bacteria is most active. Orthodox Jains of the Svetambara sect are often seen wearing masks over their mouths; this is to prevent them from accidentally inhaling insects.

ZOROASTRIANISM

Founded in Persia in the 5th century by the prophet Zarathustra, Zoroastrianism is one of the oldest religions in the world and was the majority religion in Iran prior to Islam. The followers of this faith in India are called Parsis.

Parsis believe that the world was created by Ahura Mazda and that all worship directly ends up with him. Worship usually takes place in the presence of fire, as they believe that fire, along with water, is key to ritual purification. The most widely known Parsi practice in India relates to their disposal of the dead: Instead of cremating or burying corpses, Parsis place the bodies on special structures known as Towers of Silence, where they are devoured by vultures.

Most of India's Parsis live in Mumbai and Gujarat, and many belong to successful business families. There are only about 85,000 Parsis left, however, and some worry that the culture will soon become extinct. While Parsis are expected to marry other Parsis, many don't, and only children born of two Parsi parents are allowed to enter the faith. Some of India's highest-profile industrialists, including the Tatas and the Godrejs, are Parsis, as was Freddie Mercury of the rock band Queen.

The Arts

MUSIC

Dating back to the Vedic era, Indian classical music can be divided into two major schools: Hindustani classical music in the north and Carnatic music in the south. The former is based on rhythmic patterns or talas, which are maintained by percussion instruments, most notably the tabla, and can be highly instrumental. Carnatic music is written to be sung, and instrumentalists play it in a style similar to the human voice. While classical music is still highly revered in India, the most beloved genre is the Hindi music popularized in films. Often called *filmi,* Hindi pop transcends generations, and you might even catch an elderly woman bobbing her head to the favorite tunes of her grandchildren. Contemporary pop music is not the preserve of the Hindi-speaking

© MARGOT BIGG

India has a rich classical music tradition.

regions; regional languages also have their own music scenes, such as the world-famous bhangra pop from Punjab, which employs traditional folk patterns with modern lyrics and production technology.

Contemporary music styles from the West are also popular in India, and India's huge youth population has led VH1, MTV, and *Rolling Stone* magazine to set up shop here. Electronic music has a steady following, and clubs across the country host regular nights devoted to strictly electronic sounds. Rock and heavy metal are both huge with the under-30 set, and there are plenty of Indian rock bands that have gone on to tour worldwide, such as Advaita and Indian Ocean. You will definitely notice that many Indians are very fond of Bon Jovi and Bryan Adams, and both get plenty of airtime. And if you are ever at a party and put John Denver's "Country Roads" on the stereo, you are sure to get a roomful of people crooning about West Virginia within seconds.

DANCE AND THEATER

Dance is quite popular in India, and if you live in a major city, you'll have no problem finding performances to attend. Folk dance is common in touristy areas, although the most respected dancers in India are those who work in the classical traditions. Many of India's best known classical dances originated in temples or at one of the many royal courts. Many of the dances incorporate strong elements of theater, using movement to tell stories from Indian mythology. There are currently eight forms of dance recognized as classical dance in India, the most popular of which are the Tamil Bharatnatyam, Oddisi from Orissa, Northern Indian Kathak, and Kerala's beloved Khatakali, which is a big hit with tourists for its intricate costumes and choreographed eye gestures.

India also has a strong tradition of drama and theater, much of it interwoven with dance and music. Folk theater is also popular, and NGOs across the country are increasingly using this medium to spread messages about rural issues such as health and sanitation to mostly illiterate populations.

VISUAL ARTS

Painting in India dates back to prehistoric times, and traces of India's earliest artisans remain on the cave walls of tourist sites in Ajanta and Ellora. As in Europe, much of the painting of the last few thousand years has religious themes, including the paintings of different forms of the goddess on display at Mysore Palace. The Mughals brought with them a number of art traditions from Persia that thrive to this day, such as miniature painting.

The subcontinent also has a very old tradition of pottery and sculpture, to the extent that some of India's ancient subcultures are identified by archaeologists based on the type and color of pottery that they produced. Terra-cotta pottery is still used in many villages, especially for water, as it keeps its contents cool. Sculpture, especially religious sculptures, also play an integral role in India's visual arts history, and bronze and stonework dating back as far as the Indus Valley Civilization have been uncovered. These days, collecting art is all the rage with India's well-heeled elite, and there are plenty of world-class art galleries in India's cosmopolitan cities.

FILM

India produces more films than any other country, and going to the movies is one of the favorite national pastimes. The Hindi film industry is based in the city of Mumbai and is referred to as Bollywood, a portmanteau of *Bombay* (Mumbai's former name) and *Hollywood*. The storylines of these films are usually pretty predictable, as many plots are based on either stories from Indian mythology or are near copies of some Hollywood box-office hits with an Indian twist.

Seeing a Bollywood film is an essential part of the Indian experience, and even if you don't understand Hindi, the intensive song-and-dance sequences and oftentimes slapstick action scenes are sure to keep you entertained. If you plan to see a Hindi movie in a theater, make sure to set aside at least three hours for the experience. Bollywood films are usually quite a bit longer than

© MARGOT BIGG

shopping for regional-language films in South India

their Hollywood equivalent, and screenings of all films in India, Bollywood or otherwise, generally include a 10-minute intermission.

While Bombay is the undisputed capital of India's film industry, it's certainly not the only place where movies are being made. Regional cinema is big business across India, and regional-language films are produced in most major cities, including Chennai, where the Tamil-language film industry, known as Kollywood, has been going strong for nearly a century.

LITERATURE

India has a huge literary tradition, both in regional languages and in English. Some of the oldest examples of Indian literature date back to Vedic times and were composed in the ancient Sanskrit language, which is still used today for rituals and devotional music. Great Sanskrit epics include the Ramayana and the Mahabharata, written in a form of the language known as Epic Sanskrit. Bengal also has a strong literary tradition, and some of India's most celebrated writers, including Nobel laureate Rabindranath Tagore, composed some of their works in Bengali. The market for English-language books in India is huge, and English-language publishers, such as HarperCollins and Penguin, have operations here. English-language Indian books represent a large part of the what academics call postcolonial literature, and they generally employ a version of the language similar to the spoken English used in the country, integrating Indian words and concepts without necessarily explaining their meanings. Popular writers of the 20th century include the witty Khushwant Singh, whose novels, joke books, and works of nonfiction are loved by generations of readers. More recently, the works of authors such as Arundhati Roy and Vikram Seth have gained worldwide praise. Writers from the Indian diaspora, including Britain's Salman Rushdie and Trinidad's V. S. Naipaul, are also major contributors to India's English-language literary tradition.

Sports and Games

Although India's national sport is field hockey, cricket is by far the most loved game. If you're ever in a shopping mall and see a huge group of men crowded in front of an electronics store's display window, you can be sure that a cricket match is on. Similarly, if you drive through any village or suburban lane in the afternoon, you are likely to come across a group of children playing the sport, sometimes with makeshift bats. Although cricket is originally an English sport, its following in India seems to be the largest, with cricketers such as Sachin

Tendulkar elevated to the same superstar status as Bollywood's heroes. The sport's Indian Premier League (IPL) is a multibillion-rupee business.

Badminton, which is believed to have originated in India, is another popular pastime that is often played on summer evenings. Kite-flying is also big, but it can be very dangerous—some people take the activity to the competitive level, engaging in kite fighting using glass-coated strings that can result in some very deep cuts. One of the most popular games in India is *carrom*, which looks something like a cross between tiddlywinks and shuffleboard but is actually closer to billiards. *Carrom* is played with disks on a large lacquer board that has pockets in each of its four corners. The object of the game is to get the disks into the pockets by flicking a larger cue disk across the board. If you're playing for the first time, be careful not to put too much force into your flick—the cue disks used in the game are quite heavy, and you can end up bruising your fingernail.

PLANNING YOUR FACT-FINDING TRIP

It takes a visit to India to truly understand how different the country is from the rest of the world. A good way to ease yourself into Indian life is by visiting first and exploring the area you are considering moving to. If you aren't sure of where you want to live, a trip will help you find a city that best suits your interests and lifestyle.

While a bit of sightseeing and soaking in the local culture is definitely in order, it's best if the main focus of your trip is learning about what it will be like to live in India and setting things up for when you finally do make the move. A fact-finding trip to India entails not only learning about the local language and culture but also finding out what neighborhoods you want to live in, where you want to send your children to school, and how best to structure your daily life to get the most out of your experience.

© MARGOT BIGG

Preparing to Leave

DOCUMENTS AND IMMUNIZATIONS

You'll need a visa to enter India, and it must be obtained from the embassy or consulate in your country of residence or country of citizenship before your trip. In most cases, you'll need to apply for your visa through an outside agency that has been contracted by the Indian embassy in your country to manage consular services; in the United States it is Travisa Outsourcing, and in most other countries it is VFS. It's also best to get all the recommended vaccinations for India before traveling. Carry all prescription medicines (along with a list of their generic names) in your hand luggage. (For detailed information on immunizations, see the *Health* chapter).

WHEN TO GO

Winters are always the best time to visit India, as temperatures drop across the country. In Delhi and parts of Northern India, however, December and January can get quite chilly, and houses are generally not well insulated or centrally heated, so you may find it uncomfortably cold. Avoid Christmas and New Year's if you can, as this is the time of year when many Indian families living abroad come home for a visit, driving up the cost of flights significantly. India's peak season for tourism is October–November in most of the country, and while the temperatures at this time of year can be a bit hot, they are usually bearable. You also may want to check the monsoon timing for the region you are visiting, as heavy rains can cause flooding and slow travel. In general, the southwestern monsoon starts in June, moving up from the Indian Ocean and pushing rain across the subcontinent and to the east. The northeast monsoon runs during the postmonsoon season and sometimes carries on well into December and January, dumping rain along peninsular Southern India.

WHAT TO PACK

Men and women should bring modest clothes that cover the upper arms and the knees. Bearing cleavage is a no-no unless you are in a club or restaurant frequented by foreigners or India's elite. Lightweight, breathable fabrics in light colors are much more comfortable in hot climates. India's streets are dirty, so you may feel more comfortable wearing closed-toe shoes. However, sandals are the norm here most of the year, and they are much easier to take on and off when entering temples and homes. Whatever footwear you choose, make sure it's comfortable, as you may find yourself walking a lot. Good traction is also important, as streets can be uneven and perilously slippery when it rains.

First-time visitors to India are often shocked to see cows on city streets.

If you are meeting with potential or future employers, remember to bring an outfit or two of smart business attire.

A basic toiletry kit is good to have wherever you go, and while soaps and shampoos are easy to find in India, your favorite brand of razor may not, so bring a few spares. Women may want to bring a large supply of tampons, as the kind with applicators is very hard to come by in India. A bottle of DEET-based insect repellent is also a must; it can be picked up at most camping stores. If you are prone to sunburn, make sure to bring your own sunscreen. While it is available in India, higher strengths are often incredibly expensive and may contain harsh skin-bleaching chemicals. If you have space, slip a few granola bars into your luggage—they may come in handy if you are having trouble adjusting to the food. Many travelers to India bring huge first-aid kits with them. This is not necessary if you are only visiting cities, where most medications are widely available at a fraction of what they would cost elsewhere. Keep some antidiarrheal medicine and rehydration salts on hand, but if you get more than mildly ill, it's better to seek a pharmacist or doctor than to self-medicate.

If you have infants or children with you, bring an ample supply of snacks as well as diapers, formula, and baby wipes. Although these things are available in all of India's big cities, your children may feel more comfortable with foods and products they are used to.

Finally, don't forget a small flashlight. The electricity supply in India can be irregular, and while most mid-range and luxury hotels have backup generators, streetlights generally do not, and the roads can get quite dark once the sun sets.

BEFORE YOU GO

Try to do as much research as you can before you make your fact-finding trip. Ask yourself the following questions well before you head out so that you can arrive in India both prepared and knowledgeable.

- **Where will I live?** Research the cost of living in different areas and, if you have a job secured, the distance between your workplace and the places you want to live. Before you leave, set up appointments with property dealers or relocation companies, even if you don't want to sign a lease during your fact-finding trip. They will be able to show you what kinds of properties are available in your areas of choice.

- **Where will my children go to school?** If you have children, you'll need to spend time on your fact-finding trip visiting schools. Get in touch with schools as far in advance as possible, as some may have waiting lists or may not accept students at certain times of the year (especially if you are coming in the middle of the year). Set up appointments to visit the school, and if possible, try to schedule them during school hours so you can see the school in action.

- **How will I get around?** Before you leave, read up on the transportation options available in your area. If your company will provide you with a car as part of your package, you needn't worry as much, but you still may find that one car is not enough for your whole family, so you'll want a backup. Try to spend some of your fact-finding trip using local transportation, even if you don't plan to make a habit of it. This will greatly help you get familiar with the layout of the city you are moving to.

- **What about leisure?** Research expat and hobby groups in your area before you leave. The www.meetup.com website is a good resource for people who want to gather around a common interest, and it is especially useful if you are looking for people to play sports with. Research gyms and pools in your area as well as cinemas, concert halls, and museums.

CURRENCY

There is no shortage of ATMs in India, but do bring an extra card in the unfortunate case that yours gets eaten by a malfunctioning machine. Indian cash is not always available for purchase outside of the country, but if you can get your hands on some rupees, ₹5,000–10,000 should be enough to start with. Bring some traveler's checks and cash in U.S. dollars, euros, or British pounds if you can, but remember that you may have to change these into rupees, as many shops won't accept foreign cash. All of India's international airports have money-changing facilities.

TIPS FOR LIVING OUT OF YOUR SUITCASE

India is not a place to be packing around a lot of luggage. There are a lot more stairs than elevators, and the sidewalks are bumpy and dusty, even in upscale areas, so rolling suitcases aren't much help. When packing for your trip, keep these pointers in mind:

- **Pack light.** There's no need to bring a lot of clothes and shoes to India, especially as you will be moving around a lot during your fact-finding trip. Pack as few things as possible, and pick up a few inexpensive items of clothing on your first day. Your hotel can arrange to have your clothes laundered at a very low price, or you can buy a travel-size packet of washing powder and do laundry yourself in your room (most hotels have buckets in the bathroom). Avoid packing jeans, if possible, as they take up a lot of room and dry slowly.

- **Roll your clothes.** A great way to keep your clothes compact and wrinkle-free is to roll them instead of folding them. You'll want to fold them lengthwise, and then roll them tightly, then shove them tightly into large storage bags, seal, and pack. You'll end up with fewer wrinkles than if you had packed them the old-fashioned way. Any wrinkles you do find can be easily removed by hanging the garment in the bathroom with the hot shower on. The steam will help bring it back to its natural state.

- **Bring a travel towel.** If you do need to bring a towel (a must if you are staying in low-cost guesthouses), invest in a lightweight travel towel. These towels, designed for camping and backpacking, are much more compact than their thick terry-cloth counterparts.

- **Limit your cosmetics.** Before you leave, lay out all the cosmetics and toiletries you plan

Arriving

CUSTOMS AND IMMIGRATION

On most flights, an attendant will pass out immigration forms before you enter India, so you can have your form ready when you enter the airport. If they don't, you will have to pick one up and fill it out before clearing immigration; there are desks with adequate supplies of these forms just before the immigration counters. Once you have filled out your form, proceed to immigration. There are normally separate queues for foreigners and Indians. The immigration officer will take your form, stamp your passport, and tear off a small tab at the bottom of the form where you have filled out details of any items to declare. Do not lose this, as you will have to hand it to customs officials after picking up your checked baggage from the carousel.

© MARGOT BIGG

When in doubt, travel light!

only what you need. Most drugstores sell travel bottles that you can fill with small quantities of toiletries. Buy a few of these for your major needs, and leave the rest at home. You'll not only save yourself a lot of luggage weight, but you'll also minimize the risk of your toiletries leaking into your suitcase.

to bring and ask yourself what can stay and what can go. Is that family-sized bottle of conditioner really necessary for a two-week trip? The key is to take

- **Avoid carrying a library.** If you're an avid reader, you may be tempted to bring a lot of books to while away your time on long flights and train journeys. Instead, bring one or two paperbacks that you are willing to part with, then exchange them. Many guesthouses have book-exchange libraries, or you may bump into a fellow traveler with whom you can trade directly. There are also plenty of new and used bookstores in India, so you may be able to trade in your old book for some credit toward something new.

Prohibited Items

Unsurprisingly, you will not be allowed to bring firearms or illegal drugs into India. Also note that pornography is prohibited in India. Due to high import duties, electronic items are very expensive in India, and there's a huge black market for everything from iPhones to cameras. If you have more than one such item—for example, two laptops—you may be questioned by authorities.

TRANSPORTATION

Most cities, including Mumbai and Delhi, have government-run prepaid taxi booths. Simply tell the person at the window your destination and pay the fare stated. In return, you get a slip that acts as your payment to the driver once you are dropped at your final destination.

An airport branch of the Delhi Metro is currently being built and should be operational before the end of 2011. Bengaluru has metered taxis running from the airport to the city center, operated by private companies Meru and Easy Cabs. The city's Bangalore Metropolitan Transport Corporation (BMTC) also runs air-conditioned shuttles to various points in the city.

Sample Itineraries

The following itineraries are designed to help you learn as much as you can about the area you are considering moving to before taking the plunge. They can be combined or adjusted depending on your needs and interests. A few main tourist attractions have been included for each region to give you a better idea of the history and culture of the area you might soon be calling home.

Two-week itineraries covering the main expat hubs in Northern and Southern India have also been included. If you are moving to one of the smaller cities listed in the north or the south and already know where you are going to live, you may want to adapt one of the one-week itineraries below to your own future city. If you don't have a place in mind yet, the two-week itineraries will give you the chance to see which locations suit you best.

ONE WEEK IN DELHI AND
THE NATIONAL CAPITAL REGION
Day 1

Try to arrive on a Sunday so that you have time to rest before the work week begins. India's capital can be overwhelming, so give yourself plenty of time to relax in your hotel. Chances are you will have arrived in the middle of the night and need plenty of rest. Don't push yourself, especially if it's hot outside. Instead, use this time to stroll around the area near your hotel and generally get a feel for Delhi. Call any agents, schools, or employers you have meetings with and reconfirm your appointments. In the evening, when temperatures have dropped a little bit, take an autorickshaw to India Gate, Delhi's famous arch-shaped monument. It's beautiful when lit up at night. The park around Delhi Gate is popular with picnicking families and is a nice place to walk without having to dodge traffic.

Day 2

The first thing you will want to do is visit your potential employer to resolve any questions you may have about working in Delhi. If your company has remote offices or project sites, you may want to visit these too. If they are

© MARGOT BIGG

Delhi's Defence Colony Market

far away, you may want to schedule visits for later in the week. If you are working in Gurgaon or Noida and staying in Delhi, it may take you the whole day. If your hotel is near your office, you may have some free time in the afternoon, which could be used to visit some of Delhi's tourist sites.

Day 3

If you arrived on a Sunday, Day 3 will be a Tuesday, and you will be able to drop in at the weekly newcomer's coffee meeting of the Delhi Network, one of Delhi's older expat clubs, held at the Hyatt Hotel. There you will be able to get information about joining and talk to some of Delhi's more seasoned expats. Do keep in mind that most if not all of the 60-plus members that attend these events every week are women, so men may feel a bit out of place. If you have children, spend the rest of the day visiting schools you are considering. Make sure to find out about admission requirements and the academic calendar, as these vary from school to school and state to state. Delhi's top international schools are in Chanakyapuri, the embassy enclave in the western part of Central Delhi. If you plan to live and work in Delhi or Noida, you may prefer to restrict your school hunt to those areas. If you don't have children, you can use this time to find out about any special requirements you might have, such as clubs or gyms.

Days 4 and 5

By now you should be a bit acquainted with the area and have a clear idea of where you want to move to. Try to use these days to visit apartments and houses in your chosen area. If you are working in Gurgaon, you might find it more convenient to live there, although you will miss out on some of the fun Delhi has to offer. If you don't mind a 1–3-hour daily commute, you can look for properties in Delhi, although it's recommended you limit your search to areas that are closer to Gurgaon, such as Green Park and Haus Khas. The same rule applies if you want to live in Delhi and work in Noida. Try to find places near the expressway to reduce your commuting time. New Friends Colony in southeast Delhi is a good option.

Day 6

This day can be spent exploring public transportation in Delhi. While you might prefer to avoid the bus at all costs, a short ride won't hurt and will certainly help you get a feel for Delhi's geography. Don't miss a ride on the Delhi Metro, which is reminiscent of Washington, D.C.'s underground. Try to get a spot by a window if you can, and watch the flipbook-style advertisements on the tunnel walls appear to come to life as you speed by.

Day 7

Don't forget to pick up a few souvenirs for your loved ones back home and spend your last day shopping. Visit Dilli Haat, a government-sponsored open air market featuring food and gifts from each of India's states. When you are done, head across the street to the INA Market, which has the best selection of imported foodstuffs in Delhi. This will help you get a better idea of what is and isn't available in the capital.

ONE WEEK IN MUMBAI
Day 1

Your first day in India should always be an adjustment day, even if you are on a one-week whirlwind trip. If you wake up early, grab a cappuccino at Barrista on Colaba Causweay. Then walk around the corner to the Gateway of India, Mumbai's answer to the Arc de Triomphe, which sits right next to the sea. Use the rest of the day to get a feel for South Mumbai. Hail a black cab on the street and have it drive around Mumbai's historic Fort and Churchgate areas. Get out at the famous Chhatrapati Shivaji Terminus railway station and admire the Indo-Saracenic architecture. For a full-on experience of how chaotic India's most populous city can get, step inside and get lost in the crowds of travelers from all over the world. Afternoons in Mumbai can get pretty hot and muggy, so spend this time resting in your hotel room. In the evening, head to Chowpatty Beach, a popular strolling spot for Mumbai's families and young lovers. You may see people swimming here, but the water's not clean, so resist the urge to take a dip.

Day 2

Stop by your future office and say hello to your soon-to-be colleagues. If your office is far from your hotel, take a taxi so that you don't show up sweaty and

© MARGOT BIGG

shopping in Mumbai

disheveled. Try a local train on the way back, but try to avoid the rush-hour throngs of crowds if possible. Head to a cinema in the evening and check out a Bollywood film. While you may not understand the language, the song, dance, and flashiness that characterize the Indian film industry should keep you entertained.

Day 3

Today is a good day to visit schools, but remember to make appointments first. Don't cram more than three schools into one day, and try to work your way progressively from north to south (or vice versa) in order to minimize time spent on the road. Make sure you find out about age requirements and academic schedules, as these vary greatly from school to school.

Days 4 and 5

These days can be spent looking for your future home. If you haven't decided which neighborhood to settle in, pinpoint one per day, as moving among different areas can drastically cut into your time. Be mindful of the distance and the commuting time between your office and, if you have children, their school. Mumbai's traffic means that commutes can be very long, even if you are only traveling short distances. Don't forget to find out about the minimum deposit your potential landlords will expect. Not long ago, Mumbai tenants were required to put down 11 months' rent up front as security, although many landlords have relaxed this rule in the recent past.

Day 6

Mumbai is not the easiest city to get around, so now would be a good time to explore your transportation options, especially if you have already decided where you want to live. Try out the local train if you haven't already, and hail autos and taxis on the street. If it's not too hot, try to walk around the neighborhood you plan to settle in, as this will help you get your bearings. Have a look in some of the local shops to see what kind of products they stock so you know what will be available once you move here.

Day 7

Tie up any loose ends with future employers, schools, and landlords today. If you have time, you can pay a visit to the famed Elephanta Island, home to caves full of monoliths that depict scenes from the great Hindu epic the Mahabharata. To reach the island, you need to catch a boat from India Gate, which takes a little under an hour each way. Make sure to set aside at least four hours for the trip, including travel time.

ONE WEEK IN BENGALURU
Day 1

Use this day to adjust to your new surroundings and catch up with any sleep you might have missed during your long flight over. Spend your morning resting, or go for a walk around your hotel's neighborhood and get yourself acquainted with the area. In the afternoon, you can catch an autorickshaw to Lal Bagh Botanical Gardens and explore the many varieties of flora housed in the park. Get a good night's sleep because you will have a busy week ahead of you.

Day 2

If you are applying for jobs, try to schedule your interviews for this day. If you already have a job secured, use your second day to visit the office and meet your future colleagues. This will help you get a feel for the office environment in India, which, if you work in IT, you might find a bit more formal than what you are used to back home. You'll also be able to gauge how long it will take to get to work every day.

Days 3-5

Bengaluru has a lot of expat neighborhoods scattered throughout the city; use this day to find out which one suits you best. Bengaluru traffic is really bad, so take this into account before choosing a home that's far away from your workplace. It's also a good idea to check with a couple of different agents, each of whom will likely specialize in a different area, to find your ideal home.

Day 6

By now you should have an idea of where you want to live and how much time it will take to get there from your office. If you have children, this will be the day that you need to figure out which school to send them to. Mark your office and the school on a map so that you can better decide which neighborhoods might be most convenient for you to move to. Make sure to find out if there are any waiting lists, and if so, get your children on them as soon as you can. Remember to ask about school buses and after-school child care arrangements.

Day 7

If you haven't bought souvenirs, now is the time to do so. Pay a visit to the hectic City Market for an authentic Indian shopping experience. You'll be able to buy anything from silk saris to plastic lunchboxes. If you have a spouse or children who will be joining you, take pictures of the city for them. This will help them get a better feel for life in Bengaluru and is much more personal than downloading stock images from the Internet. You can also use this day to visit some of Bengaluru's famous sites, such as the Bull Temple, fashioned in the Dravidian style and dedicated to Nandi, the steed of Lord Shiva.

COMMERCIAL_ST.JPG © GATESPLUSPLUS, COMMONS.WIKIMEDIA.ORG

Commerical Street, Bengaluru

TWO WEEKS IN NORTHERN INDIA
Days 1-4: Kolkata

Start your Northern India trip in Kolkata, taking it easy on your first day in order to get used to being in India. Check ahead so that your trip does not coincide with Durga Puja, an annual religious festival, dedicated to the goddess, that brings Kolkata to a standstill. If you come during the summer or monsoon seasons, it's imperative that you get an air-conditioned room, as it can get quite hot and muggy and you don't want to shock your system. Use this day to go on a walk down Park Street. Pop into Oxford Books for a great selection of books about Kolkata and India. You can browse through your choices at the in-store coffee shop upstairs.

Spend your next few days traveling around Kolkata, checking out sights and neighborhoods as you see fit. You can easily hail taxis on the street to get around, or take the tram. There is no central hub for expats in the city, so it's best to explore different area to get a feel for the city overall, but Sudder Street has a lot of travelers from abroad who may be able to give you tips about the city. The Salt Lake area, a bit farther out, is worth a visit as it's one of the more comfortable parts of town and many large companies have operations there. If you have time for tourism, make sure to visit the famous Kalighat Kali Temple, but be prepared for a lot of pushing and shoving inside. The adjacent Missions of Charity, Mother Theresa's organization, is also a popular place to visit.

Days 5-9: Jaipur

Once you've got a feel for Kolkata, you'll want to move on to Jaipur. Low-cost carriers such as SpiceJet and IndiGo offer direct flights to the city, so unless you want to stop in Delhi, it's best to fly directly. Spend your first day in Jaipur leisurely wandering around the old Pink City, Jaipur's historic section. If your India plans involve handicraft manufacture or export, you will want to spend a lot of time here, talking to the many jewelers and crafts dealers in the area. Otherwise, try to avoid the many touts who will try to get you into their shops, and head to the Hawa Mahal (Palace of Winds), an ornate structure covered with miniature windows that were once used by the ladies of the court to observe daily life on the street below from a safe distance.

The next day, explore the city's neighborhoods. It's possible to hire an autorickshaw for a day and have the driver take you around the city. Jaipur is very small, so it's easy to do this all in one day. As Jaipur is very popular with tourists, most autorickshaw drivers will speak a fair amount of English, which makes the city a lot easier than other places for newcomers to navigate. C-Scheme

WWW.FLICKR.COM/CREATIVECOMMONS © RUSS BOWLING

the Hawa Mahal in Jaipur

is a good place to start, and there are plenty of shopping complexes and stand-alone restaurants where you can grab lunch. Then head to Tilak Nagar and Bapu Nagar, which are next to each other, and have a look around.

Once you have decided on areas, you can contact real estate agents who will be able to show you specific properties the next day. Otherwise, spend a day visiting some of Jaipur's many sights, such as the Amber Fort, on the outskirts of the city, and the City Palace. If you have time, take one day to visit the Taj Mahal in Agra. It's only a few hours' drive from Jaipur, and it is well worth a visit. There are plenty of buses leaving for Agra, and you shouldn't have to pay more than a few hundred rupees for a seat on an air-conditioned coach. Just make sure you arrive early in the morning, preferably by sunrise, to avoid long queues and large crowds.

Spend your last day in Jaipur shopping for souvenirs for your friends and family. Even if you don't think you will move here, it's one of the best places in India to pick up anything from bangles to bedspreads. Just remember to bargain—shopkeepers here are used to tour buses full of visitors with lots of cash to spare, so you'll have a good opportunity to hone your haggling skills, which will come in handy once you make the big move. In the evening, catch the 8:45 P.M. *Ashram Express* train to Ahmedabad (book ahead). You'll arrive the next morning in Ahmedabad around 8 A.M.

Days 10-11: Ahmedabad

Once you've checked into your hotel, it's time to explore. Hop in an autorickshaw and head to the Satellite area, the main hub for expat housing. In fact, you may want to contact an agent directly to show you a few properties, especially if this city is high on your list of possible new homes. This may take all day. In the evening, you might get a kick out of seeing a Gujarati film at the nearby Sunset Drive-In Cinema, which claims to be the largest of its kind in

Asia, although you'll need to book a taxi to do this. The next day, visit schools (if you have children) and try to meet with others working in your field to assess the opportunities for you in Ahmedabad.

Days 12-13: Gandhinagar

Take a bus out to Gandhinagar, the capital of Gujarat and a possible place to live. Admire the leafy avenues and their sprawling bungalows. While you are here, pay a visit to the huge Akshardham Temple, one of the city's main tourist sites. Return by bus in the evening. Spend your last day visiting Mahatma Gandhi's ashram, Sabarmati, to learn about the life of the father of modern India. In the afternoon, visit the National Institute of Design (NID), India's top arts college, where many of the students' works are on display. There's even a boutique selling books and home decor that you won't easily find in other shops. Then head for an evening stroll in Law Gardens, where many local families go to play badminton or jog when the sun sets.

Day 14: Return Home

Return to Kolkata to catch your flight home. If you have decided that Kolkata is the city for you, you may want to return from Ahmedabad earlier to tie up any loose ends.

TWO WEEKS IN SOUTHERN INDIA
Days 1-4: Chennai

Arrange to arrive in Chennai and give yourself the first day to get over any jet lag and adjust to being in a new country. On your second and third days, visit some of Chennai's attractions and neighborhoods using a combination of autorickshaws and the local trains. This will give you a feel for Chennai's size and allow you see Chennai life from a perspective that you wouldn't get if you only took taxis. Don't miss a stroll on Elliot's Beach and a coffee in Amethyst Café; these are good places to find other expats who might be able to give you some helpful advice. If you have time, you can spend your fourth day on a day trip to the 7th-century monuments of Mahabalipuram, a UNESCO World Heritage Site about 40 miles south of Chennai. Whatever you do, don't leave Chennai without sampling some of the local specialties, such as the ubiquitous masala dosa, a thin pancake stuffed with lightly seasoned potatoes.

Days 5-7: Hyderabad and Secunderabad

Fly to Hyderabad in the morning and settle into your hotel. Spend the rest of the day exploring some of the major sights of the city, such as Hussain Sagar, the city's giant lake. Have a famous Hyderabad *biryani* for dinner, and call it a night. The next morning, wake up early and head to the Jubilee Hills and Banjara Hills neighborhoods, which are a hub for Hyderabad's expats. Visit the many malls and shops, and if it's not too hot, take a walk through the leafy backstreets to get a better idea of what the neighborhoods look like. In the afternoon, take a car out to HITEC City and Gachibowli to see where most of the city's techies work. If your visit falls on Friday, head to the Walden Club at 7:30 P.M. for the weekly Twin-cities Expatriate's Association meeting. The next morning, take a taxi ride around Secunderabad before heading to the airport and flying to Goa's Vasco de Gama airport.

Days 8–11: Goa

Settle in to your hotel and go see the beach. If you are staying in the north, rent a motorcycle or scooter on your eighth day and explore. If your visit is on Wednesday or Saturday, be sure to attend one of the famous Anjuna markets. On your ninth day, make a trip out to Old Goa and visit some of the old churches and squares of this historic part of the state. Your 10th day in Goa can be spent visiting the south of the state. You may prefer to take a bus or taxi for this part of the journey as getting from north to south can take quite a bit of time. Now that you've seen most of the state, spend your last day relaxing on the beach and soaking up Goa's relaxed atmosphere. In the evening, catch an overnight bus to Pune; they usually leave around 6 or 7 P.M. from Mapusa, Margao, or one of the other bustling inland cities.

ARAMBOL BEACH 2009.JPG © RIDINGHAG, COMMONS.WIKIMEDIA.ORG

a tropical beach in Goa

Days 12-14: Pune

You'll arrive in Pune early in the morning on Day 12. After checking in to your hotel, head out and explore the city. Your first stop will be Koregaon Park, where you can visit Osho's ashram, one of the major attractions in Pune. After your tour, head across the street to the German Bakery for a coffee or some lunch. You might run into a few expats as well as plenty of tourists. The nice thing about this part of town is that it's a hub for both tourists and expats, so you will get a feel for what to expect living in Pune while still being in a tourist-friendly area. In the afternoon, head to Kalyani Nagar, home to a few malls and a few more expats. The next day can be spent exploring some of the outskirts, such as the popular student areas in Aundh. Make sure you give yourself plenty of time to fly back to your final departure city.

Practicalities

The notion that India is a land of extremes extends to its accommodations options. You can find some of the world's most luxurious hotels as well as some of the most modest, and some might say rustic, places to stay. If you're on a budget and don't mind sharing your room with a family of insects, you can easily get a room for a few dollars a day. If this is your first time to India, you may want to splurge a bit. The same rule applies to restaurants. In most of India's major cities, you can spend a small fortune on lobster and champagne, or feast on rice and curry for under a dollar. Below you will find a variety of hotels ranging from simple to ultraluxurious, as well as a selection of restaurants offering everything from local dishes to more familiar pastas and sandwiches.

HOTELS VERSUS GUESTHOUSES

Guesthouses are often smaller, more intimate, and cheaper, while hotels tend to have more rooms and a larger staff. Larger properties are not always cleaner than little guesthouses, nor do they necessarily offer better service, unless they fall into the five-star category. Most places in India offer room service or can order food for you from reputed restaurants outside. If you are staying in budget accommodations, however, you may want to bring your own towel and toilet paper.

SAFE EATING

India can be a bit rough on the stomachs of first-time travelers. To minimize your risk of "Delhi belly," you should follow a few guidelines. First of all, have your drinks without ice unless you are at an upmarket eatery. Avoid eating street food until you are well adjusted to the country, especially during summertime, when meats, dairy products, and potatoes can easily become breeding grounds for bacteria. My personal, and completely unscientific, rule of thumb is never to eat anything that hasn't been refrigerated once the outside temperature has risen above my body temperature. Crowded restaurants are generally safe as they make their foods fresh, as are restaurants frequented by families with small children. While the filtered water offered by restaurants is usually fine to drink, visitors are best to stick to bottled water. Trusted brands such as Bisleri, Kinley, and Aquafina are your best bet. It's normal to feel off your feed for the first few days of your trip while your body is still adjusting to jet lag and possibly a hotter climate. However, if you have digestion problems or a lack of appetite that lasts for more than a couple of days, seek medical help.

DELHI AND THE NATIONAL CAPITAL REGION
Accommodations
Accommodations in Delhi range from hole-in-the-wall guesthouses to extravagant five-star luxury properties, with very little in between. The cheapest options are in Paharganj near the New Delhi train station, although they are generally not very good quality. Staying in a property in and around Delhi's central Connaught Place is your best bet if you want to get a feel for the city.

The **Imperial Hotel** (Janpath, near Connaught Place, tel. 11/2334-1234, www.theimperialindia.com, ₹11,500–17,500 d) is the most luxurious and classic option, with prices to match. If you plan to spend most of your time in Delhi house hunting, you may be interested in staying somewhere a bit farther south, closer to the neighborhoods most popular with expats.

Sunder Nagar has a few comfortable guesthouses, of which **Jukaso Inn** (49–50 Mathura Rd., Sunder Nagar, tel. 11/2435-0308, www.jukasohotels. com, ₹7,000 d) is the most popular.

Farther south, the **InterContinental Nehru Place** (Nehru Place, tel. 11/4133-1916, www.ichotelsgroup.com, ₹7,500 d) is a comfortable option popular with business travelers. From Delhi, it's easy to go to Noida or Gurgaon for a few hours and still stay in Delhi.

If you prefer to stay in Gurgaon, the **Bristol Hotel** (108–110 Sikanderpur, off MG Rd., tel. 124/435-1111, www.thebristolhotel.com, ₹12,000 d) is the most convenient, and it has a cooling rooftop pool and small gym.

In Noida, the boutique **Mosaic Hotel** (C-1, Sector 18, Noida, tel. 120/402-5000, www.mosaichotels.co.in, ₹13,500 d) has sleek, spotless rooms in the center of commercial Noida.

Dining

Delhiites are notoriously fond of food, and there's no shortage of places to feast on both international cuisine and local specialties. Defence Colony Market is chock-full of good places to eat, including **Moet's** (50 Defence Colony Market, tel. 11/4655-5777, www.moets.com), which houses four slightly upscale restaurants serving everything from Northern Indian cuisine to seafood.

South Delhi's bohemian Hauz Khas Village has a few excellent dining options; try **Gunpowder** (22 Hauz Khas Village, 3rd Fl., tel. 11/2653-5700) for authentic Southern Indian food with a home-cooked flair. **The Living Room Café** (31 Hauz Khas Village, tel. 11/4608-0533) is among Delhi's most popular expat haunts, thanks to its regular live-music nights, a good selection of beer and wine, continental dishes, and laid-back environment—it even has pub quizzes on Sundays.

If you want to try Delhi's favorite street food, a collective variety of spicy snack items known as *chaat,* you can brave eating from one of the many roadside vendors set up across the city, or you can head straight to **Haldiram's** (45 Ring Rd., tel. 11/2517-1946, www.haldiram.com), to pick up local varieties of *chaat* prepared in a sanitary environment.

In Gurgaon, your best bet for variety is to head straight to the long strip of shopping malls on MG Road. The food courts and restaurants sell everything from smoothies to sushi. Don't miss **Rajdhani** (Metropolitan Mall, MG Rd., tel. 124/437-9001, www.rajdhani.co.in), where you can get humungous platters of traditional Rajasthani cuisine for a few hundred rupees.

Most of Noida's best places to eat are in the Sector 18 area; try the Noida branch of **Punjabi by Nature** (P-19, Sector 18, tel. 11/4532-2222, www.punjabibynature.in) for high-quality Northern Indian meat-based and vegetarian dishes.

MUMBAI
Accommodations

Like almost everything in Mumbai, accommodations are expensive. The crème de la crème of Mumbai hotels is the **Taj Mahal Palace and Tower** (Apollo Bandar, Colaba, tel. 22/6665-3366, www.tajhotels.com, ₹21,000 d), a historic hotel complex adjacent to Mumbai's India Gate, just a few minutes' walk from the sea.

The Shalimar Hotel (August Kranti Marg, tel. 22/6664-1000, www.theshalimarhotel.com, ₹6,700 d), in South Mumbai's trendy Kemp's Corner, has contemporary furnishings and solid on-site facilities, including a beauty salon, a bakery, and a pub.

A bit farther south, **The Regent Hotel** (Best Marg, Apollo Bandar, tel. 22/2282-5696, www.regenthotelcolaba.com, ₹4,200 d) is another good mid-range option and is conveniently located in the touristy hub of Colaba.

If you are trying to keep costs down, the **YWCA International Guest House** (18 Madame Cama Rd., Fort, tel. 22/2202-5053, www.ywcaic.info, ₹2,100 d) is a good choice—they keep their rooms in tip-top shape and even have an in-house dining hall with cheap buffet meals.

If you are on a strict budget, the starkly furnished **Salvation Army** (Ormiston Rd., Apollo Bandar, Colaba, tel. 22/2284-1824, ₹1,200 d) is a good bet. While it's certainly nothing special, it's safe and well-maintained, although you may have to share a dorm room if the few single and double rooms have already been taken.

Dining

Mumbai has a great selection of restaurants and pubs representing food from all over the world. The best breakfast spot in Bandra is **Theobroma** (29/30 Link Square Mall, Linking Rd., tel. 22/2646-9010), a Parsi-owned establishment famous for its great coffees and sumptuous pastries. They also have a branch in Colaba.

Trendy **Blue Frog** (Senapati Bapat Marg, tel. 22/4033-2300, www.bluefrog. co.in) is definitely worth a try for its delicious continental dishes and sleek interiors that appear to have been plucked straight out of a James Bond film. The restaurant doubles as a nightclub, showcasing everything from live jazz to electronic music.

A little farther south, in the Kemp's Corner neighborhood, is **East Pan Asian** (76 August Kranti Marg, tel. 22/2381-1010), a pan-Asian fusion restaurant with creative takes on well-known East Asian fare.

In South Mumbai, try the Southern Indian treats at **Kamat** (opposite Electric House on Colaba Causeway, tel. 22/2287-4734). If you are in the mood for something more familiar, **Moshe's** (7 Minoo Manor, Cuff Parade, tel. 022/2216-1226, www.moshes.in) has delicious Italian and deli food as well as a good selection of homemade jams.

BENGALURU
Accommodations

Accommodations in Bengaluru vary a lot. If you are on a strict budget, you are best staying in one of the many cheap guesthouses on SC Road near the train station, such as the **Royal Regency Lodge** (251 Subedar Chatram Rd., tel. 080/4113-0202, www.royalregencylodge.com, ₹400 d), a simple guesthouse popular with the foreign backpacker set.

If you plan to base yourself out of Whitefield, you might consider the Bengaluru branch of the **Ginger Hotel** (128 EPIP Phase II, Whitefield, tel. 80/6666-3333, www.gingerhotels.com, ₹2,200 d). The furnishings here are a bit on the generic side (if Ikea did hotels, this is what they would look like), but it's clean, well-staffed, and has Wi-Fi.

Another mid-range option with Wi-Fi is **Hotel Ganga Sagar** in Koramangala (3 YSR Mansion, Koramangala 8 Block, tel. 80/2570-4880, ₹1,000 d). Although the service here is nothing special, the hotel's location, smack in the middle of Koramangala, will give you a good feel for what life is like in one of Bengaluru's most popular expat neighborhoods.

A more upscale suburban choice is the comfortable **Hotel Royal Orchid** (Airport Rd., Kodihalli, tel. 80/2520-5566, www.royalorchidhotels.com, ₹6,500 d) just south of Indira Nagar.

However, if you want to be in the center of the action, your best bet is **The Gateway Hotel** (66 Residency Rd., tel. 80/6660-4545, www.thegatewayhotels.com, ₹10,000 d), an upmarket business hotel just a few minutes from Bengaluru's main strip on MG Road.

Dining

Bengaluru is often called India's pub town, and there are plenty of places across the city to enjoy libations with your meal. For great views of Bengaluru's city center, head to **The 13th Floor** (Barton Centre, 84 MG Rd., tel. 80/4178-3355). This indoor-outdoor penthouse lounge has a decent selection of Indian and continental dishes as well as cocktails, mocktails, beers, and wines.

For classic Southern Indian food, try **Mavalli Tiffin Rooms (MTR)** (14 Lalbagh Rd., tel. 80/2222-0022, http://mavallitiffinrooms.com), Bengaluru's best known breakfast joint.

Lumiere (27/7 Sri Kote Ashirwad Towers, Doddanekundi, Marathahalli, tel. 80/6534-1133, www.lumiere.co.in) is the place to go for fresh, organic cuisine—the restaurant even has its own poultry and vegetable farm.

If you're in the mood for coffee, skip one of the many Café Coffee Days that dot the city and head to **Mocha** in Koramangala (No. 577, Kalyana Mantapa Rd., 80 Ft. Rd., 8th Block, Koramangala, tel. 80/2660-1236, www.mocha.co.in). This Middle Eastern–themed café-restaurant has delicious sandwiches and platters plus some of the best milk shakes in the country.

Children will love Indira Nagar's **Claytopia** (318 6th Main Rd., HAL 2nd Stage, tel. 80/4126-7283), a two-in-one café and pottery workshop where you can paint on prefired pottery while enjoying pastas and desserts in the garden café.

NORTHERN INDIA
Accommodations

If you start your trip in Kolkata, you may want to indulge in a stay at the luxurious **Park Hotel** (17 Park St., Kolkata, tel. 33/2249-9000, www.theparkhotels.com, ₹5,500 d) in the center of the action.

If you are considering a move to the Salt Lake City area, you might prefer to stay in the **Hyatt Regency** (JA Block Salt Lake City, Kolkata, tel. 33/2335-1234, http://kolkata.regency.hyatt.com, ₹6,500 d).

Given its status as a major tourist spot, Jaipur has no shortage of great places to stay. The regal **Samode Haveli** (Gangapole, Jaipur, tel. 141/263-2407, www.samode.com, ₹6,000 d) is a good heritage option.

If you are on a budget, you might prefer the clean, centrally located **Gangaur Guest House** (Near Khasa Kothi, MI Rd., Jaipur, tel. 141/237-1641, ₹950 d), run by Rajasthan Tourism Development Corporation.

Ahmedabad's **Lemontree Hotel** (434/1 Mithakali Six Cross Roads, Ahmedabad, tel. 79/4423-2323, www.lemontreehotels.com, ₹2,900 d) is a good option with pristine rooms, a small gym, and an extensive breakfast buffet that includes everything from rose-flavored yogurt to baked beans on toast, plus an array of interesting Gujarati specialties.

Dining

Kolkata's **Blue Sky Cafe** (Sudder St., Kolkata, tel. 33/2252-2958) is an institution among hungry travelers and locals alike, and it's a good place to meet other foreigners, although many of them will be tourists rather than expats.

The historic **Flury's** (Park St., Kolkata, tel. 33/4000-7453, www.flurysindia.com), Kolkata's most famous tea room, is also worth a visit, even if just for a cup of tea and a pastry.

Jaipur's **Cafe Kooba** (F-40, 1st Fl., Jamna Lal Bajaj Marg, C-Scheme, Jaipur, tel. 141/511-6343, www.cafekooba.com) is a popular expat hangout; grab a seat on the rooftop for great views of the city.

For authentic Rajasthani cuisine, you may prefer to head out to **Chokhi Dhani** (12 Miles Tonk Rd., Jaipur, tel. 141/222-5002, www.chokhidhani.com), a kitschy artificial village for tourists that redeems itself with an all-you-can-eat buffet of everything Rajasthani.

Swati Snacks (opposite Law Gardens, Ellisbridge, tel. 79/2640-2185) offers a range of home-style Gujarati dishes in a very clean environment. The helpful waiters speak enough English to help explain what to expect from each dish.

SOUTHERN INDIA
Accommodations
Chennai has a good selection of hotels near the Egmore train station, and you may find this more convenient if you plan on taking the commuter train around town. One of the nicer options in this area is the spotless **Hotel Victoria** (3 Kennet Lane, Chennai, tel. 44/2819-3638, www.empeehotels.com, ₹3,000 d), with its friendly staff and no-nonsense service.

In North Goa, you can easily find a nice guesthouse or beach hut for a few dollars a day. If you are visiting during the busy tourist season, however, it's best to book ahead. In Anjuna, the family-run **Anjuna Beach Resort** (De-Mello Vaddo, Anjuna, tel. 832/227-4499, www.goacom.org/hotels/anjuna-beachresort, ₹600 d) is ideal for travelers on a budget.

If you are interested in moving to South Goa, you may find Palolem's quaint **Chattai Beach Huts** (Ourem, 81/5 Palolem Beach, Palolem, tel. 9822/48-1360, www.chattai.co.in, ₹1,200 d) more convenient.

In Hyderabad, the recently renovated **Peppermint Hotel** (6-1-1063/C Lakdikapool, Hyderabad, tel. 40/4435-1234, ₹3,500 d) is a good choice for its proximity to both the city center and the major expat neighborhoods.

Pune's **Hotel Sunderban** (19 Koregaon Park, Pune, tel. 20/2612-4949, www.tghotels.com, ₹3,500 d) is an intimate heritage hotel in the heart of Koregaon Park. The hotel also has a few studio rooms (₹5,500) that come equipped with kitchenettes.

Dining
Chennai's Tamil cuisine is best experienced at the vegetarian restaurant **Hotel Saravana Bhavan** (21 Kennet Lane, Chennai, tel. 44/2819-2055, www.saravanabhavan.com), popular with visitors and locals alike. Although this branch in Egmore might be the most convenient, they have plenty of branches scattered throughout the city.

Amethyst (Padmavathi Rd., Gopalapuram, tel. 44/2835-3581), a lovely little café in an old colonial house, has good coffees and great pastries as well as a small boutique selling jewelry and knickknacks. It's also a popular hangout spot for expats and a good place to meet new people.

In Goa, Anjuna's beautiful garden restaurant **The German Bakery** (east of

Anjuna Market Ground, Anjuna, tel. 9623/27-0417, www.german-bakery. org) is a favorite with travelers for its great espresso, huge salads, and platters of fresh seafood. There are occasional movie nights and other events that can be a great place to meet long-term residents of Goa.

No visit to Hyderabad is complete without trying one of the city's famous *biryanis,* and the 24-hour **Bawarchi Restaurant** (Plot No. 66, RTC Cross Roads, Hyderabad, tel. 40/763-4494, http://hydepages.com/bawarchi) is just the place to do so. They also have a good variety of kebabs and meat dishes, plus a few vegetarian versions. Make sure to tell your waiter if you don't want your food to be too spicy.

To get a sense of Pune's youthful vibe, don't miss **Kavi Restaurant** (70/2 Govind Chambers, Karve Rd., Pune, tel. 20/2544-9621). The drinks here are strong and the food fresh, although you may find the music a little on the loud side.

DAILY LIFE

MAKING THE MOVE

Moving to another country requires a lot of planning and foresight, and in the case of India, you'll need to do even more preparation. Of course, there's only so much groundwork you can do before you finally set off, and a big part of the experience of moving abroad is about learning to go with the flow and be open to surprises. However, while flexibility and openness are key to making your transition a success, there are a few things you'll want to take care of before making the big move. You'll have to secure visas for yourself and your family, and decide what to bring and how to bring it. If you have children or pets, you will also have to ensure that their move goes smoothly. If your employer is working with a relocation company, this process will be a lot easier, as you will likely get support on everything from handling visas to importing your furniture. If you are coming to India independently, you will need to handle everything yourself. Things may seem bureaucratic at first, but once you have all your documents in place, the process of moving is quite straightforward. Try to get started on your planning as soon as you decide to move, as the process can be time-consuming.

© MARIYA ZHELEVA

Immigration and Visas

Before you enter India, you have to get prior approval from the Indian embassy or consulate in your country. If you have Indian ancestry as close as a great-grandparent, you can apply for a Person of Indian Origin (PIO) card, which allows you to work and live in India on a long-term basis. If your spouse is Indian or of Indian origin, you are also eligible for the card. You may also qualify to become an Overseas Citizen of India (OCI), the closest thing India has to a dual-citizenship scheme. For everyone else a visa is necessary, and these are not issued on arrival for nationals of most countries.

GETTING YOUR VISA

Visa applications are dealt with at local consulates, and your place of residency will determine which consulate will process your application. In most countries, Indian visa services are outsourced to private companies that collect relevant information, forms, and fees from applicants and then send it on to the local consulate or embassy. In the United States, visa services are outsourced to Travisa Outsourcing. In Canada, the United Kingdom, and Australia, visa services are managed by VFS Global.

To get a visa, you must submit a valid passport with at least two blank pages and at least six months' validity, two passport-sized photographs, a copy of your birth certificate, and proof of your residency (such as a photocopy of your driver's license or electricity bill). Additional requirements vary based on the type of visa you need to get. Note that visas are normally valid from the date of issue, not the date of expected travel, so it's better to avoid applying too far ahead of your trip. Processing times can vary tremendously, however, depending on the type of visa you are getting and where you are obtaining it, so make sure you know how much time your specific type of visa will take before you apply. Indian visa rules and requirements can and do change on short notice, so it's a good idea to check the website of the Indian embassy in your country regularly.

COMMON TYPES OF VISAS
Tourist Visas

If you are going to India for tourism purposes rather than to work, volunteer, or study, you should apply for a tourist visa. Tourist visas are issued for a period of six months to most nationals, although U.S. passport–holders can also apply for five- and 10-year multiple-entry tourist visas. In most cases, tourists will not have to register their presence on arrival in India.

Although tourist visas are usually good for multiple entries, a new law has recently come into effect that restricts the amount of time a foreign national can spend in India on one visit. The rule states that if you leave India, you have to stay out of the country for two months. The issue many tourists face is that if they are traveling in the region, they may want to visit other countries as part of their trip. For example, if you have a visa that is valid January 1–June 30 and you want to travel to Nepal on February 1, you will be required to wait until

the U.S. Embassy in Chankyapuri, Delhi's diplomatic enclave

© MARGOT BIGG

April 1 to reenter India. If you want to leave and reenter, you can either apply for a Permit to Reenter India or just show a copy of your itinerary to immigration.

The Permit to Reenter is useful for people who are unsure of their exact itinerary or are traveling by bus or other means of transportation that cannot be booked in advance. However, those with the permit are required to register with the Foreigners Regional Registration Office (FRRO) within 14 days of their arrival in India.

Business Visas

If you are traveling to India to set up a joint venture or do business on behalf of a company in your home country, a business visa may be the most appropriate visa for you. Business visas are valid for at least one year and up to 10 years, with a provision for multiple entries. Note that a business visa will not permit you to work, so if you are coming over for any type of job or volunteer position, you should apply for an employment visa instead.

In addition to the basic requirements, if you are applying for business visa, you have to furnish sponsor letters from an organization in India as well as from a company in your country of residence. Those working in specialized areas of science and technology also have to furnish an additional form that outlines their experience and qualifications in their field.

Employment Visas

If you plan to work or volunteer in India, you have to get an employment visa. Employment visas are normally issued for one year, but can be extended in India at the Foreigners Regional Registration Office (FRRO) or the Ministry of Home Affairs (MHA). If you have an employment visa, you are required to register at the local FRRO within 14 days of your arrival.

Those seeking an employment visa must furnish the basic documents and proof of identity required for all visas as well as information pertaining to their employment, including proof that the hiring company is registered in India, a contract, a letter of appointment (offer letter), and a copy of their résumé. The amount of paperwork necessary to obtain employment visas has recently increased, and now employment visa seekers must also send over a tax liability letter that states that the hiring company will take responsibility for the employee's taxes and that the company employs less than one percent foreigners as part of their total workforce. Other new requirements include forms and letters that outline details of the project and give background information on the employee's skills and qualifications.

In late 2010, a new law came into effect restricting employment visas to people earning at least US $25,000 per year. The law has come under scrutiny from the business community and may not stay in effect for much longer. Please check with the Indian mission in your home country for up-to-date information on visa requirements, as they are known to change frequently.

Student Visas

If you plan to move to India to study, be it at a university, a language school, or a yoga ashram, you are supposed to apply for a student visa. Student visas are normally valid for the duration of your course and allow multiple entries. To apply for a student visa, you need an admissions letter from a recognized school as well as proof that you have the means to support yourself during your stay. If you are studying medicine, you first also have to obtain a "no-objection certificate" from the Indian Ministry of Health. If you plan to study engineering or another technical subject, you need prior approval from the Indian Ministry of Human Resources Development (Department of Education).

Journalist Visas

If you are a professional journalist, you are expected to apply for a journalist visa, even if you are visiting the country for nonwork-related purposes. The only exception to this rule is if you are coming to work for an Indian publication, in which case you have to apply for an employment visa. Journalist visas are valid for three months but can be renewed once you enter India.

Research Visas

Scholars coming to India to work on independent or sponsored research should apply for a research visa. If you apply for this type of visa, you are expected to send an original copy of your university admission letter, details of the research project, an invitation from a recognized university in the case of visiting professors, and invitations to any conferences or seminars you might be attending in India. You also have to furnish seven copies of a "research pro forma," available from visa centers.

Medical Visas

If the primary purpose of your trip to India is to seek medical care, you should apply for a medical visa. Along with the standard documents required for all visas, you also need a medical certificate from your home country that contains a recommendation from a medical practitioner that you seek treatment in India. Up to two blood relatives can come with you by applying for medical attendant visas.

Missionary Visas

Missionary work is frowned upon in India, and this type of visa is often denied. If you do want to go to India for this reason, you need to apply well in advance—at least six months—and provide a letter of sponsorship from the organization sending you over.

FAMILY MEMBERS
Entry Visas

Spouses and dependents of people moving to India for employment, business, research, or studies have to apply for entry visas, sometimes referred to as X visas for the code used for this type of visa. Normally, the primary visa holder should apply first, and once his or her visa has been processed, only then should family members apply for entry visas. Proof of relationship (i.e., marriage certificates for spouses and birth certificates for children) and a photocopy of the primary visa holder's visa must be submitted. Spouses and dependents of Persons of Indian Origin (PIOs) and Overseas Citizens of India (OCIs) are expected to apply for this kind of visa in all situations, even if they only plan to come to India for tourism, and must also submit proof of their relationship with the PIO or OCI in question.

THE WORKING SPOUSE

The spouses of people in India on employment, business, and student visas are normally issued entry visas and are not legally entitled to work in India. Unless you are willing to work under the table, there's no real way around this, except applying for a job and then returning to your home country to apply for a separate employment visa linked to your job.

Now imagine this: A married couple both work for the same company, and both are offered positions in India. Both go to apply for visas at the same time, but only one, let's say the husband, is granted an employment visa, while the wife gets an entry visa. The situation might sound hypothetical, but it has happened before, much to the frustration of the applicants. If this happens to you, you will need to contact your local consulate or embassy directly to inquire about the confusion. If you want to be sure to avoid it, apply separately.

CHANGING VISAS

If you want to change your visa type, you usually have to leave India. In some cases, the Ministry of Home Affairs can give you permission to stay on in India after a job contract ends for tourism purposes, although usually only for a short period. If you have an employment visa and want to change jobs, you have to return to your country of citizenship or permanent residence and apply for a fresh visa.

THE FOREIGNER REGIONAL REGISTRATION OFFICE (FRRO)

If you are on a long-term visa such as an employment or student visa, or if you plan to stay in India for longer than 180 days (even as a PIO cardholder), you have to register your presence in India within 14 days of your arrival and obtain a residential permit. In major cities, this can be done at the city's FRRO. In smaller cities and towns, you must register with the local Foreign Registration Officer (FRO), usually the superintendent of police. If you fail to register within 14 days of your arrival, you could be subjected to a late fee.

Obtaining Your Residential Permit

The FRRO is notorious among foreigners for its long lines and endless red tape. Some people go through agents to make the process easier, although you often still have to be present at the time of registration, so it might not be worth it.

If you live in a bigger city, there will be lots of people registering every day—not just expats, but Indians with foreign passports, refugees from Burma and

Tibet, and Afghanstan nationals, all of whom are required to register regardless of the length of their stay. You have to show up at the FRRO bright and early and join the line (sometimes there is a separate line for Afghani citizens, so make sure you join the correct line). As the line moves up, eventually you come to a desk where you are given a registration form and a number. You are required to fill out the form and make two additional photocopies of it; this often involves leaving the FRRO and finding a place that does photocopies. You have to be back with your completed forms when your number is called, at which poin you submit them. The officer at the window verifies that all your documen are in order. If anything is missing, you may have to come back later.

Different documents are required depending on what type of visa you hold. All foreigners will need to bring four passport-sized photos, a photocopy of their passport and visa, and proof of residency in India, usually in the form of a notarized rental agreement. In many cases, you may not have found a place within two weeks of having moved to India, so you have to register using your temporary address. Once you move into a permanent home, you must notify the FRRO immediately. If you entered on an employment visa, you have to submit a copy of your contract, a letter from your employer requesting the FRRO to register you, and a "certificate of undertaking" signed by your employer that states that they will be responsible should anything adverse happen to you in India (the template for this is available online).

Business visa holders must prove the authenticity of their business. If you are starting a joint venture with an Indian citizen or entity, you also have to produce permission from the Reserve Bank of India and the Indian government at the time of your registration. Students need certification of their enrollment at school, and scholars on research visas need a certificate from the agency or ministry sponsoring their visit. Journalists need certification from the Press Information Bureau and the Ministry of External Affairs.

Once you have registered, you are given a document called the Registration Report & Residential Permit. The appearance of this document is a stamped and dated form with your photo stapled to a small booklet about the size of a passport. The permit contains details about your visa, passport, and address, and it is useful in situations such as opening a bank account. When you leave India permanently, or if you plan to reenter on a different visa, you have to send your residential permit back to the FRRO/FRO that issued it, or simply give it to the immigration officer at the airport.

FRRO SURVIVAL TIPS

All foreigners planning to stay in India more than 180 days will need to make at least one trip to the Foreigners Regional Registration Office (FRRO) nearest to them. The long lines, confusing documents, and lack of central air-conditioning at most offices have given the registration process in India a horrific reputation in expat lore. But guess what? It's really not that harrowing an experience, especially if you know what to prepare for. Here are a few tips to ease the burden of your FRRO experience:

- Arrive as early as possible. The FRRO reaches its maximum workload for the day and may start turning people away before lunchtime. To avoid having to come back the next day and start the waiting process all over again, try to reach the office at least half an hour before it opens.

- The lines at the FRRO are on par with those at Disneyland, only without an exciting ride to anticipate, so make sure you bring a snack and some water, as you may be waiting longer than expected.

- If you are asked to furnish additional documents, try to obtain them and return them to the same counter on the same day. If you come back the next morning, you will have to line up all over again to regain entry.

- Before you go, make sure you have all the required documents in order. Up-to-date details of requirements can be found at the Bureau of Immigration's website at www.immigrationindia.nic.in.

© MARGOT BIGG

You'll need to report to the FRRO within 14 days of arrival in India.

DAILY LIFE

Extending Your Residential Permit

If you plan to stay in India longer than the duration of your initial visa, you must apply for an extension of your residential permit and visa. Normally you must submit all the same documents you used for your first registration, and in the case of employment visas, a letter from your employer extending your contract for up to a year. In most cases, you can apply for visa extensions directly at the FRRO/FRO. The FRRO can extend student visas and medical visas for up to a year at a time, but employment visas are routed to the MHA the first time they are extended (subsequent ex-

A residential permit is necessary for all foreigners officially residing in India.

tensions can be processed directly at the FRRO). If you have an employment visa and want to extend it for another year, the FRRO will give you a three-month extension stamp in your passport while your case is submitted to the MHA for consideration of extension. However, if your visa has expired and you only have this approval, you may be denied entry to India if you go home for a visit during the consideration period. Sometimes it's easier just to apply for a new visa in your home country, even if your job has not changed.

Moving with Children

Although moving to a new country is an excellent way to broaden your children's horizons, parents naturally worry about moving to India with young ones. Not only must children adjust to cultural and educational differences, they will also have to get used to a different climate and a more careful approach to health and safety. Fortunately, India is a very child-friendly place, and you will find that your children are showered with adoration by many people you meet. Moreover, children from most educated urban families are fluent in English, which makes communicating and adjusting a bit easier for international kids.

Before you move, it's a good idea to familiarize your family with Indian culture. Going out for an Indian meal before you leave is also a good idea. Although a lot of younger children from the West don't take well to Indian food, it's a good idea at least to have them try it at home first. Many parents have found it useful to rent Indian children's movies and buy children's books that are set in India. You can also contact your nearest Indian cultural association and ask to attend some events before you leave. When children are exposed to different cultures in their home environment first, it can lessen the culture shock that they may experience when they arrive in their new home.

MOVING WITH BABIES AND TODDLERS

Many parents report that babies and toddlers adapt and adjust shockingly well to new countries. You'll probably find that your toddler loves all the attention that little ones get in India, and you may end up with a multilingual kid in a matter of a few months. In many ways, parents of babies and small children find life easier in India, where good nannies are affordable and children are welcome almost everywhere.

However, India can be difficult for parents of infants and toddlers in a number of ways. First, you may have difficulty finding the same brands of disposable diapers you are used to back home, and don't count on a cloth diaper service. The same goes for baby food and infant formula. While you can get formula in India, finding your brand might not be easy. The same goes for baby food. Many Indian children start eating adjusted versions of mushy grown-up food from a very young age, and while baby food is available, don't expect to find it in most local shops. Bottles, clothes, toys, and other accessories are easy to find in major cities, and if you are looking for imported maternity and baby products, the British retailer Mothercare has a growing presence in India.

MOVING WITH SCHOOL-AGE CHILDREN

Moving to India with school-age children can be quite a challenge, but it will surely be a memorable experience for your kids. Not only will they have a chance to learn about new cultures and traditions, they will also have the opportunity to make friends from around the world, and maybe even pick up some new language skills in the process. However, most expat children in India live quite differently than they would in their home countries.

It's common for expat families in India to have a number of people working for them, such as drivers, cooks, nannies, and maids. Many families worry that with all the extra help around, their children may end up getting spoiled and not learn the same amount of responsibility that they would back home.

DAILY LIFE

© MARGOT BIGG

Convent schools are popular among India's educated elite.

Many parents ensure that their children maintain responsibility for putting their toys away or setting and clearing the table just as they would in their home countries. If your children have chores back home, try to make sure they maintain them in India. This will not only help them maintain a sense of routine when they move, it will also make moving back home a lot easier.

Food is also a big issue for school-age children moving to India. At many school cafeterias, Indian food is the only thing on the menu, and many non-Indian children find the food too spicy, oily, or "funny-looking" to stomach. Some schools also insist that children eat from the cafeteria instead of bringing a packed lunch, and for many families this is a battle worth fighting. If your child refuses to eat or simply doesn't like Indian food, insist that the school allows you to send sandwiches from home.

MOVING WITH TEENAGERS

It's not easy being a teenager anywhere in the world, and moving away from your friends to a new country can be upsetting to even the most well-adjusted teenager. Fortunately, kids in international schools tend to be more understanding of what it feels like to be the new kid, and many have spent their lives moving from one country to the next. This makes making new friends a bit easier for many teens.

In some ways, teenagers in India have more freedom than they would back home. Alcohol is easy to buy no matter what your age, and although the minimum drinking age can be as high as 25 in some cities, very few bars and clubs strictly enforce this rule. It's also easy to get a tattoo or piercing without parental permission. However, in many other ways, your teenager will have less freedom than he or she might have back home. The minimum driving age in India is 18, and traffic is considerably more hectic and cutthroat than it is in most other countries, so even if your child is old enough to drive, it's not recommended. Furthermore, you may need to impose earlier curfews than you would back home, especially for girls, who are more likely to face harassment than they would back home. Remember that the teenage years are when many people attempt to assert their independence from their parents and forge the foundations of an individual identity, and teenagers often express this through fashion. Clothing that would be acceptable, even normal, back home might not fly in India. In some regions this includes short skirts and tank tops for girls and even shorts for boys.

Moving with Pets

If you plan to spend a significant amount of time in India, you may want to bring your pet along. Moving abroad with pets used to be very difficult and required months of quarantine and heaps of documentation. While bringing animals across borders is still no cakewalk, microchip tracking technology has made the process a bit easier. However, you'll want to have a long think about how making such a move will affect your pet's health and well-being. He or she will be subjected to long flights in the luggage hold of an airplane and come to a very hot and humid country, all of which can cause your pet a lot of trauma. Moreover, ensure that your country will allow you to bring your pet back when you want to move home, and if so, how long you will need to keep your animal in quarantine. The following information applies to dogs and cats. Birds, reptiles, and exotic pets may require additional certification and may not be allowed into the country (especially if they are considered wildlife in India).

PREPARING YOUR PET'S MOVE

Before you leave for India, the first thing you need to do is to have a microchip implanted into your pet's body. This simple procedure involves the injection of a numbered microchip under the skin and can be done at your local veterinarian's office. Your will also need to obtain a rabies vaccine certificate, which must contain a note of the chip number. Finally, you will need a health certificate approved by the government of your home country that states that your animal is free from Aujeszky's disease, distemper, rabies, leishmaniasis,

DAILY LIFE

leptospirosis, and tuberculosis. If you are traveling from the United States, you will need to obtain this document from a USDA-authorized veterinarian, and then submit it, along with all other documentation about your pet's health, to the USDA for stamping.

You will also need to book a flight for your pet, if possible on the same flight you are taking. Try to get a direct flight if possible. As your pet will be kept in the cabin of the plane, make sure that there is enough pressure for your animal to get an ample supply of oxygen. Your pet will need to travel in a crate large enough for him or her to stand up and turn around. You must also make sure your animal will have access to water throughout the duration of the journey. Finally, you have to attach your pet's microchip tracker and copies of documentation to the outside of the crate. It's a good idea also to put a collar on your pet and a tag with your contact information in case he or she breaks loose in the airport.

© MARGOT BIGG

Pet shops are easy to find in India, although they are not always of good quality.

DAILY LIFE FOR PETS

In upscale Indian neighborhoods, many people keep dogs as pets, and dalmatians and pugs are particularly popular. Very few people let their dogs out of their homes unaccompanied, usually because of fears of traffic or attacks by packs of street dogs. Instead, they take them on regular walks or even hire a dog-walker to do the work. If you are taking your dog out, remember to carry a large stick to scare off other animals, especially at night, when street dogs are at their most territorial. In many parts of India, especially the north, pet cats are not as common, although you will still be able to find litter boxes and cat toys at any urban pet shop. Also, many Indians, especially those from more traditional backgrounds, are superstitious about cats, and some will not drive down a street if any cat (black or otherwise) crosses their path.

Pet food is commonly available in pet stores and some larger supermarkets, although it will be relatively much more expensive than in your home country. Many people instead choose to feed their animals cheaper varieties of rice mixed with soy protein nuggets and some meat. Also, it's a good idea to filter or boil the water you feed your pet, as animals can also fall victim to "Delhi belly."

What to Take

Many people come to India loaded with everything they've ever owned, only to find that they can buy equivalent products in India for less than they spent on shipping. The old adage that "everything is possible in India" should be extended to "everything is available in India." I personally arrived in India with only two suitcases, and I never felt that I should have brought more. However, there are a few things you may want to bring from home, especially specialty products.

AVAILABILITY
Foods
In large Indian cities, imported foods are widely available in specialty shops. Expect to find imported cereals, sauces, condiments, and junk food. However, if there's something you absolutely can't live without, bring a large supply from home. The most popular cheese in India is the processed variety, and while you can buy overpriced cheddar at upscale supermarkets and specialty shops, most of it is imported from the Middle East and is not nearly as good as you get back home.

Toiletries
International standard toiletries are widely available in India, although your favorite brand may not be. Not all major perfume and makeup brands are available, so you may want to stock up at duty-free on your way out. Certain shaving supplies and hair gels, tampons with applicators, and strong mosquito repellent are also harder to come by in India.

Clothing
If your shoe size is much larger than average, you may have trouble in India and should bring a few pairs of shoes to get you going. Fortunately, you can have footwear custom-made in most Indian cities. The same applies to clothing—plus sizes are easy to find in major cities, and if there's something you want that you can't find in your size, you can always have it stitched up by a local tailor.

It's not a good idea to bring your nicest clothing to India, unless you plan to trust it only to the hands of a reputable dry cleaner. Water in India can be harsh, and washing techniques nearly violent. Moreover, dust and pollution will shorten the lifespan of your clothes considerably. Instead, buy inexpensive clothes locally for daily use and save nicer garments for special occasions.

SHIPPING OPTIONS

It's not unheard of to move to India with only the luggage you take on the plane, especially if you plan to move into furnished accommodations. You can also send boxes of your favorite items through the mail or courier services, although this will end up costing you a fortune. If you plan to move with a lot of furniture or household goods, you may instead want to use a shipping company.

Relocation and Shipping Companies

Shipping companies usually send representatives to your house to see what you need to ship, then give you a quote based on the size of the shipment you want to make. Most offer a number of different options, including the less expensive surface options that use ships, which can take months. Some companies can also get everything to you within a few days, although this will be very expensive. When choosing a shipping company, you want to research prices and timelines as well as the range of services offered. Some shippers will send people to your home to pack and unpack for you and provide support for bringing the items through customs. Others will limit their involvement to simply getting the goods from point A to point B, leaving you to deal with the bureaucracy in between. It's also a good idea to find out if your shipping company has local offices at both your point of departure and your final destination, as many of them outsource shipments to local companies in your arrival city, which can make tracing a shipment more challenging.

HOUSING CONSIDERATIONS

The first thing you need to sort out when you move to India is where to live. Some companies offer housing for their employees, and if you are on a short-term contract, you will probably find this the easiest option. However, many expats arrive in India only to find out that the housing selected for them by their employer is not up to their expectations. Others, especially those staying for more than a year, prefer to find a home that suits their personality and lifestyle.

Alternatively, you may have a contract in hand but no place to live, or you may be a student who prefers to live off campus. In these cases, you should act quickly to secure a place, and it's advisable to try to sort out your housing before you move to India. Make sure to do a lot of research before you arrive about what neighborhoods you want to live in, how much you want to pay, and what amenities you can and cannot live without.

Currently, foreign nationals (with the exceptions of PIO card holders and

© MARGOT BIGG

OCIs) are not allowed to buy property in India. In fact, some states don't even allow Indians from other states to buy property. While there are tried and tested ways around this, such as tying up with a trusted Indian partner and having the deed put in his or her name, it is neither legal nor advisable.

Finding a Home

Finding the perfect place to live in India can be hit or miss. India's cities are crowded, and apartments are the norm here, although if you have a large family and don't mind living in the suburbs, you should be able to find a house or villa to suit your needs. If you opt for an apartment, you have a number of options.

Short-term residents may prefer to stay in service apartments, which are ready-to-lease apartments that can usually be rented on a short-term basis, usually by the week or month. They can range from a hotel room with a kitchenette to a deluxe furnished apartment that feels a bit more like a home. The benefits of living in a service apartment are that you do not need to deal with landlords, furnishings, and general maintenance, and you have access to a staff that can help you with everything from grocery shopping to getting your dry cleaning done. Service apartments can cost quite a lot—sometimes as much as hotel rooms—and renting one isn't really worth it if you are staying for more than a month or two.

One of the most common options is to rent an apartment in a divided house. Many of India's houses are divided into apartments, one per floor. The nicest units are normally on the ground floor, and these tend to stay cooler than the upper floors in the hot summer months. With a ground-floor apartment, you often get a small patio or garden included in the price. If you rent the top floor, however, you usually get access to the roof along with it. In some cases, house owners build a small studio known as a *barsati* on the rooftop.

If you want a place with secure parking, you may be better off with an apartment complex, also known as a "housing society," as on-street parking is not always available and you may find that your neighbors are territorial about parking spaces they have claimed as their own. Many modern complexes also have swimming pools, fitness centers, and on-site grocery stores as well as security guards and backup electricity.

Both furnished and unfurnished apartments can be rented, although the concept of what defines furnished and unfurnished is a bit hazy. An unfurnished apartment is not only free of furniture but may also lack appliances (such as a refrigerator), cupboards, and closets. A furnished apartment generally

COMMON HOUSING TERMS

- **almirah:** a commonly-used Indian English word for cupboard or closet, which comes from the Hindi-Urdu word *almaari.*

- **barsati:** a rooftop apartment (usually a studio). It gets its name from the Hindi word *barsaat,* which means rain, and these apartments often have tin roofs, so you can listen to the rain during the monsoon.

- **BHK:** stands for bedroom, hall, kitchen, and the B is usually preceded by a number indicating the number of bedrooms. For example, a 2BHK is a two-bedroom.

- **builders flat:** a flat in a house that has been converted into apartments.

- **bungalow:** a detached house. This word originally came from *bangla,* the Hindi word for house (and for Bengali). In many other English-speaking countries the word *bungalow* refers to single-story houses, but in India a bungalow can have any number of floors.

- **farmhouse:** a large house or mansion with a large lawn, usually on the outskirts of the city. Farmhouses do not necessarily have anything to do with farming or agriculture.

- **geyser:** a small water heater that can be mounted on kitchen and bathroom walls.

- **PG:** short for paying-guest accommodations. PGs are single rooms, usually with shared bathrooms, that are rented to students and young single professionals. A meal plan is normally included in the price. PGs are usually single-sex and can be rented on a per-room or shared basis.

- **terrace:** flat rooftop area.

- **twin-sharing:** indicates that a room will be shared with another person. For example, a PG room rented out on a twin-sharing basis will have two twin beds and will be shared.

- **unfurnished:** usually means that there are no appliances (major or otherwise) or furniture in the house, although it can also indicate that the home is absent of light fixtures and basic fittings.

has all of these, as well as furniture, and often a television, water filter, and even a backup electricity source.

When looking for an apartment or house to rent, the Internet is a good place to start. The best websites for finding a rental property are www.sulekha. com, www.magicbricks.com, and www.99acres.com. These sites are used by both landlords and agents to recruit tenants, and even if none of the listings catch your eye, you can at least get a general idea about rental costs in your chosen neighborhood. Another good way to find a place is through word of mouth. Most expat clubs have a Web presence, and expats who are leaving the country often post ads for the apartment they are vacating, especially if they have had a positive experience with the landlord. Otherwise, you may need to go through an agent.

© MARGOT BIGG

India's locksmiths (in Hindi, *chhabi wallahs*) can make you a set of spare keys in just a few minutes.

THE AGENT SYSTEM

Most properties in India are leased through agents, who act as a liaison between landlords and potential tenants. Agents generally stick to a given geographical area, so if you know where you want to live, a single agent should be able to show you a number of different properties. You do not normally have to pay a fee to use the services of an agent, but once you sign the lease to an apartment that the agent has found for you, you are expected to pay a commission equivalent to one month's rent. The landlord is also expected to pay the same fee to the agent, so it's actually in the agent's best interest to get as much rent as he can from you.

RENTAL AGREEMENTS

The first thing you have to do before moving into your new home is to sign a rental agreement. Standard rental agreements, referred to as lease deeds, are for a period of 11 months, and the first page needs to be typed on government-issued stamp paper valued at ₹50. These are available from notaries public. Once the deed has been typed up, you and your landlord must take it back to the notary public and sign every page in his or her presence. Additional notarized photocopies can be made at this time, and they are considered as good as the original.

Settling In

FURNISHING YOUR HOME

Depending on how furnished your apartment or house is when you move in, you may have a lot of shopping to do. While you can bring furniture from home, it's often more cost-effective to pick up furniture locally and sell it when you leave. You can also have furniture custom-made in India at a fraction of what it would cost back home. However, due to strict deforestation regulations, most wood in India is imported, so if you are having wooden furniture made, you will spend on materials what you save on labor costs. A cheaper alternative is getting cane furniture made or just buying ready-made pieces.

The first thing you will want to buy is a bed, or at least a mattress, and you will certainly find a variety to choose from. The cheapest mattresses are best described as a cotton-stuffed cross between a futon and a mat, and usually only cost around ₹500 for a single. Mattresses made of coir fiber are also popular, although proper spring mattresses are more comfortable and last a lot longer. It's common practice in India to put two twin mattresses on a double frame, and double mattresses are not as easily available as they are in the West. Taller people might consider having beds and mattresses custom made, as most are only six feet long.

Some people like to bring linens from home, although again this really isn't necessary. You can have curtains custom made for little more than the price of the material, and fabric shops can usually provide you with the contact details of specialized tailors who are adept at curtain-making and upholstering. You may want to bring fitted bedsheets from home, however, as it's much more common in India just to buy flat sheets and tuck them under the mattress. However, leave your duvet covers at home and invest in some of the beautiful handmade silk bedspreads available in India.

You will also probably want an air conditioner or at least a desert cooler, and as central air-conditioning is still rare in Indian homes, you will probably have to install one. Air conditioners come in two varieties: split and window. Window models have to be fitted in a window or in specially designed air conditioner nooks, which allow the back of the air conditioner to push hot air outside. In many homes there is already a boarded-up space in the window where you can install an air conditioner. If not, carpenters and air conditioner vendors in India are adept at removing windows to make space for the unit. Split air conditioners are divided into two parts, one that cools the room and the other that pushes the hot air outside. The two parts are connected by tubes. Split units are generally more expensive than window units.

DAILY LIFE

DAILY LIFE

© MARGOT BIGG

a window air conditioner with a voltage stablizer

Air-conditioning units are measured in tons, and although 1-ton models are available, you need at least a 1.5-ton system to cool a small room. You also need a power stabilizer to control its intake of electricity. Air conditioners also need a drainage system, especially during monsoons when they collect a lot of extra water. You can either let the water drip outside or have a hose attached that directs excess water into a drain. Although many expats who plan to stay in India for a few years end up buying a new air conditioner, you can also rent one (starting at around ₹6,000 per year for a 1.5-ton window model).

The desert cooler is a common alternative to an air conditioner and consumes less power. However, because coolers work using water, they are not very effective during the muggy monsoon months. Moreover, they are quite noisy, so few expats choose this option unless they are on a very tight budget.

Electricity Concerns

One of the first things you will notice in your new home in India is that there are two types of electrical sockets on the walls, and that different appliances use different plug sizes. Small appliances, such as blow-dryers, lamps, and phone chargers, are equipped for the smaller sockets and have either two pins or are grounded with a third pin. Appliances from parts of continental Europe that use the two-pin system can also be plugged into India's smaller plug points. Larger appliances, such as space heaters and some electric kettles, use the three-pronged M-type plug.

No matter where you live, India will make you realize how much we take for granted in the West, especially when it comes to electricity. Power cuts are a regular occurrence across India, especially in the summers when everyone turns on their air conditioners, creating a huge strain on an already strained grid. Even if you live in a swish apartment complex with its own backup power station, you still have to deal with power cuts to some degree, either at local shops or during the period between when the power goes out and the backup kicks in. Moreover, backup supplies do not necessarily extend to heavy appliances such as air conditioners and hot-water heaters, or appliances that use large plugs. Electricity in India runs on 220–240V AC, 50 Hz.

If your apartment or house does not come equipped with a backup power supply, you'll need to get one yourself. One option is a generator, which is loud and polluting (they run on diesel) but very efficient for backing up heavy appliances such as air conditioners. The size of generator you need depends on the size of your house and the number and types of appliances you want to back up. They are generally better for larger appliances. Another option that is easier to maintain is the uninterruptible power supply (UPS), essentially a battery that keeps electrical items going when the power goes out. The UPS switches on within a few milliseconds of the electricity going out, which means that if you have a computer hooked up to it, you won't lose your work.

Bathrooms

When you move into your new home in India, you may not notice many differences. Many Indian homes used to be constructed around open courtyards, often with the kitchen separate from the living quarters, although most of the newer apartments in metropolitan areas are similar to what you find anywhere in the world. That is, until you get to the bathroom.

Not long ago, most homes were equipped with toilets of the squat variety rather than the "Western style" (as they are called in India) sit-down toilets that are the norm in the West. Rest assured that these days, most modern homes are equipped with sit-down toilets, which often

Showers are generally not sequestered from the rest of the bathroom.

DAILY LIFE

© MARGOT BIGG

STAFFING YOUR HOME

Labor is inexpensive in India, and it is very common for people to have domestic help. The best way to find staff for your house is either through a respected agency or through word of mouth. Ask your landlord, neighbors, and other expats for recommendations, or contact your local expat club, which might have a roster of trustworthy staffers. They can also help you get an idea about what salaries are appropriate in your area, as this varies greatly across the country. If you want English-speaking staff, expect to pay a premium.

Some houses come with servants' quarters, and you may choose to have live-in help. It's also common to have people who come in for a few hours a day. Depending on the size of your house and whether or not you have a garden, you may want to hire extra help, from gardeners to swimming-pool maintenance staff. Here are some of the basic types of help you may need:

- **ayahs (nannies):** Ayahs are basically nannies who also often take care of other chores around the house, such as cooking and clean-

ing. People with newborns and small children often employ two nannies, one for the night shift and one for the daytime. Some ayahs can be quite subservient to the children they're looking after, which can make it difficult for parents. Talking down to staff is accepted in many circles in India, even though it would be considered very rude in the West. Moreover, the concept of children doing chores and even cleaning up after themselves is not common in middle-class Indian households when there is hired help. Parents are advised to brief their ayah on what behavior is expected from their child and not to let their children get complacent about keeping their rooms and play areas tidy. An ayah can charge ₹5,000-10,000 per month for a 50-hour work week, and even more if they are expected to cook and clean.

- **drivers:** With India's traffic as hectic and unpredictable as it is, many people prefer to hire a driver. Drivers are generally not live-in staff. Instead, they

come equipped with built-in bidets. Other bathrooms have a small hose on the wall that's used for the same purpose. And to dispel a common myth, toilet paper is widely used and available in urban India, although in rural parts of the country it's a good idea to bring your own.

Unless you live in an ultramodern and luxurious property, you probably won't have a bathtub. You may not even have a separate divided shower with a shower curtain. It's very common simply to have a showerhead and a tap sticking out of the wall, positioned a strategic distance from the towel rack so that you don't soak the entire room. The drain is built into the bathroom floor in a corner of the room (which makes mopping a breeze). Some people prefer the Indian "bucket bath" system, where you simply fill a bucket with water and use a small jug to pour water from the bucket over your head. This

will come to your house in the morning (usually by motorbike or public transportation) and leave again in the evening, usually, but not always, with a weekly day off. Having a driver is definitely a good idea in cities where there is a lot of morning traffic, and many people who drive themselves still like having a driver for the commute to and from work. A driver will cost you ₹4,000–8,000, depending on what city you live in.

- **guards:** Also known by the Hindi word *chokidar*, guards are a must if you have a large house to yourself. It's normal to have one at night and one during the day, split into two 12-hour shifts. In the case of split housing, the guard's salary will normally be split between you and the other people on your plot. In some areas, neighbors pitch in together to pay for a guard who watches over the whole street. It's best to hire a guard through a company, who will take care of training, screening, and uniforms on your behalf. Budget at least ₹12,000 per month for 24-hour service.

- **maids:** Most people in India have a maid, even if she only comes for a couple of hours per week. A maid's duties range from simply sweeping, mopping, and washing dishes to cooking full meals every day. Maids will also do your laundry, either in the machine (if you have one) or in a bucket. Some maids also iron clothes, although its common to outsource this service to the local *dhobi*, or washerman. Each neighborhood has a few *dhobis* – they usually have a small stand on the roadside, where you'll see them ironing away with large, old-fashioned irons filled with hot coals. Indian maids commonly have an aversion to daily dusting, which in most cities is an absolute necessity. Be firm about this or you will end up doing it yourself. A maid will cost anywhere from a few hundred rupees a month to ₹15,000, depending on location, responsibilities, hours, and language ability. As salaries vary greatly, it's best to ask your neighbors or another expat in your area about what prices are fair.

is a much more ecofriendly way to bathe than using a water-wasting shower, and it is also a good way to bathe the little ones. In fact, the Indian version of bath-time baby photos usually involves a small child sitting in a brightly colored bucket.

As water in most Indian homes is stored in large black containers on the roof, in the summer you will likely have hot water coming out of the cold tap. In the winter, however, especially in the chillier northern cities, you definitely need a hot-water supply. Large hot-water heaters are not the norm in India. Instead, bathrooms are fitted with a small water heater, known as a geyser (GEE-zer), that needs to be turned on about 15–20 minutes before your shower. Many houses and apartments that are advertised as unfurnished still have geysers installed, but if yours does not, it's easy enough to buy one at any home appliances shop and have it installed by a local plumber. Just make sure that the inlet and outlet valves are built in, which they almost always are in newer homes. Some people also use immersion rods, electric heating devices with coils at the end that can be submerged in a bucket of water. However, these devices can be a bit dangerous, and touching the water while the rod is in it can give you a shock.

Another thing to keep in mind is that bathrooms are not commonly equipped with fans, so you may end up creating a bit of a steam room every time you take a hot shower. The easiest solution to this problem is simply to open the window. If you don't have a window, you will probably want to keep your bathroom door open for a while after your shower, or open and close the door quickly a few times to air out the room. Unless you have a fully tiled bathroom, you will have to deal with some mildew.

Kitchens

Depending on how furnished your house is, your kitchen may be fully functional at the time you move in, or it may be nothing more than a room with a sink and a few electrical sockets. If this is the case, you have to buy your own fridge, stove, and possibly cabinets, as well as various cutlery, dishes, and pans. Refrigerators in India cost around what they do in the West (or even more for imported brands). They're available in a range of sizes, measured in cubic liters. Local brands such as Kelvinator are good buys, as they are made for the Indian market and thus can handle electricity surges. With cheaper models, however, you have to defrost the fridge yourself, possibly quite often depending on how hot it is outside. Brands like Whirlpool and Samsung are also popular, and the appliances they produce for the Indian market take the climate into consideration. Some fridges have special "monsoon" settings for when it's hot and muggy out; others play a song (usually "Jingle Bells" or a classic Bollywood Song) if you leave the door open for too long. It's also common for fridges to come with built-in locks, in case you want to keep something off-limits to your household staff or children.

If you plan to learn how to cook Indian food or have someone do it for you, you will probably need to invest in a few bits of crockery that you may find unfamiliar. In Northern Indian homes, you need a *tawa,* a flat, round pan with a handle that looks like a cross between a frying pan and a griddle. The *tawa* is used to cook staple breads such as the unleavened *roti,* which is often eaten with Indian food instead of rice. You also need a pressure cooker, as this seriously speeds up the time it takes to prepare pulses such as dal and beans. For meat and vegetable dishes, you need a type of wok known as a *kadai.*

© MARGOT BIGG

Pumped-in gas is a rarity in India; instead, you'll need to buy it by the canister.

You may also need to install a place to store your dishes. Cabinets can be custom-made by carpenters for a small fee, or you can buy readymade ones and have them installed. Many people also like the two-in-one drying rack–storage space. These large metal contraptions are basically drying racks that can be mounted on the wall, and they can be bought from any home-furnishings market.

If your kitchen is not equipped with a cooking range, you will need to buy one of these too. Gas ranges are not very expensive, starting at around ₹1,500 for two burners, although you need to use a match to get the fire going unless you buy a fancier self-lighting model. Cooking gas in India is rarely piped in, so you also need to obtain a "gas connection," which essentially means access to a cylinder. To do this, you have to apply to a local gas supplier, with a notarized affidavit stating that you do not already have a cylinder licensed under your name (the supplier can provide you with a template for the affidavit). You are entitled to two gas cylinders per residence, but waiting lists for cylinders are often quite long. In the interim, you can buy small refillable cylinders from most local markets specializing in home furnishings and appliances. Once you do get a cylinder, make sure that the valves and tubes are properly fitted, and notify the supplier immediately if you smell a leak.

If you'd prefer to avoid the bureaucratic headache of obtaining a gas connection, you can always buy an electric stove instead. Just bear in mind that you won't be able to use yours during power cuts unless you have them connected to a backup source of electricity. Exhaust fans are not that commonplace in the Indian kitchen, although you usually have a chimney of some sort that allows smoke out of the house. Ceiling fans, however, are common in larger kitchens and are much needed during the hotter months. It's also not a bad idea to pick up a small fire extinguisher. Smoke detectors are not common fixtures in Indian homes, although they are available.

Finally, you have to secure your drinking-water supply, as tap water in

If you don't have a filter, you can still buy drinking water by the 20-liter barrel.

most of India is not potable. Your options are either buying a water filter or simply setting up a bottled water account with a water supplier or a nearby shop. Bottled water comes in 20-liter barrels, which can be tipped over onto a dispenser (either a proper heating and cooling dispenser akin to the ones found in offices in the West, or a more rudimentary plastic dispenser). Popular bottled water brands include Bisleri, Catch, Kinsley, and Aquafina. Less expensive local brands are also available and are generally safe, although sometimes the water sold by unknown brands is of questionable origin. If it tastes funny, don't drink it.

The best-known home water filter on the market is called Aquaguard, and it uses the reverse osmosis (RO) process, which is also employed by many bottled water companies, to filter water. If you plan to stay in India for a while, installing a water purification system in your home may turn out to be more cost-effective than buying bottled water. However, the filters do not work during power outages (unless they are connected to your backup electricity supply), so it's a good idea to keep a few bottles of filtered water on hand for such cases. Moreover, some organisms can pass through filters, and while most expats drink filtered water regularly with no problems, some people are nervous about any water that does not come from a sealed bottle.

Cleaning Supplies

Most expats, even students and those on limited budgets, hire a maid to come in daily for basic cleaning (your landlord may even require this). Maids can charge as little as ₹400 per month (in smaller cities) for only sweeping and mopping, or as much as ₹15,000 per month for full-time service that includes cooking and grocery shopping, especially if they speak English. Whether you opt for a maid or not, you have to buy a variety of cleaning supplies, a few of which are different from what you are used to back home. As your house will probably have either marble or linoleum floors and no carpets (a common situation in hot climates), you need a big bottle of floor cleaner to get started. While regular floor-cleaning solution is available, people in India often use phenol to wash the floors instead. Although this definitely does the trick and helps keep pests away, it smells horrible and is not a good idea if you have toddlers in the house. Indian brooms are usually short, with a handle and a long set of soft bristles (hard bristled brooms are also available), and this is what most cleaning staff are used to. You should get one of these right away, as well as a bucket for mopping and a *pochha,* a soft cloth that's used for scrubbing the floors instead of a mop. Dishwashers are rare, and Indian cleaners usually prefer bar dish soap instead of liquid detergent. If you don't have a washing machine, you also need a bucket, laundry detergent, a scrub brush, and a bar of blue-colored laundry soap that your cleaning staff will use on tough stains and to get your garments extra clean. While you may not be used to all of these additional bars of soap, you'll soon realize that they are very effective at getting clothes and dishes very clean and are a real blessing in India's dustier cities.

UTILITIES

When you move into your new house, be sure to clarify what utilities you are expected to pay for. Bills often come in the name of your landlord, who will give you a photocopy of the bill for reimbursement.

Water

Generally, your landlord charges you a set monthly fee for water, although if you have a large house, you may have a separate supply all to yourself that is billed based on usage. Water rates vary from city to city, and rates are often raised and adjusted, so budget at least ₹500 per person per month. In most homes, water is stored in large underground tanks and then pumped to smaller rooftop storage barrels. If your landlord's home is on-site, he may just deal with pumping the water himself, which only involves flipping a switch and remembering to turn it off when the upstairs tank is full. However, the city only supplies water at certain times of the day to each neighborhood, so if you are responsible for pumping the water yourself, you have to find out when to switch it on.

Water shortages are common in many Indian cities, especially during the summer months. It's a good idea to buy a large plastic garbage can and use it to store extra water in case you run out. Just make sure you keep it covered, as still water can attract mosquitoes. If water shortages persist, you can also buy water from private water suppliers, who come to your house with a large truck full of water and sell you the precious resource at an inflated price.

Electricity

Your electricity bill is normally in your landlord's name, so you won't need to establish a connection yourself. Billing is monthly for large properties with three-phase meters, and every other month for smaller apartments with single-phase meters. You are billed a fixed "demand" charge, a consumption charge based on the meter reading, and an additional 5 percent tax. Per-unit electricity charges are calculated in slabs, but expect to pay an average of around ₹4 per unit. In the event that your meter is not accessible when the power company comes to read it, they approximate your bill based on previous consumption. You are expected to pay this amount, even if it is considerably higher than what you actually consumed. The money paid is adjusted to your bills for the months that follow.

Garbage

India's system for getting rid of garbage is very different than in most other countries. Instead of garbage trucks coming around your neighborhood at a scheduled time, your neighborhood will probably have a local garbage collector who collects garbage from you for ₹50–150 per month, depending on the size of your household and the economic level of your neighborhood. This person may also be the local toilet cleaner, who offers to come to your house a few times a week to clean your latrine. This position is necessary in India, as many maids will not clean toilets, although many expats prefer just to do the dirty work themselves. The garbage collector is often also responsible for sweeping the streets, which involves nothing more than kicking up big clouds of dust into the air with a broom. These people take your garbage to local sorters, or sort it themselves for bits and pieces that can be sold to recyclers and for food scraps that can be sold to livestock owners for feed or turned into compost.

Many people are surprised to learn that recycling is actually huge in India. It doesn't take the same form as it does in Western countries, where bottles and cans are rinsed and sorted into different bins and later picked up by recycling companies. Instead, it relies on a network of smaller contractors, known as *raddiwallahs* and *kabriwallahs,* who eke out a living by acting as middlemen between consumers and recyclers. You can hear them in the streets, zipping by on bicycles and announcing their presence with nearly intelligible cries of *"raadi, raadi." Raddiwallahs* deal in paper, mainly old books and newspapers. *Kabriwallahs* buy anything from jars and scrap metal to old appliances. They will happily take your recyclables off your hands and will even pay you a few rupees in return. If you don't have the time or energy to sell your old newspapers and bottles to these men, just throw them out with your trash. The garbage collector takes them to the recyclers and will surely be thankful for the small addition to his or her measly salary that this transaction will provide.

DAILY LIFE

LANGUAGE AND EDUCATION

India's official language is Hindi, written in the Devanagari script, and English has secondary official-language status. After independence, India had originally planned to phase out the use of English for official dealings, although public outcry from southern states where Hindi is not known or used by a large part of the population prompted the government to reconsider its Hindi-only policy. English serves as a lingua franca in India, and the fact that the language is not geographically rooted here allows it to be used by members of different communities to communicate. In India, a person's ability to speak English is inextricably linked to social status, and the middle and upper classes make a point of sending their children to schools where the language of instruction is English.

Although India's schools where the language of instruction is English are often of very high quality, expats usually prefer to send their children to international schools, which offer instruction and a learning culture similar to what

© MARGOT BIGG

one would find in the West. University students who want to study in India also have the option of enrolling directly in an Indian university or studying at a study-abroad center affiliated with an overseas university.

Learning the Languages

Depending on where you live, you may want to learn a bit of Hindi, another local language, or both. Hindi is the primary language in cities such as Delhi and Jaipur and is widely used and understood in Mumbai, Bengaluru, Ahmedabad, Pune, Goa, and even Kolkata. If you move to Chennai, you are better off learning Tamil. In Kolkata, Hindi is used and understood, although you will make a better impression on local people if you pick up a bit of Bengali instead.

Many people come to India specifically to learn Indian languages, especially Hindi. However, it's more common that people who have moved to India for other reasons, usually a job, end up wanting to learn a bit of the local language. Most larger cities have at least one institution offering language training, although many expats prefer to get an individual tutor, which costs in the range of ₹400–1,200 per hour.

IS ENGLISH ENOUGH?

You will find that in most social and professional situations in India, knowing English is enough to get you by. Most of your colleagues will be fluent

DAILY LIFE

ENGLISH WORDS OF INDIAN ORIGIN

You may know that many words used in modern English derive from French and German. South Asian languages, especially Hindi and Urdu, have also left their mark on the English language. Here are a few common words that entered the English language via the subcontinent:

• avatar

• bandana

• bungalow

• calico

• cheetah

• cot

• jungle

• khaki

• loot

• pundit

• shampoo

• thug

• veranda

INDIAN ENGLISH

The type of English used in India is quite different from what you hear in North America, Australia, or even the United Kingdom. Many Indian English expressions that sound odd to native speakers are actually direct translations of Hindi or regional-language sayings. Certain words that have been archaic for over a century in other English-speaking countries are still used in everyday speech in India, and they can sound theatrically comical at first. Then there are the scores of words that emerged from Indian languages but are still used, sometimes in a slightly anglicized way, in regular English conversation. There are enough Indian English words and expressions to write volumes on the subject, and people have. Here is a small selection of some of the most common, and amusing, Indian English utterances:

- **artiste:** an artist of any sort, from a singer to a painter. Like many phrases and words borrowed from French, *artiste* sounds affected and pretentious to native speakers of English, but it's the norm in India.

- **batchmate:** classmate or person who graduated in the same year, or batch.

- **pass out of:** to graduate from; "I passed out of Delhi University in 2008."

- **do one's graduation:** to study at the bachelor level; "I did my graduation in engineering."

- **time pass:** pastime.

- **thrice:** three times. Rarely used in U.S. English, but as common as the word *twice* in India.

- **senti:** short for *sentimental*, used to refer to a person.

- **funda:** short for *fundamental*.

- **the needful:** the thing that needs to be done; "I would like you to fill out this form. Kindly do the needful before 3 o'clock."

- **revert back:** respond to a letter or email.

- **What to do?** expression of resignation.

- **Why like this?** similar to saying "What's the matter?" Translation of the Hindi expression *aise kyun*.

- **after some time:** a long and fancy way of saying "later." Translation of the Hindi expression *bad mein*.

- **do one thing:** a way of suggesting you do something or try something, not a command.

- **just like that:** for the heck of it. If you ask why someone did something, and they don't really have any clearly defined motive behind

in English, and all written correspondence and formal discussions happen in English, even between two people who are native speakers of another language. However, outside the office, a little knowledge of the local language will get you a very long way, and it is useful when talking to autorickshaw and taxi drivers, shopkeepers, and household staff. However, it's customary in upscale shops, cafés, and restaurants to use English, even if the staff member is not 100 percent fluent. If you only speak a little bit of the local language, these

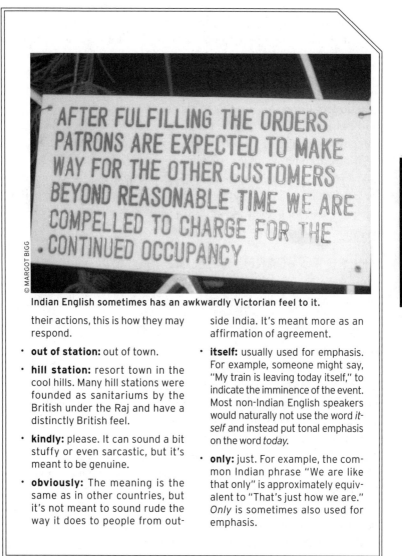

AFTER FULFILLING THE ORDERS PATRONS ARE EXPECTED TO MAKE WAY FOR THE OTHER CUSTOMERS BEYOND REASONABLE TIME WE ARE COMPELLED TO CHARGE FOR THE . CONTINUED OCCUPANCY

© MARGOT BIGG

Indian English sometimes has an awkwardly Victorian feel to it.

DAILY LIFE

their actions, this is how they may respond.

- **out of station:** out of town.

- **hill station:** resort town in the cool hills. Many hill stations were founded as sanitariums by the British under the Raj and have a distinctly British feel.

- **kindly:** please. It can sound a bit stuffy or even sarcastic, but it's meant to be genuine.

- **obviously:** The meaning is the same as in other countries, but it's not meant to sound rude the way it does to people from out-side India. It's meant more as an affirmation of agreement.

- **itself:** usually used for emphasis. For example, someone might say, "My train is leaving today itself," to indicate the imminence of the event. Most non-Indian English speakers would naturally not use the word *itself* and instead put tonal emphasis on the word *today*.

- **only:** just. For example, the common Indian phrase "We are like that only" is approximately equivalent to "That's just how we are." *Only* is sometimes also used for emphasis.

establishments are not the place to practice, as attempting a few words in the local language to a person who knows English, albeit not perfectly, can come across as condescending.

Important Things to Know

The nice thing about most Indian languages, especially Hindi, is that you can throw in an English word here and there if needed and still be understood.

People often use English numbers when discussing prices or even phone numbers, and in cities, most people understand the English words for things like fruits and vegetables. Taxi and rickshaw drivers also generally know words like *left, right,* and *straight* (although not *forward*), and many people understand basic English a lot better than they speak it. However, it's still a good idea to learn the local-language names for foods and directions, as well as basic questions such as "how much" and "where is." It's also helpful to learn the script of your city's local language, especially if you plan to drive or take buses.

Visitors to India are often shocked at the lack of the use of "please" and "thank you" by the general population. Don't mistake this for bad manners. Some Indian languages, including Hindi, use different verb forms to indicate politeness, and while there are words for *please* and *thank you,* they are not peppered in conversation as frequently as overseas.

WHERE TO LEARN

If you are serious about studying an Indian language, here are a few places you may want to consider.

Hindi

There are many Hindi language courses available in India, the most reputable of which is the Landour Language School near Mussorie, north of Delhi. This school was established back in the Raj era and continues to offer individual tuition to students from around the world. They also teach Punjabi, Urdu, and Garhwali. In Delhi, the East West Language Institute (EWLI) is run by a former teacher from Landour and uses the Landour textbook. In Delhi, there's also Hindi Guru, which is more expensive and does not have the reputation of EWLI, at least among scholars. Many foreign students also head to Varanasi to study at Bhasha Bharati, which offers long-term Hindi courses as well as short intensive courses aimed at students. In Jaipur, the American Institute for Indian Studies offers full-time courses in Hindi language and Indian studies, which are especially popular with U.S. study-abroad students.

Bengali

Bengali, also known as Bangla, is the second-most spoken language in India and is the primary language of the state of West Bengal and the country of Bangladesh. If you are based in Kolkata, a little knowledge of Bengali can make a lasting impression on people you meet and make day-to-day tasks a bit easier. The Ramakrishna Mission Institute of Culture in West Kolkata's

Golpark offers six-month and year-long courses in Bengali as well as a long list of other Indian and non-Indian languages. Their group courses are shockingly affordable, and if you prefer one-on-one instruction, you can also contact them for references of private tutors.

Tamil

If you are moving to Tamil Nadu, forget about Hindi and instead start learning the local Dravidian language of Tamil. Tamil is spoken throughout Tamil Nadu and some parts of Sri Lanka and is much more useful (and appreciated) than Hindi if you live in Chennai or elsewhere in the state. The Institute of Asian Studies in Chennai offers four-

Underprivileged children gain access to learning through "Hole-in the-Wall" education kiosks.

month introductory courses and six-month advanced courses in Tamil. They also have condensed intensive courses, which last one or two months, for foreigners who are short on time.

Education

Education in India has a long history dating back to ancient times. The system of education used today was modeled after the British system in the 19th century. Schools are divided into three levels: primary (or elementary), secondary (high school), and tertiary (college).

Education in India is intense and very competitive. It is also a huge business, and the variety of education options is phenomenal. At the primary and secondary level, you can find everything from the most basic one-room rural schools that operate more like day cares to world-class institutions with ultramodern facilities. At the postsecondary level, options range from colleges that seem to be more in the business of selling degrees than actually providing education to schools and colleges that are recognized as some of the world's finest.

COLLEGES AND UNIVERSITIES

Indian colleges and universities offer degrees similar to what you get in the West. Most bachelor degree programs last for three years, and masters last for one or two years. Competition to get into India's best tertiary schools is fierce, and many schools only offer places to a small percentage of applicants. A quota system is used to secure places in universities and government jobs for people from minority cultural groups and castes, although as a foreign student this does not apply to you.

If you have come to India to pursue higher studies, you have an overwhelming choice of institutions. If you want to study engineering, you will want to consider one of the many Indian Institutes of Technology (IIT) scattered across the country. For business, you could opt for one of the country's many Indian Institutes of Management (IIM) or head straight to the ultraprestigious Indian School of Business (ISB) in Hyderabad. Students of humanities and social sciences have a number of options—popular schools among foreigners include Delhi University (DU) and Jawaharlal Nehru University (JNU), both in Delhi, and Symbiosis in Pune.

Direct Enrollment Versus Study Abroad

Once you have decided where you want to live or what you want to study, you have to decide whether to enroll directly or to enroll in a study-abroad program. Many students, especially those who have never been to India, prefer

भारतीय प्रौद्योगिकी संस्थान दिल्ली

INDIAN INSTITUTE OF TECHNOLOGY DELHI

© MARGOT BIGG

The Indian Institutes of Technology produce some of the world's finest engineers.

to do a study-abroad program. These programs are designed for foreigners, and many of them allow you to earn credit that you can transfer back to your home institution. These programs are especially useful for U.S. students receiving financial aid, as they allow you to maintain the minimum enrolment requirement to receive aid and, in some cases, you may qualify for higher loan or grant amounts to offset the cost of traveling and living in a foreign country. Another plus of going through a study-abroad program is that they normally provide you with housing and cultural-adjustment support, and they usually host an orientation program that gives you the chance to meet other students while learning about India. Some programs even offer travel programs that allow you to see India and study different regions with the rest of your group.

If you opt for direct enrolment, you should start the registration process quite early. Many schools ask for certified copies of your transcripts and any other degrees or certificates obtained, and may even require you to take an entrance exam. While the process for applying for direct enrolment can be quite bureaucratic, there are a number of advantages. First, you will save a lot of money compared to those who opt for study-abroad programs, as you are charged in rupees rather than dollars or pounds. Moreover, you will be immersed headfirst into India's educational system, and you are bound to meet a lot more local people than you would if you went through a study-abroad program. Finally, direct enrolment is useful if you want to pursue an entire course of study in India leading to a degree, as study-abroad programs don't generally last for more than one year.

Postgraduate Research

Some students and scholars also come to India to conduct research for their master's or doctoral degrees or to conduct postdoctoral research. While you can simply show up and begin your research, many people find it useful to come as a visiting scholar in conjunction with an Indian university. This allows you access to library resources and makes getting into conferences a bit easier. If your home institution has an affiliation with an India-based university, it's usually easiest to apply to visit that school. If not, the easiest way to get in is first to contact a professor or department head of the school you are interested in visiting. Professors naturally occupy a high place in the university hierarchy in India, and they can help you jump through whatever bureaucratic hoops the university's admissions department might have set up.

ELEMENTARY AND SECONDARY SCHOOLS

India's childhood education system is enormous and complex, and the quality of education in the country ranges from pitiable to top-notch. At the low end of the scale are the government-run free schools, which have such a bad reputation that even low-wage laborers often go without meals just to send their children to private schools.

Indian schools generally run January–December, and children are admitted depending on the year in which they are born. This varies a lot, however, and you may find students born in different years in the same class. Some parents go so far as providing false birth date information for their children in order to get them into a preferred class, and you will likely meet quite a few people with both real and fake birthdays.

Admissions into the top schools of India can be quite difficult, and some schools request that you put your children on waiting lists while they are still in the womb. Your social background, job, and whether you or your spouse attended the school play a large role in determining your child's admission. Foreigners may have an easier time gaining admission, although many of the top schools do not accommodate people who start class in the middle of the school year. If you are sending your child to any type of school except an American or Canadian international school, school uniforms are also required.

Boarding school is also quite popular in India, and, as in the United Kingdom, sending your children (or at least your sons) to boarding school used to be the norm for the country's business elite. These days, more and more parents prefer to keep their children at home, sending them to local schools that offer the same standard of education.

The traditional teaching methods used in India are dramatically different from the methods used in most Western English-speaking countries today. The focus is on memorizing and regurgitating information, and many schools put math and sciences on a pedestal high above the humanities. The result is generations of scientists with very sharp memories and the ability to synthesize data quickly and methodically. Moreover, the coursework is far more demanding than in many Western countries, especially the United States, and people who have been educated in this system often find university in the United States and Britain laughably easy. Because the focus is on memorization rather than critical thinking, however, students who have been taught in more traditional or old-fashioned ways tend to find arguing their own opinions, especially those that go against the status quo, more challenging. They also might come across as a bit ignorant about the arts and culture (Indian or otherwise) simply because so much of their schooling revolved around crunching numbers and learning formulas. For this reason, many parents prefer to send their children to international schools or schools that pride themselves on alternative approaches to learning.

As the state-sponsored educational institutes are far below par, you will have to fork out some cash for your child's education in India. While you can always home-school, there are enough high-quality schools in India that you should be able to find a school that is suitable for your child's needs. You just have to figure out whether an international school or a more Indian private school is better for you.

International Schools

International schools may be the way to go if you want your child to be in a similar social and educational environment to what he or she would experience back home. International schools attract teachers and students from all over the world, so your child will not feel like an outsider the way he or she might in a predominantly Indian school. However, these schools are expensive, sometimes costing upward of ₹1 million per year per student. Interestingly, unlike top private schools in the West, where the students are almost exclusively from wealthy backgrounds, India's international schools are mixed. In most cases, employers pay tuition as part of a relocation package.

There are a few important things to find out when selecting an international school. First, make sure that the school has air-conditioning and a backup electricity supply. Find out about food options and whether they allow children to carry a packed lunch—most international schools have Western options on the menu to accommodate kids who haven't acquired a taste for Indian food. Also ask if there's a school bus or any aftercare services, especially if you are a single parent or if both you and your partner are working. Finally, ask to speak to other parents of foreign children, as they will be able to give you the best insight into the pros and cons of the school.

© MARGOT BIGG

School uniforms are the norm.

Although most top international schools in India only admit day students, two of the very best are boarding schools. These are Kodaikanal International School in Tamil Nadu and Woodstock School in Landour, near Mussoorie. These schools traditionally served the children of missionary families, and these days they attract students of all faiths and cultural backgrounds.

Plenty of schools in India add the tag "International School" to their names simply to make the school look more attractive, especially to Indian families. Do not be misled; many of these so-called international schools have nothing international about them except the foreign-looking children they hire to model as students for their brochures. Yes, they usually have air-conditioning, shiny facilities, and clever English names, but if they are not using course methodology that would prepare your children for a Western university, you probably want to avoid sending your kids there.

Good international schools have tie-ups with either the Switzerland-based International Baccalaureate (IB) or the United Kingdom's University of Cambridge International Examinations (CIE). The IB is an organization whose standardized method of education is recognized by universities and schools worldwide. IB is helpful for students who have to move a lot, as it helps them pick up in a new school where they left off in their previous school. The IB program is divided into three levels: the Primary Years Programme (PYP), the Middle Years Programme (MYP), and the Diploma Programme (DP). Only a handful of schools in India offer all three, but most good international schools offer the DP, which is spread over the final two years of secondary school. The

students at one of India's popular convent schools

program covers math, sciences, English (or the primary language used in the school), foreign languages, arts, humanities, and social sciences. The IB diploma is awarded based on exams that are conducted simultaneously around the world in either spring or autumn.

The CIE equivalent to Britain's GCSEs (formerly O-levels) is known as the International General Certificate of Secondary Education (IGCSE). This certificate is especially useful for British students or those who want to attend university in Britain, and it also acts as a good foundation for students carrying on to study for the IB diploma or their A-level and AS-level examinations.

Private Schools

Another, sometimes more affordable alternative to international schools is Indian private schools. Students in private schools may or may not have the option of taking their A-levels or IB examinations, but most students in private schools are expected to take examinations run by the Council for the Indian School Certificate Examinations (CISCE). Tenth graders take the examination for the Indian Certificate of Secondary Education (ICSE), which shows their aptitude in seven key subjects and allows them to continue on to the last two years of secondary education. In 12th grade, known as class 12 in India, students must pass another exam in order to obtain the Indian School Certificate (ISC), which is designed so that students can seek direct admission to British universities without having to complete their A-levels

© MARGOT BIGG

school buses that run on Compressed Natural Gas (CNG)

first. Students may also have to take exams administered by the government's Central Board of Secondary Education (CBSE).

PRESCHOOLS

India has an abundance of preschools, or nursery schools, and crèches; some are more like playgroups, and others are closer to preelementary schools. The quality varies, and it's best to find one that's closest to what you might have at home. It's also best to try to find one that is located close to your home, in case you need to go in on short notice (although this is generally advisable in any country). Bear in mind that a large percentage of Indian preschools only run for half a day, usually mornings, and many do not provide after-school care.

When visiting a nursery school, it's a good idea to ask if you can stick around and observe the day-to-day activities of the children. Are there other international students enrolled? Do the teachers and children communicate in English? Does the school provide an outdoor area to play in that includes adequate shaded space? Is the school air-conditioned? Most importantly, do the children look happy? Go with your gut instinct.

HEALTH

Health and safety are among the top priorities for most visitors to India—not surprising when others return from India with tales of violent bouts of "Delhi belly" and roller coaster–like traffic. While there is no denying that you have to take extra care to ensure you stay healthy in India, bear in mind that living in India is very different than traveling as a tourist, and most of the restaurants you frequent will be as hygienic as in Western countries. It's also true that at first glance, the traffic in Indian cities can seem a bit less predictable than what you are used to back home, but once you recognize the order in the chaos on the roads, you will find that with a little bit of strategic planning, getting around safely is possible.

Living in India does put you at risk of contracting communicable diseases that have long been limited or eradicated in the West. However, most of these are prevalent only in rural areas or in very poor conditions, which you won't come in contact with unless you are an aid worker. In fact, most of the common ailments in India are easily treatable and easy to prevent. If you do fall

© MARGOT BIGG

ill, rest assured that India has some of the finest doctors and medical staff in the world.

The information in this chapter is intended only as a guideline and should not be taken as a substitute for advice from a qualified medical professional. This is especially crucial if you have a compromised immune system or any allergies. Remember that the public health situation may change during your trip. For up-to-date information on outbreaks, consult the U.S. Centers for Disease Control and Prevention (CDC).

Hospitals and Clinics

India has some excellent medical facilities, as well as plenty that look like they would do you more harm than good. No matter where you go, remember that India has some of the best doctors in the world, and you will usually be in safe hands. However, the sanitation in some of the more basic hospitals is not always up to Western standards, so it's better to opt for one of the more modern private hospitals when possible.

PRIVATE HOSPITALS AND CLINICS

Most expats would agree that private hospitals and clinics are the way to go. Because the fees are higher, private institutions have lower caseloads and can offer more attentive and timely services to patients. Larger private hospitals also have newer equipment and are just as good as anything you will find back home. There are also many chains of high-quality hospitals in India, such as Fortis, Max, and Apollo. Emergency care (known in India as urgent care) in private hospitals is at the same standard as in Western countries, although it will cost you about 20 percent of what it would cost in the U.S. In the event of an emergency, call the hospital directly for a hospital-operated ambulance.

GOVERNMENT HOSPITALS

India's government hospitals are best avoided. While they may have some of the best doctors, the patient loads are often unreasonably high, and the conditions are often poor. The costs at government hospitals are usually lower than at private clinics, but long waits and often substandard conditions simply do not justify the money saved.

MEDICAL TOURISM

India is increasingly becoming a hot spot for medical tourism, and it is no surprise why. India's doctors are among the best in the world, and their rates are some of the lowest. India's recent boom in private health care also means that there are now scores of modern hospitals across the country with facilities on par with what you would find in the United States with rates that are less than most people in the States have to fork over in co-pays.

Medical tourists are now coming to India for treatment that they may not be able to afford in their home countries, including cardiology and plastic surgery. India also has some great bargains on routine medical services, such as dentistry, and it's a great place to get new glasses at a fraction of what you would pay back home. Medicines are also much cheaper in India than in other countries, so if you are currently footing the bill for expensive drugs, you may want to consider getting your prescription filled in India instead.

© MARGOT BIGG

India's major cities have ultra-modern hospitals with international standards of care.

DAILY LIFE

SPECIALISTS

Specialists are quite common in India, and you can usually approach a specialist directly without seeking prior referral from a primary doctor. Dermatology is a huge industry, and there are many skin clinics in large cities offering everything from wrinkle reduction to hair removal. These clinics have dermatologists who can also help you with noncosmetic issues such as acne. There are also plenty of specialist hospitals that deal with everything from

DAILY LIFE

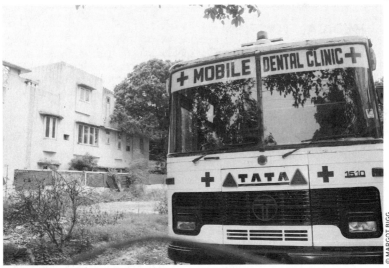

© MARGOT BIGG

an innovative way of getting dental care to the masses

heart disease to obstetrics. If you wear corrective lenses, you can usually get a vision test at a local optician or glasses shop. Mental health is not focused on in India as much as in many Western countries, although psychiatric services are available.

DENTISTS

Dental services are high quality and inexpensive, and a branch of medical tourism related to dentistry is booming in India. A routine cleaning and checkup at a good clinic costs around ₹600–1,000, and a root canal costs ₹4,000–5,000. Some dentists are not as good as others, however, and botched jobs are not uncommon. Ask around before settling on a dentist.

Insurance

Many visitors to India purchase traveler's insurance, although you may not be covered if you plan to stay long-term. Your insurance may also be limited to certain parts of the country; for example, some insurance policies do not cover you if you are vacationing in areas where there are government-issued travel advisories. You may also want to take out special expat coverage from an international insurance company or even purchase additional insurance

AYURVEDA

Ayurveda, the Indian subcontinent's traditional system of health care that dates back to Vedic times, continues to play an important role in keeping much of India's population healthy. The system relies primarily on plant-based treatments and incorporates a number of other practices, such as diet regulation and massage, to keep patients in tip-top shape.

One of the key concepts in ayurveda is that everyone's body is a combination of three humors, or *doshas,* namely *vata* (wind or air), *pitta* (bile or fire), and *kapha* (phlegm or water). Ayurvedic medicines are prescribed for both preventive and curative purposes, and treatment courses are tailored to the patient based on the composition of his or her *dosha.*

While ayurvedic medicine can be helpful for a number of health concerns, the medicines are not always that effective against serious ailments that may have evolved in modern times. Also, remember that just because something is natural does not always mean that it is appropriate for everyone, and it's always important to seek professional medical advice before starting any course of treatment.

from an Indian provider, such as ICICI (which is perhaps the most reputable). Private policies in India are comprehensive, and many policies are free of co-pay stipulations. However, some policies only cover hospitalizations, although coverage usually extends nationwide. A family of two adults in their early to mid-forties with two children can expect to pay around ₹8,000–10,000 per year.

EMPLOYER COVERAGE

Large employers offer medical reimbursement and insurance as part of their package, although normally these policies only cover you if you are hospitalized for longer than 24 hours. Even if you do have coverage, you will often have to pay out of pocket first and seek reimbursement from your insurer later, which can turn into a lengthy and bureaucratic process.

HOSPITAL INSURANCE PROGRAMS

Some hospitals offer private insurance packages that work almost like a membership. Fees vary, and family plans are available, although you will only be covered by the hospital you have "joined."

DAILY LIFE

Pharmacies and Prescriptions

Pharmacies, also called chemists, are everywhere in India, and many offer extras such as home delivery and on-site nurses. Most pharmacies sell a range of over-the-counter and prescription drugs as well as toiletries, condoms, and ayurvedic medicines. Chain pharmacies, such as those operated by health care companies like Fortis and Guardian, are popping up across the country, although these sometimes only sell expensive brand-name versions of medicines.

DISPENSING MEDICINES

Medicines in India are very inexpensive and can be purchased per pill (bubble-packed) or in strips. Although you technically need a prescription for a wide range of drugs in India, not all pharmacists will ask for one. In fact, psychoactive substances such as codeine can easily be purchased without a prescription. Even more frightening is that if you go to a pharmacy and tell them you have a common symptom, such as a cough or stomach upset, they will likely hand you a strip of antibiotics without a prescription. This is dangerous and can lead to antibiotic resistance, or worse. No matter what your pharmacist may tell you, always see a doctor before taking antibiotics.

If you need a vaccination, you may have to buy the vaccine, along with a syringe, from a pharmacy. Most vaccines need to be refrigerated, and not all pharmacies have backup electricity supplies; it is best to buy vaccines only from pharmacies located inside hospitals.

long lines at the pharmacy

Diseases and Preventive Measures

The first thing you need to do before going to India is consult with a travel clinic. A nurse or doctor will be able to give you specialized information about India and advise which vaccinations and medications are appropriate. Remember to inform the travel clinic if you will be working with animals, in conditions of extreme poverty, or in rural areas, as these factors may affect the advice they give you.

DISEASES AND ILLNESSES

Many diseases that are prevalent in India are rare or no longer exist in the developed world. It is important to understand how these diseases are contracted and how best to prevent them.

Mosquito-Borne Illnesses

Diplomats in days of yore used to refer to hardship postings as "mosquito countries," and itchy bites were the least of their concerns. Diseases transmitted by mosquitoes are still quite common in tropical countries, especially after heavy rains, when breeding is at its highest.

The two most common mosquito-borne diseases to watch out for in India are malaria and dengue fever, which are both treatable but can be fatal if not identified early on. Malaria is the best known of the two, and there are preventive medicines available for it, although they have side effects and are thus not always advisable for long-term visitors.

Commonly prescribed antimalarial medications include doxycycline, Lariam, and Malarone. Doxycycline is a broad-spectrum antibiotic that is relatively inexpensive, although it must be taken daily. However, it has some side effects, including photosensitivity of the skin, and it can cause yeast infections in women. If you are prone to sunburn or have had any issues with antibiotics in the past, this may not be the pill for you. Lariam (mefloquine) is taken weekly, although some travelers have reported scary side effects, including nightmares and even psychological breakdowns. You should steer clear of this medicine if you have a history of psychological illness, depression, or epilepsy. Malarone (atovaquone and proguanil) is the most expensive of the lot and has the fewest reported side effects. However, it's very expensive and usually only used by short-term travelers.

Dengue, also known as break-bone fever, is common in the postmonsoon season, especially in metropolitan areas. The only way of avoiding it is to avoid getting bitten. The disease comes with symptoms such as severe and sudden fever, achy joints and muscles, rash, and pain or pressure around the eyes. However, these symptoms are common in other types of viral fever, so if you feel hot and achy, don't jump to the conclusion that you have dengue. Instead, head straight to the doctor, who will administer the necessary blood tests before diagnosis. Dengue symptoms are similar to those of chikungunya, a more recently discovered mosquito-borne illness that has been found in some parts of South Asia.

The best ways to prevent any mosquito-borne illness is by avoiding bites. Mosquito sprays containing DEET are recommended, especially in humid climates and seasons. The most popular insect repellent in India, marketed under the brand name Odomos, is not as effective as stronger DEET-containing formulas. Natural formulas, such as those containing citronella oils, smell nice but don't always keep insects away. You can also burn mosquito coils or use plug-in mosquito repellents (All-Out and Good Knight are popular Indian brands). Ceiling fans and air conditioners also help keep mosquitoes at bay, and if you are in the humid south, you may want to sleep under a mosquito net.

Waterborne Illnesses

Waterborne illnesses are very common in India, and its important only to drink bottled water or water that has been properly filtered and food that is fresh, well cooked, and prepared in sanitary conditions. Typhoid is a waterborne illness, and common symptoms include headache and fever. Fortunately, there is a vaccination for it, although if you develop symptoms, you should still get checked out, as the vaccine is not infallible. Other common waterborne illnesses in India include amoebic dysentery, which can lead to fever and diarrhea or bloody stools. Dysentery is treatable with antiparasitic drugs, but it needs to be diagnosed by a doctor (and not just a pharmacist). Giardia is another common parasite that is also common among campers and hikers in the West. Symptoms are often mild and can include severe gas, bloating, diarrhea, and a loss of appetite. The symptoms can last for months and fluctuate in their intensity, and although giardiasis usually goes away on its own if you wait long enough, it's better to get it dealt with as soon as you can.

HIV/AIDS

HIV is prevalent in India, especially among intravenous drug users and sex workers. Like anywhere in the world, the best way to avoid HIV infection is to avoid contact with bodily fluids. If you are HIV-positive, bear in mind that there are still many misconceptions about the virus and its spread in India, and many people, even educated ones, believe that the virus can be caught through simple contact with infected individuals. You are not legally allowed to live in India if you are HIV-positive, and you will need to prove that you are HIV-negative if you plan to stay in the country for more than one year.

VACCINATIONS

You have to get a series of vaccinations well in advance of leaving for India. First, make sure you are up-to-date on common vaccinations (the ones that you should have no matter where you live). One of the most important routine vaccinations is against tetanus. In the United States this is normally administered as a combined vaccine called DPT, which also aids in immunity against diphtheria and whooping cough, and it is good for 10 years. It is also important to make sure you and your children are up-to-date on other standard vaccinations, such as the MMR vaccine against measles, mumps, and rubella.

Along with routine vaccinations, travelers to India are advised to get vaccinations against hepatitis, typhoid, and polio. Although all types of hepatitis can be found in India, including the relatively new hepatitis E strain, there are not currently vaccines against all of them. The hepatitis A vaccine is administered in two sessions, during your first visit to the clinic and followed by a booster 6–12 months later. You may find that you need to get the booster after arriving in India, especially if you are sent over on short notice. Make sure to keep all records of your shots, including the name of the vaccine, the manufacturer, and the batch number.

Hepatitis B vaccine is also recommended. Given in a series of three doses, it is now routinely administered to children in the United States. If you are older than 25, however, it is unlikely that you received this vaccination during childhood or adolescence. As hepatitis B is contractible through bodily fluids, the vaccination is strongly advised for people who may have sexual contact with local people and for anyone who might need to seek medical treatment involving a blood transfusion. If you haven't been vaccinated for either strain of

DAILY LIFE

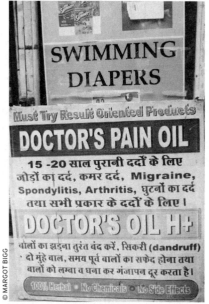

Natural medicine is very popular in India.

hepatitis and are age 18 or older, you can opt for a combined hepatitis A and B vaccine.

Typhoid is very common in India, and it is easy to contract through contaminated foods. It is also easily preventable, and inoculations against the disease can be administered orally or intramuscularly. The vaccine wears off after three years, so if you plan to stay for a long time, you may need to get revaccinated in India. Polio also still exists in India, and if you haven't had an adult booster, it's recommended you do so before moving.

Tuberculosis (TB) is also a serious problem in India, although most strains are treatable in patients whose immune systems are not compromised. There is a vaccine against TB, known as Bacillus Calmette-Guérin (BCG). The efficacy of this vaccine is questionable, however, and you can still contract TB whether you have been vaccinated or not. Moreover, those who have been given BCG can end up giving false positives on TB skin tests, which is a major reason why routine BCG vaccination is not recommended in the United States. Some other countries do routinely administer BCG, and if you have a small circular scar on your upper left forearm, you have probably had this vaccine in the past.

Special Cases

Your doctor may suggest additional vaccinations depending on where you plan to live and the type of activity you will engage in during your stay. If you are going to be working with animals or spending a lot of time in the wilderness, your doctor may want you to get a rabies vaccination. If you plan to work or live on a farm or in an area where there are many pigs, hogs, or wading birds present, your doctor may also recommend inoculation against Japanese encephalitis.

Environmental Factors

India is harsh to the senses, and environmental factors will play a large role in how you approach your health and well-being.

POLLUTION

Air pollution is a huge problem in India, and asthma is common in many of the larger cities. A number of factors contribute to this, including widespread cremations and, most notably, a huge road transportation system filled with diesel-powered trucks. While some efforts have been made to curb air

It's best to avoid buying water and ice from street vendors.

pollution, such as encouraging the use of natural gas instead of gasoline or diesel, most large Indian cities have a long way to go before they will be breathable places to live. If you travel by motorcycle or autorickshaw, you may want to invest in a small mask or a bandana to tie around your mouth and nose. Although this won't make a huge difference in reducing the amount of fumes you breathe in, it will help keep your lungs relatively free from dust and other nasty particulates.

FOOD AND WATER

Food poisoning and waterborne illnesses are a fact of life in India, and much of the food and water available is contaminated. Never drink municipal water without boiling it or filtering it first, and it's best to order mineral water in restaurants, unless you are in an upscale eatery and have verified that the water is potable. Street food is an important part of the Indian culinary experience, but you may prefer to avoid it. If you do eat street food, avoid carts along busy roads, where dust is often kicked up into the food, and look at the clientele. If most of the cart's customers are men in unkempt clothes, you might want to avoid eating there. If you see middle-class families eating from a cart, however, or if the cart is in an upscale market, you should be OK. The same goes for restaurants: If the place is empty or looks dirty, don't eat there. If it's busy, that means the turnover is high and the food will likely be freshly made. Avoid ice unless you are in a nice restaurant, and if you order juice on the street, instruct the vendor not to add water or ice to the mix.

DAILY LIFE

HEAT AND SUN

India can get very hot, and you need to remain vigilant to keep yourself healthy during hot spells. Indian offices are notoriously overly air-conditioned, and you can easily get sick if you go from a freezing office to a furnace-like environment outside. While you are more likely to suffer from heat exhaustion, a fever, or general malaise, actual diagnosable heatstroke is a serious possibility and requires immediate medical attention. Symptoms of heatstroke include body temperature over 105°F, dizziness, and disorientation.

The heat can also wreak havoc on your skin and cause prickly heat, or miliaria, an itchy rash that some-

Hand fans are especially helpful in hot climates.

times feels like pins and needles. Prickly heat occurs when sweat glands get blocked or infected. The best way to prevent this is to stay in air-conditioning when possible, wear loose-fitting breathable clothes, and apply talcum powder. Those with lighter complexions need to be very careful in India as the sun is strong. Sunscreen should be applied to exposed areas, and it's a good idea to carry an umbrella on sunny days to prevent your scalp from burning. Fair-skinned people also need to be aware of polymorphous light eruption (PMLE), a skin allergy that develops with repeated exposure to the sun and results in an itchy rash. PMLE usually affects women under age 40.

Finally, make sure to drink a lot of fluids, as dehydration is common in the summer months. Symptoms include headache, dizziness, and swelling of the extremities. Dehydration is usually treatable with rehydration salts, although if your case is not too severe, you can also just pick up a large bottle of *nimbu paani* (lemon water), a popular Indian lemonade that often contains enough sugar and salt to get you back on your feet.

HUMAN WASTE

There is a serious shortage of public restrooms in India, and some people, especially the poor and impoverished, have no choice but to relieve themselves anywhere and, seemingly, everywhere. If you take an early-morning train through the Indian countryside, you might pass gender-segregated groups of people relieving themselves near the tracks. Spend any time in a major Indian city and you will see that walls are commonly used as makeshift urinals. To prevent this, some home owners install tiles depicting images of different gods and holy figures on the walls in front of their houses, as it is sacrilegious to relieve yourself on or near a divine image. Spitting is also common in India, and although "No Spitting" signs are posted all over the place, they are rarely obeyed.

Safety

By and large, India is a safe country, although it's always a good idea to exercise common sense. Always be aware of your surroundings, and if you ever feel unsafe, don't hesitate to ask for help. Most Indians are hospitable people and will go out of their way to assist you.

TRAFFIC AND DRIVING

India's roads are often likened to war zones, and blasé attitudes toward things like drunk driving and giving others the right of way don't make things any easier. Always err on the side of safety when crossing busy roads, and try to use an underground walkway instead of crossing directly when at all possible. If you do drive, remember that larger vehicles generally get the right of way.

WOMEN'S SAFETY

Although India is generally a safe place for women, there are a few things that women need to keep in mind. First, when out in public, it's best not to smile or make casual chitchat with adult men you don't know, unless they are very old or with a family. Your friendliness can easily be misinterpreted as a come-on. India is home to plenty of lecherous men, and it's not uncommon to get stared at, often in a sexual or demeaning manner. Sexual harassment (known locally as "Eve-teasing") is also prevalent, although such behavior is criminalized and frowned upon by most of society. Groping and "accidental" slips of the hand are also more common than in Western countries. If someone touches you inappropriately, don't be afraid to slap him hard or make a lot of noise to draw attention to the perpetrator's actions.

If you are waiting alone for a train or bus or looking for an empty seat, always opt to stand with women or families. Some trains and buses have women-only compartments or seating areas, which are great if you are traveling on your own.

Crime

As a foreigner, the crimes that will concern you most are those that involve trying to separate you from your money, and you may be seen as an easy target for criminals. The general perception is that foreigners have more money than sense, and there are plenty of people who earn a living by conning others out of their cash. Common scams range from trying to sell you fake gems to forcing you to pay for services or "gifts" you didn't ask for. In some cases, it's easier to just bite the bullet and pay up, especially if it's no more than a couple of rupees. However, if someone is trying to pull a fast one on you, don't have any qualms about asking them to sort out the issue at the local police station. There is a common fear of police brutality in India, and mentioning the police is usually enough to scare people off.

THEFT

Theft is common in India, and if you need to let plumbers, repairmen, or other unknown characters into your house, watch them like a hawk. Women should avoid wearing flashy jewelry in public, as "chain snatching," where an assailant passes a woman on a motorcycle and quickly rips the chain from her neck, is a common crime in India. If you have domestic help, keep valuables hidden away from them, preferably under lock and key.

VIOLENT CRIME

Reports of violence against foreigners are rare, and there are usually enough people around to answer your cries if you feel you are in danger. Women should avoid walking alone at night when possible, and those who do need to be alone after dark should make sure to dress modestly. Avoid verbal confrontation with people as it can lead to violent altercations if emotions flare up. Gun violence is not unheard of, and while nowhere nearly as common as in the United States, shootings do occur.

COMMON SCAMS

As a foreigner, you automatically become an easy target for scam artists, from the small-scale street kid trying to get a few rupees out of you to full-fledged racket-running criminals. Here are a few to watch out for:

* **goo on the shoe:** This oft-mocked scam sounds absurd, but it's actually quite common. Imagine you are strolling through a busy market when suddenly an unidentifiable wad of gunk splats onto your shoes. Just as you are trying to discern what the new addition to your wardrobe could be, a young man approaches and begins to clean your shoes. You're relieved to get the stuff off of your shoes and still shocked enough that you let the shoeshine man do his work without bothering to haggle for a price. Within the blink of an eye, your shoes will be like new again, and the person responsible for their salvation will be demanding a hefty fee for his services.

* **the gem scam:** Perhaps India's most notorious scam, plenty of tourists fall victim to the gem scam every year, especially in touristy cities such as Jaipur and Agra, where it's most active. This is how it works: You are approached by a friendly local who builds a rapport with you, perhaps taking you out to eat and generally trying to, as they say in India, "make friendship." Once you have reached a certain level of comfort with your newfound friend, he will pop the big question: Would you like to earn some money delivering precious gems – think diamonds and rubies – to his partner in your home country? You will be offered excellent pay for this service, as you will help your new friend circumvent import taxes. There's just one catch – upon receipt of the diamonds, rubies, and other gems in question, you will need to provide some form of collateral – a bank account number, a blank check, or, most commonly, credit card details. By the time you realize that the gems you have been given to smuggle are nothing more than cut glass, your newfound friend – and your money – will be gone forever.

* **fake international tourist bureaus:** The train stations in larger Indian cities usually have a sales office specifically intended for use by foreign tourists. These offices are set up to sell tourist-quota train tickets and provide a slightly less harrowing ticket-buying experience for overseas visitors. Touts often congregate near train stations and try to steer tourists away from the genuine international tourist office toward a travel agency nearby, which may have a misleading signboard that reads something along the lines of "Indian Government International Tourist Bureau." Remember that bona fide Indian Railways offices are inside the train station or on the station grounds.

REPORTING CRIME

If you are the victim of a crime, head to your nearest police station and request to file a complaint, known as a First Information Report (FIR). A copy of this will be necessary if you need to claim damages related to a crime from your insurance company. The police in India are usually very helpful to foreigners, although the system is slow and corruption is commonplace. If you are having trouble navigating the system or feel that something is not quite right, you may also want to contact your embassy for support. Note that some cities have special tourist police forces and women's cells.

People with Disabilities

India does not have much infrastructure for the disabled, and if you have compromised mobility, you may struggle a lot, especially if you use a wheelchair. Sidewalks don't have built-in ramps, and only a handful of public restrooms in upscale shopping malls have special toilet facilities. Elevators are not found in most older buildings. You will probably need to hire a medical aid in order to help you get around, and if you are used to living independently, you may find that it is not an option in India.

Blind people in India normally use a white cane, and the concept of service dogs is virtually unheard of. Some ATMs have audio options, though few have instructions in braille.

The deaf population in India is considerably more literate than the general population, and Indo-Pakistani sign language is the common method of communication. Unfortunately, illiteracy is high among the general population, and those who are literate often can only read the alphabet of their native language, so writing things down won't necessarily get you very far.

EMPLOYMENT

The majority of people who move to India do so for work. India's job market is huge, and finding a job in India is fairly easy for highly qualified foreigners with skill sets that are not widely available within the general population. Until recent years, most foreigners who landed a job in India were provided with a slew of benefits and incentives, such as free housing and education for their children, chauffeur-driven cars, extra days of annual leave, and additional income in the form of "hardship allowances." This trend has changed over the past 5–10 years, and these days plenty of people who move to India do so on salaries that would be considered a pittance by Western standards but are still decent for living in India. This shift indicates not only that India is becoming a more popular and intriguing place for foreign nationals, who no longer have to be coerced with extra perks to move to India, but also that living standards in metropolitan India are much more comfortable than they were in the past.

If you want to seek out work in India, you must accept that in many cases,

your salary will be much lower than in the West. People in high-level management and IT positions may earn equivalent salaries, and diplomats and educators in international schools can expect "Western salaries." If you are young or making a job switch, however, or if you are applying directly to Indian companies as opposed to asking an overseas company to send you to India, then you are more likely to earn a local salary. You will also need to prepare yourself for a culturally different approach to working life.

The Job Hunt

Although India does have high official rates of unemployment (around 9 percent in 2010), finding a job here is still very easy, especially if you can leverage skills you have acquired by virtue of having grown up outside of India when you apply, such as fluency in European languages other than English. People with excellent foreign-language skills are always in demand, especially with companies that deal a lot with overseas clients. Technical skills are slightly less in demand simply because there are a lot of highly skilled tech workers in India. However, if you have high-level management experience with technology providers, you may find yourself in very high demand.

APPLYING TO INTERNATIONAL COMPANIES

If you want a high salary, a plush relocation package, and all the other perks that once were the norm for Western expats, you're best off applying to an international company or organization. If you already work for a company with operations in India, you may be able to apply for a position internally. Keep in mind that most companies send seasoned employees overseas, so it's not easy to apply to a new company for an overseas posting. However, if you have experience in nonprofits and international organizations, or if you have a health care background, you will have an easier time finding an employer in your home country who will send you to India.

APPLYING TO LOCAL COMPANIES

If you want to work for a local company, you'll have many more options than if you are trying to get an assignment from overseas. You'll need to have a contract letter secured before you can apply for an employment visa, so for most people, it makes sense to go through the entire interview process on the phone or online, and most employers are willing to be flexible with the interview process when dealing with candidates based abroad. You can also come to India for your job hunt, although you will have to return to your home country and apply for a new visa, and few employers will be willing to pay for this.

The easiest way to find work in India is through word of mouth. Nepotism is less frowned-upon in India than it is in the West, and few companies have policies about placing an ad if a suitable candidate has already been found internally or through contacts. If you let Indian and India-based people in your network know that you are looking for work, they'll often be able to help. If you don't have any contacts in India, or if you are looking for a post in a large company, you might want to start your search online.

The most popular employment websites in India are http://naukri.com and http://monsterindia.com. The *Times of India* also has a job site, http://timesjobs. com, which serves as an online alternative to the traditional newspaper-based job classifieds of days past. Different industries also have specific portals. For example, those seeking jobs in the nonprofit or development sectors may want to start searching at http://ngojobs.in, whereas those in media and advertising might find http://exchange4media.com more relevant.

INDIANIZING YOUR RÉSUMÉ

Before you begin applying for jobs, you will probably want to adjust your résumé, or CV, to make it more suitable for the Indian market. Unlike in many Western countries, where one-page or at most two-page CVs are preferred, the Indian CV often reads like a small novel, with paragraphs of information covering every last detail of a candidate's work experiences. While it's best not to go overboard, many Indian employers may find a one-page résumé too short, especially if you have a lot of experience. Instead of bullet points, you may want to write small paragraphs covering each past job. It's also common for employment seekers to include their age, photo, and the details of their marital status, and although you may not feel comfortable including such personal information, don't be surprised if a potential employer asks you to send such details. At the time of your interview, you may also be asked personal questions, ranging from your age to your father's profession. To many Westerners such questions feel intrusive, but it's something you have to get used to, so try not to take offense. Personal questions may be used simply to break the ice, but they usually serve a double purpose of sizing up your personality and family background to see if you are suitable for the company's culture.

EXPAT PROFILE: NATHAN STEELE

PHOTO COURTESY OF NATHAN STEELE

Nathan Steele founded Escape Delhi.

The following is from an interview with Nathan Steele, founder of travel company Escape Delhi. Steele first came to India in 1998 to teach English to monks in the Himalayas. Over the next decade he continued to visit India for travel and work, and he ended up setting up his own business, a travel company offering short breaks out of Delhi that's especially popular with the capital's expat crowd.

Why did you decide to start Escape Delhi?
I had worked a lot in the Indian travel business, and I saw there were not many good companies offering weekend trips out of Delhi, and there was a big demand for this kind of thing. I also noticed a lot of people, particularly short-term expats, wanted to get away and didn't want to travel alone, but they couldn't always easily find other people to travel with.

What were some of the challenges of setting up a business in India?
Apart from the fact that I am not a particularly good businessman, I haven't had any problems starting up in India. Of course, you have to deal with things working quite slowly, but anyone thinking of setting up a business here would probably already be familiar enough with how things work to get around it. The best thing has been the number of return customers and referrals we have had since getting started, which has taken a lot of strain off the marketing.

Do you have any advice to give to entrepreneurs looking to set up a business in India?
I would say, have a good think about whether you are in it for the long haul, and get first-hand advice from people who have done it themselves. It's also important to get a good accountant, so ask around for recommendations. Try to make sure you don't get stuck here 12 months of the year, as it's important to get away once in a while. I wish that following this advice was as easy as it is to give.

Self-Employment

Unless you have PIO or NRI status, you can't legally work as a consultant in India. Instead you will need to start your own business or tie up with an already-established company in India. The one exception is accredited journalists affiliated with overseas publications or bureaus, who can apply for journalist visas.

STARTING YOUR OWN BUSINESS

Plenty of expats start their own businesses in India, but few find it easy or straightforward. Foreign-owned companies in India are usually run as joint ventures with an Indian partner, and most people seek the advice of a lawyer to set up a company. Alternately, if you have a company established in your country of origin or residence, you may be able to set up a branch office in India. The following information is intended to be indicative of the process for setting up a company in India, but should not be used as a replacement for the advice of a good lawyer.

To form a company, you first need to obtain a registration number. Once you have this, you have to register the company's name with the Registrar of Companies (ROC), ensuring that your company's name doesn't resemble that of another company. If the name is taken, you need to think of something else (three additional backup names are advised). Once your company's name has been approved, you have to get your documents officiated with—you guessed

© MARGOT BIGG

Many people earn a living by hawking snacks and wares at traffic signals.

DAILY LIFE

it—a rubber stamp. Then you can take your documents to the ROC, which will give you a certificate of incorporation, which proves your company's existence and is necessary for all foreigners holding employment visas to obtain residence permits. Now you have a company. The next step will be obtaining a Permanent Account Number (PAN), the Indian equivalent of a Social Security number, for your business. This allows you to pay taxes and legally employ personnel and contractors. You also have to register your company as a payer of different taxes, such as Value-Added Tax (VAT), and apply for special permits depending on what type of business you are starting (for example, import/export permits).

Business Culture

Many Western visitors and expats don't experience extreme culture shock in India until they enter into some sort of business relationship with an Indian person. This could range from buying a banana from a roadside vendor to setting up accounts with Indian clients, but at some point during your business interactions in India, you are likely to pinch yourself and ask yourself if you are dreaming.

The first thing you may notice is that there's a certain mix of formality and familiarity in Indian business interactions that seems the near opposite of what happens in the West. On one side, Indian people are very formal with each other when it comes to using last names and honorifics, and they hold meetings that are so rigidly formal that they can sometimes come across as parody. Indian cultures are much more oriented toward the group than Western cultures are, and maintaining the status quo often takes precedence over individual growth. That's not to say that cutthroat office politics don't exist in India. Rather, people won't be as likely to openly challenge ideas, and those who do are more likely to be viewed as rebels than as leaders, at least in more traditional work environments.

Although Indians can be very formal with their business dealings, there's a simultaneous familiarity that might confuse some Westerners. Your Indian colleagues may call you "sir" and avoid chitchat when discussing work-related issues one moment, and the next moment inquire about your family and how your stomach is taking to Indian food, sometimes asking very personal questions that might seem intrusive to Westerners. Just remember that food and family are both held with high regard in Indian culture, and asking questions about these two topics is a way that people express that they care.

YOUR NEW OFFICE: WHAT TO EXPECT

As is the case everywhere in the world, office culture in India varies drastically from industry to industry and even city to city. If you work in a large corporate setup in Delhi, expect a much more formal environment than you would find at a small start-up in San Francisco. Wherever you end up working, there will probably be a few surprising differences between your new workplace and what you have been used to in the past.

Indian offices often open a little later than in the West, and 10 o'clock is not considered a late start time. The Indian attitude toward punctuality is not as rigid as in the West, so if your office opens at 10 A.M., don't be surprised if people are still flowing in as late as 10:30. You may also find that the workdays are longer but more laid-back then in the West, with lots of breaks to compensate for the longer official office hours. Many people also work on Saturday – sometimes only a half day – or every other Saturday.

It's common for colleagues in Indian offices to greet each other in the morning through rounds of handshakes, and contrary to popular and outdated belief, women and men in business situations are expected to shake hands with one another. People in India normally use first names with each other and add formality by prefixing the first name with a Mr. or Ms. – if your name is Lisa Smith, you'll hear Ms. Lisa much more than Ms. Smith.

Food plays a big role in bonding in India, and this extends into the office. People often bring packed lunches in lunch boxes and end up having not more than a couple of bites of what they brought. It's customary to share your lunch with everyone around you, even waiting for others to try before you taste your own food. Your colleagues will also offer you bites of their lunch, and it's polite to have a bite, even if you are not hungry. Larger offices also have canteens that serve basic Indian vegetarian meals at low cost, usually around ₹30-40 per meal. Meat options are sometimes available for a few more rupees.

DAILY LIFE

Indian attitudes toward time are also considerably more flexible than in the West, which can be frustrating to Western-born managers, most of whom have been raised to value promptness and strict adherence to deadlines. It's always a good idea to set deadlines for much earlier than when you actually need results, to allow a buffer in case your colleagues or subordinates are running behind schedule.

Another big shocker for a lot of Westerners is the devotion that employees in India are supposed to have to their companies. Workaholics will revel in how loyal people in India are to their companies, but if you are the type who works to live and likes to keep work time and private time strictly delineated, you might find working in India a bit suffocating. This doesn't mean that Indian employers don't value and respect family obligations. In fact, if a family member falls ill, your employer will likely grant you a leave period that would be unheard of in the West. However, there are also times when you may be asked to stay late without extra pay, especially if a project is due. You may even need to stay if you don't specifically have work to do, as moral support for your colleagues if nothing else. This is especially annoying for Westerners working at companies that follow a six-day work week.

HOW TO DRESS

Many offices have strict dress codes for men and women. In stricter environments, men may be required to wear a collared dress shirt with a tie, and women may also be required to wear collared blouses. Women can also wear ethnic clothing, such as saris and Punjabi suits, whereas men are usually required to wear Western office wear. Women are usually allowed to wear dressy sandals, but men must wear closed-toe shoes. You may also want to keep a sweater or shawl in your desk drawer year-round. Indian offices are often air-conditioned to the point of feeling like walk-in freezers, and it's important for your health to be prepared for 50°F inside temperatures when its 110°F outside.

In more laid-back environments and in smaller offices, you can usually wear jeans and other types of casual wear, although men may still be expected to wear closed-toe shoes. Women should always cover themselves up a bit more than in the West, and normally dresses should cover your knees and tops should cover your shoulders, at least partially. Women should note that tight clothes and low-cut necklines are not really approved of, although

Although it's not common, some expat women opt to wear elegant saris to the office.

most people will be too shy to say anything to you about it, especially if you work with men.

OFFICE HIERARCHY

Indian society is strictly hierarchical, and nowhere is this more obvious than in the professional world. You'll notice it right away, no matter where you fall along the pecking order. You may also notice that the same person who is humble and deferent to his superiors is bossy and arrogant toward those under him, much as a teenage bully might pick on younger kids but will turn into a nervous wreck when a teacher calls him out on his behavior. While many people are able to get their needs met by being very gracious and kind, most people are used to taking an aggressive approach with their subordinates or constantly teetering between offering praise and threats instead of simply reasoning with them. Many Westerners managing Indian employees come in with their own cultural notions of hierarchy that are, at least outwardly, more egalitarian than what goes on in India. While Western-style management works in some cases, many Indian employees are more comfortable with a stricter form of management.

Another thing you will notice, and probably appreciate, is that even small Indian offices have low-level staff, known as "peons" or the more politically correct (sort of) "office boys," sometimes in the form of 40-year-old men. These staffers do in India what interns do in the West: They make coffee, photocopy documents, stuff envelopes, and pretty much do simple but time-consuming tasks for executive employees. Sometimes their presence can be a little overwhelming, such as when you spill your coffee and go to mop it up only to find them doing it for you. Usually, however, their presence is invaluable, at times when you might have 2,000 envelopes to stuff and an annual report to finish on the same day.

BUSINESS CARDS

Business cards are loved in India, and because they are so cheap to produce, even entry-level employees who have little or no interaction with the public are given their own cards. When you meet new people, even socially, they may ask for your card with no intention of contacting you. When you receive the business card, look at it, read it, admire it, and then put it away. Invest in a Rolodex, because you never know when you might want to contact one of the many people with whom you will exchange cards.

Labor Laws

Labor laws in India are strict but not always enforced. Executive expats won't have much to worry about as long as they follow the terms of their contract; they can expect similar laws to what's found in any other democracy. Informal, under-the-table labor is very common, and India's poorest and hardest workers generally fall into this category. As of 2010 the base national minimum wage in India is ₹100 per day, although different states also have minimum wages that usually depend on whether the work is considered unskilled, semiskilled, skilled, or highly skilled.

CONTRACT AND NOTICE PERIODS

Contracts in India are generally very long documents full of legalese about everything from probation periods to intellectual property. They can be a lot to digest at first, but at the same time they provide a certain level of relief for many an apprehensive expat. Contracts also generally come with an annex that breaks down the employee's total monthly earnings into the following categories: basic pay, housing rental allowance, conveyance (transportation) allowance, and special allowance. By funneling some of your salary through allowances, employers reduce both your tax liability and theirs, but at the end of the month your total salary remains the same, so it's not something to worry much about. Employers deduct taxes from employee's paychecks, known as Tax Deducted at Source (TDS). When you negotiate your salary, make sure to specify whether you are talking about your "in-hand" or take-home (net) salary versus the CTC (cost to company, or gross salary). You also may need to contribute to a retirement fund known as the Provident Fund (PF). Your contributions will be matched by your employer. If you change jobs,

© MARGOT BIGG

Certain trades, such as tailoring, are passed down through generations.

your PF will need to be transferred to your new employer. If you don't initiate this, you'll loose whatever money you have contributed.

Most contracts have a probationary period of 3–6 months built in. During the probation period, the employer or the employee can terminate the contract without notice or reason. Some companies also make employees sign a document stating that they will not take up new employment with a competing or similar company for a certain amount of time after terminating their contract.

There's no legal minimum notice requirement for any category of employment in India. When you sign a

A *dhobi* woman irons clothing.

© MARGOT BIGG

contract, your employer will require you to give notice of normally 1–3 months, depending on the type of position you have and your company's policies. If you or your company wants to terminate the contract earlier, the terminating party is required to compensate the other party as per the agreement (one month's salary is common). It's common that if one person leaves, especially if that person is a manager, many loyal staff members might leave too, sometimes even following their manager to a new place of employment.

In some cases, companies make each new hire sign a Legal Monetary Bond, a document that states how much the employee will have to pay if he or she breaches the contract. Very few companies extend the practice of bonded labor to their expat employees, and it's best to avoid signing any such document, especially if you aren't sure how long you want to remain in India or with your company.

SICK LEAVE AND VACATION LEAVE

Indian companies grant a lot of leave, but policies on how and when leave can be taken vary greatly from company to company. Most companies grant 4–10 days of sick leave per year to their employees, and it cannot be carried over. This is sometimes mixed with what's known as casual leave, days off used for reasons other than illness, akin to personal days in the United States.

Most companies grant two days of paid holiday for every month worked. During an employee's probation period, paid leaves are normally accumulated but cannot be used until the probation period is up. Domestic servants, in theory, are entitled to four days off per month, plus 20 days of holiday per year, although this is not enforced and is usually at the discretion of the employer.

Almost all companies close their offices on national holidays and major religious festivals. Depending on the customs of the state you live in, your office may be closed on additional holidays (for example, Maharashtra offices are often closed for Ganesh Chaturthi, but Delhi offices are not). Some offices grant employees one or two "floating holidays" per year. These are essentially religious holidays of lesser significance to the general population but which may be important to an individual employee or his family. Your company will provide a list of such holidays, and you will need to inform HR ahead of time about which holidays you plan to take off.

Volunteering

Volunteering is a rewarding way of experiencing life in India, as well as a good way to interact with local people and experience Indian culture firsthand. There are plenty of organizations in India that can use extra help, so if there's an area that you want to volunteer in, a simple Internet search is usually the only thing standing between you and a nonprofit organization that's perfect for you. Some people also go through volunteer placement agencies, most of which charge a fee to place you with an organization for a short-term project. While these "volunteer tourism" organizations are helpful in that they offer support services such as airport pickups and housing assistance, some of them are clearly in the business for the money, so it's important to be careful which organization you sign up with if you do choose to go this route. Cross-Cultural Solutions and Volunteers for Peace (VFP) are some of the better-known volunteer tourism organizations. If you plan to volunteer in India, you will need an employment visa, despite the fact that you won't be working for pay.

FINANCE

India's foreign population can be divided into expats on "foreign salaries" and people earning rupee salaries based on the local economy, sometimes referred to as "inpats." Not long ago, people used to get hardship allowances for living in India and actually made more than they would in their home country for the same work. These days, more and more people come to India for the experience rather than for the money, and they are paid about 25–35 percent of what they would make in the same position back home.

One of the first questions people ask when they decide to move to India is how much it will all cost. Unfortunately, there's no straightforward answer to this. If you are an NGO worker or teacher in a small village in rural Bihar, you will be able to live comfortably on a monthly salary that wouldn't even buy you a meal in a fine restaurant in Delhi.

Once you arrive in India, you have to figure out how to manage your money wisely. That entails getting used to the currency and understanding how much things *should* cost. In most cases, you will want to get a bank account, which,

© MARGOT BIGG

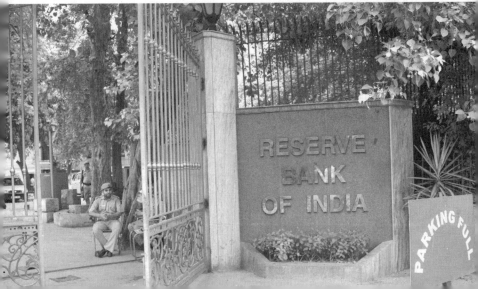

like many processes in India, can be time-consuming and bureaucratic. You will also need to pay taxes in India and possibly in your home country. You may even want to invest in the local stock market.

Cost of Living

Overall, India is a much cheaper place to live than any Western country. If you live a simple life in a middle-class neighborhood and eat only at home or in inexpensive restaurants, you can easily live on a few hundred dollars per month anywhere in the country. At the other end of the spectrum, you can easily live a life of luxury in India, and many people, expat and local, do.

MONTHLY EXPENSES

If you live a simple life in a smaller city, you can get by on as little as ₹10,000 per month, plus rent and utilities. This means eating at home or in inexpensive roadside eateries, limiting your clothing and toiletries shopping, and traveling on public transportation. You will need at least twice that much to lead a comparable lifestyle in larger cities like Delhi and Mumbai, and remember that this number does not include rent, which can get quite expensive depending

AVERAGE PRICES IN INDIA

Most everyday items in India cost considerably less than they do in Western countries. Here are the average prices of a few common items that you might need to buy on a regular basis.

Item	Cost
Pound of tomatoes	₹15-20
Ice cream bar	₹10
34-ounce bottle of water	₹15
Tube of toothpaste	₹35
Cappuccino	₹46
2.2-pound bag of laundry powder	₹81
Pack of cigarettes	₹100
Paperback novel	₹100-295
Bottle of Indian-made red wine	₹500
Dental cleaning and checkup	₹500-1500

Imported food products are available in India, but expect to pay a hefty premium.

on where you are staying. Your major monthly expenses will be housing, utilities, food, domestic help, and entertainment. You may also have additional unexpected expenses, such as health care costs, as well as planned costs such as educational expenses for your children.

Housing and Utilities

The cost of housing varies greatly from city to city and neighborhood to neighborhood. If you rent a room in a shared house in Bengaluru or in a modest Delhi neighborhood, you can get by on around ₹5,000–6,000 per month in rent. You could also rent a palatial property in Delhi or a decent-sized well-appointed flat in Mumbai and end up shelling out as much, if not more, as you would in places like London and New York. The *Prime Living Locations* chapters have detailed information on housing prices in different cities.

Utilities in India are quite expensive relative to the economy, and electricity rates are on par with those in North America and Britain. It's a good idea to budget about ₹1,000 per person per month in your household for electricity, although if you have air-conditioning, you can end up spending a lot more in the summer months. Water rates vary from city to city, but expect to spend a minimum of around ₹200–300 per person per month.

Food and Household Expenses

India is frequently referred to as a land of extremes, and food prices are no exception to this. Convenience food in India is a reserve of the middle and upper classes, and if you want something imported (think fruit roll-ups and cans of baked beans), expect to pay double what you would pay at home for the same product. Eating a diet based on fruits, vegetables, rice, flour, and legumes is a much more affordable (not to mention healthier) way of living in India. Keep in mind that certain "exotic" vegetables (such as broccoli and lettuce) cost far more than vegetables that are commonly used in Indian dishes (think cauliflower and eggplant). Locally made toiletries and household cleaning products cost more than you would expect based on the overall cost of things in India, but they are still much cheaper than in Western countries.

Entertainment

The cost of entertainment in India naturally varies depending on what you like to do for fun. Satellite television can cost as little as ₹200 per month for a basic package, although installation will cost over ₹1,000. Film rental is not common, and most people simply buy the films they want to watch, which can cost as little as ₹30 for pirated copies and around ₹250 for authentic high-quality DVDs. Going to an English-language film in a modern air-conditioned cinema will cost you ₹150–250 per person. The cost of tickets for theatrical and dance performances ranges ₹100–500 in most large cities.

If you like clubbing or drinking, expect to pay more in India than you would back home. It's not uncommon for nightclubs to charge upward of ₹2,000 per couple, which is sometimes redeemable against drinks. Many clubs don't allow single men (referred to as "stags") to enter, and those that do charge lone males as much or more than they do couples. High taxes on alcohol and

Never pay more than the printed maximum retail price (MRP).

imports make drinking a very expensive hobby in many Indian cities, and you can expect to pay as much, and often more, for a beer or cocktail than you would in the West.

Domestic Help

The cost of domestic help varies tremendously, not only from city to city but neighborhood to neighborhood. You pay more for a maid in a middle-income part of Delhi than you would for someone in a more upscale part of Ahmedabad. If you want to hire English-speaking help, expect to pay a premium, especially if the people you are hiring have worked for expats in the past. A full-time (six days a week) maid-nanny who cooks, cleans, and takes care of one or two children costs ₹5,000–15,000 per month, although if you provide on-site accommodations for her and her family, you will pay quite a bit less. If you have a larger house, extra cooking duties, and more than two children to take care of, you may pay even more. Alternately, if you just need someone to come in a few times a week to do the laundry and dishes and mop the floor, you could pay as little as ₹400 per month. If you aren't sure how much to pay, ask other expats living in your neighborhood what kind of salaries they are paying their staff.

Banking

CURRENCY

India's official currency is the rupee, which can be divided into 100 paise (plural of paisa), although whole rupees are normally used in pricing and paisa coins are nearly obsolete in much of the country. Coins are used for lower denominations of rupees, and bills are used for higher denominations, with some overlap. Rupee coins come in denominations of 1, 2, 5, and 10, although 10-rupee coins are fairly new, and bills for this denomination are still far more common. Bills in denominations of 5, 10, 20, 50, 100, 500, and 1,000 are commonly used, and you may occasionally be offered a now rarely used one-rupee or two-rupee bill as change. Five-rupee coins are becoming increasingly preferred over the paper version, and bills in this denomination will likely be discontinued.

The rupee bills currently being printed all have Mahatma Gandhi's face on the front, and each denomination has a different symbol on the back. The size and color of bills differs depending on the denomination, ranging from the small green five-rupee bill to the larger (and wider) red-hued thousand-rupee

DAILY LIFE

© MARGOT BIGG

fronts and backs of ₹10, 20, 100, 500, and 100 notes

bill. Beware that bills that are torn or otherwise heavily damaged may not be accepted by merchants, even if they've been patched up with a bit of tape, so always check your change thoroughly to make sure you haven't got any bills that appear to be disintegrating.

The Indian rupee is listed as INR and is commonly abbreviated "Rs." and occasionally as "Re." In July 2010 the Indian Ministry of Finance introduced an international symbol for the rupee, ₹.

EXCHANGING CASH AND TRAVELER'S CHECKS

It's easy to exchange cash in India, especially U.S. dollars, British pounds, or euros. Some banks and hotels offer this service, and most touristy parts of India have scores of shops with people anxious to exchange money. There are also plenty of black-market money changers who will offer to take your foreign currency off of your hands. If you want to go the legal route, you should ask for a receipt. This will make it easier for you to exchange your money back into a foreign currency later if you need to.

INTERNATIONAL WIRE TRANSFERS

Some banks also offer international wire transfers to or from India, and this can be an efficient and easy way of getting money in and out of the country. However, the fees are often high, and processing times are slow. If you want to transfer money out of India on a regular basis, you may need to set up a bank account with one of the larger international banks, or find an Indian bank that offers transfer services, as not all banks do.

ATMS

There are ATMs seemingly everywhere in India, and if you live in a city, you will have plenty to choose from. If you have an Indian bank account, you will normally be allowed to use the ATMs of other banks a certain number of times per month without getting charged. There are armed guards stationed at most ATMs. Many ATMs have an upper limit of ₹10,000 per withdrawal. If you need to get a lot of cash, you have to make multiple withdrawals in a row, and your bank may charge you a service fee for each transaction. Alternately, check around for ATMs with high withdrawal limits, often posted on the wall next to the machine. Citibank ATMs often let you withdraw ₹20,000 or more per transaction.

There's no shortage of reliable banks and ATMs in India.

THE ART OF BARGAINING

Bargaining is necessary in India. People bargain with everyone from fruit and vegetable hawkers to the clerk at their local clothing shop. And while you might feel that haggling over a few rupees here and there feels like a tiresome chore, you will soon gain a deep appreciation for one of India's favorite national pastimes, and possibly develop some techniques of your own. Until then, here are a few tips to get you started:

- **Know what you are dealing with.** Ask around at a couple of shops selling similar products to get a general idea of how much the product you are looking for should cost before you begin the bargaining process.

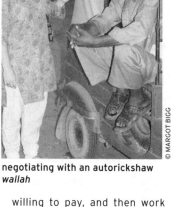

negotiating with an autorickshaw *wallah*

- **Go early.** The first customer of the day is considered auspicious, and it's important for sales for the rest of the day that this customer makes a purchase. Arrive before anyone else and you are likely to be given a very good deal.

- **Make the seller name the price.** You might ask how much something is, only to get the question "How much do you want to pay?" thrown right back at you. If this happens, either insist that the shopkeeper gives you a price or quote something so absurdly low, perhaps with a smile, that it's clear that you are joking. This will force your interlocutor to name some price.

- **Start low.** Always name a price that's lower than what you are willing to pay, and then work your way up. For example, if a shopkeeper asks for ₹300, and you are only willing to pay ₹200, offer ₹150 and let the shopkeeper bargain you up to ₹200. Asking for the "best price" before going into bargaining is another way of cutting the process short and indicating that you'd prefer to avoid engaging in a lot of back-and-forth price discussions.

- **Don't act too interested.** This may seem obvious, but if you act too interested in something, the shopkeeper will leverage this to charge you as much as possible for the object of your desire. Be casual.

© MARGOT BIGG

CREDIT AND DEBIT CARDS

Credit and debit cards are widely accepted in Indian cities, although not to the extent that they are in high-income countries. You are normally able to pay with a card at larger supermarkets, upscale restaurants, coffee shops, and chain clothing stores. However, it's always a good idea to check, just in case. Note that the concept of asking to be charged extra and then getting cash back has not caught on in India, and considering that fraud is rampant here and difficult to detect, it probably won't for a long time.

Signature verification is not common, which means that if you loose your credit card, someone else may be out there using it without any problems. Debit cards issued by Indian banks are usually PIN protected, and you will need to enter your number even if your card is endorsed by Visa or MasterCard. It's difficult to use non-Indian debit and credit cards to make purchases on Indian websites. Instead, you will need to ask your bank to send you login details for their direct-debit transfer service, usually known as net banking.

INDIAN BANK ACCOUNTS
Setting Up an Account

In most cases, your employer will be able to help you set up a bank account linked to their payroll, known as a salary account. Otherwise, you will need to set up an account yourself. To open a bank account you have to bring in a copy of your passport's identity and visa pages, a copy of your residency permit, details of your income (including contract details, if you are employed), and proof of your address. You will also need to provide a sample of your signature, which is used to verify your identity if you come into the bank to make a withdrawal. Note that every time you sign your signature it must match this original signature to the last letter. Tourists and short-term visitors can open a special Non-Resident Ordinary Rupee (NRO) account, although such an account can only remain valid for six months.

Salary Account

Most employers have a bank that they use to pay salaries via direct deposit, and if you want to get paid, you need an account with whatever bank your employer has chosen. This type of account is called a salary account. Your employer will be able to help you set up the account when you join your company, and a bank representative will normally come by your office to make sure all of your details and documents are in order. It may take a few weeks or even a month to get your salary account set up, so you will probably receive your first month's pay by check or in cash.

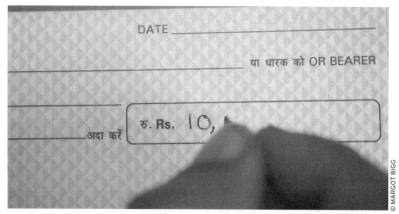

Checks in India are often printed in both English and Hindi.

Checks

Checks are still frequently used in India for paying rent and bills. Writing a check is pretty straightforward, and the format is similar to what you find in other English-speaking countries. It's common to have the words "or bearer" printed next to the "payable to" line on a check. This allows the person who is in possession of the check to cash the check directly. If you want your check to be cashable only by the person you've named, make sure to cross out this line.

When depositing checks in the bank, you don't need to endorse the back the way you do in the United States. ATM-based check-deposit schemes are still uncommon, so you either need to cash your check directly at the bank or drop it in a drop box. Drop boxes are normally divided into "local" and "out of station" sections—the latter refers to checks issued by banks in other cities. Simply fill out a deposit slip, pin it to your check (pins are provided), and drop it into the box. Make sure you record all check details on your deposit slip and keep a record for yourself in case the check and the slip get separated.

Taxes

TAX LIABILITY IN INDIA

If you are a resident of in India, you are expected to pay taxes on your income. Foreign nationals who are in the country for more than 183 days in a year are considered resident and thus tax-liable. In most cases, you are taxed at the same rate as your Indian colleagues. Some tax is usually deducted directly from your salary, which you can claim when you file your return. This is called Tax Deducted at Source (TDS).

In order to pay taxes in India, you need to possess a Personal Account Number (PAN) and accompanying PAN card. PAN cards are issued by UTI Technology Services Limited (UTITSL), a financial consultancy services provider, on behalf of the Indian government. PAN cards also double as ID cards, as they include basic details, such as your full legal name, your father's name (or husband's name if you are a married woman—shocking, isn't it?), your date of birth, your signature, and a small photo. If you are visiting Indian monuments, it's a good idea to carry your PAN card with you, as this may entitle you to local rates on admission.

The rate at which you are taxed is determined by what bracket your annual salary falls into. Taxation rates for men and women of working age are slightly different, and senior citizens get additional concessions. If you earn less than ₹160,000 per year and are a man or under ₹190,000 per year and are a woman, you are not expected to pay taxes, although most expatriates earn more than this. The next bracket, up to ₹500,000 per year, is taxed at 10 percent, and if you make between ₹500,000 and ₹800,000 per year, you can expect to pay 20 percent. Anything above that is taxed at 30 percent. India's agency for taxation is called the Central Board of Direct Taxes (CBDT).

The tax year in India runs April 1–March 31, and you have to file by July 31. To pay your taxes, you need to obtain a Form 16 from your employer, which details your salary and taxes paid by your employer on your behalf. You also need proof of any investments in India as well as summaries of any bank accounts you have in the country. It's recommended that you hire an accountant to file taxes on your behalf. If you really want to file yourself, you can do so at http://incometaxindiaefiling.gov.in.

TAX LIABILITY IN THE UNITED STATES

While in India, you are naturally still responsible for taxes on your property and investments in your home country. You may also be required to pay income taxes in your home country, especially if your salary is above a certain level. If you make US$9,350 per year or more (2009 revised rates), you are required to file a U.S. tax return reporting all earnings, in most cases based on the yearly average exchange rate. However, the first US$91,400 that you earn may be eligible for exclusion from U.S. taxation. The IRS publishes a number of guides to help U.S. citizens and residents understand their tax liability when they are overseas, including *Publication 54: Tax Guide for U.S. Citizens and Resident Aliens Abroad*. More information is available at www.irs.gov.

DAILY LIFE

Investing

Investing in India can be a tricky business for foreigners. If you are of Indian origin and hold a PIO or OCI document, you are allowed to invest and trade in the Indian stock market. Overseas Corporate Bodies (OCBs), or companies owned primarily by Indians or people with Indian ancestry, can also invest directly in India. However, if you don't have any familial ties to India, you are not allowed to invest directly in the stock market. Instead, you can invest in mutual funds or in American Depository Receipts (ADRs), which are essentially shares in a foreign company issued by a U.S. depository bank. Although this does limit your options somewhat, plenty of large Indian companies do trade on the New York Stock Exchange and NASDAQ.

THE STOCK EXCHANGE

Asia's oldest and largest exchange is the Bombay Stock Exchange (BSE) in Mumbai. Nearly 5,000 companies and almost 8,000 scrips are listed on the BSE. The Bombay Stock Exchange Sensitivity Index (SENSEX, also referred to as the BSE 30) is the major index on the BSE, made up of the top 30 stocks in India. Also in Mumbai, the National Stock Exchange (NSE) is the first debt market in the country. This is where to invest in private bonds and government-issued treasury bills. Other cities and states have their own local stock exchanges—the second-largest is Kolkata's Calcutta Stock Exchange (CSE).

OTHER INVESTMENTS

India's banks offer excellent return rates to their clients, especially compared to what banks in the West are currently able to offer. Investment products and funds are available through most banks, although you may feel more comfortable dealing with a bank that has branches in your home country, especially if you are looking at fixed-term investments but are not sure how long you will stay in India. Your banker will be able to advise you about what packages you are legally eligible to invest in.

COMMUNICATIONS

India has a well-developed communications infrastructure, with an advanced telecommunications industry, a reliable national postal service, and a huge selection of English-language media. It's true that getting a telephone line or a cable or Internet connection is still more bureaucratic and time-consuming than it would be in the West. However, while the processes necessary to get services set up still bear traces of old-school bureaucracy, the end results are worth it. Internet, phone, and cable TV services are as reliable as anywhere else and are a much better value than in other countries. The Indian Post is another example of a service that, despite being bureaucratic and a bit old-fashioned, works remarkably well.

If you like to read, you will likely be delighted by India's extensive selection of English-language reading material. Many Indians are more comfortable reading in English than in local languages, which means you will likely have at your disposal a larger selection of English-language newspapers than in your hometown. There are also plenty of locally published versions of

© MARGOT BIGG

international magazines, most of which are readily available at local newsstands. Most bookstores are dominated by English-language literature, with selections ranging from contemporary chick lit by local authors to English classics. While much of Indian television has a distinctly Indian feel, there are still plenty of English-language entertainment and news channels, both locally produced and from abroad.

Telephone Services

Until the 1990s India's telephone services were atrocious. The process of setting up a phone line involved a lot of rubber stamps, waiting lists, and red tape, all for services and connections that would be considered substandard in more developed countries. The services were also expensive, and most lower-income people did not have phones in their homes. These days, telephone services are widely available throughout the country, and even the most rural and isolated places have at least some access to telephones. Low-cost plans and no-frills budget phone models mean that these days even underpaid menial workers can be seen chatting away on their cell phones. India's telecommunications industry is growing quickly, and some analysts believe that India could become the world's largest telecom market in terms of subscriber numbers within the next decade. The percentage of people who have cell phones has risen dramatically in the past few years, and in some places it's easier to get a cell signal than it is to find a landline.

BSNL is India's national communications service provider.

STD? IT'S NOT WHAT YOU THINK

If you spend any significant amount of time in India, you will notice how much people love abbreviations. The "STD" signs you see from Kashmir to Kanyakumari stand for standard trunk dialing, which allows you to make domestic calls. International calls can be made from international standard dialing (ISD) providers. These are often booths in shops or standalone facilities, called public call offices (PCOs) and are India's answer to the pay phone. While some STD phones are coin-operated, most public phones in India are metered – it's best to ask the rate to the destination you plan to call before dialing.

© MARGOT BIGG

Look for these abbreviations when you need to make a phone call.

CELL PHONES

India has some of the world's lowest cell phone rates coupled with a very well-developed telecommunications industry. Unlike in the United States, where subscribers pay for both incoming and outgoing calls, you only pay to make calls and send texts (unless, of course, you are roaming). The largest cell phone providers in the country are Bharti Airtel, Vodafone Essar (formerly Hutch), and Idea Cellular. The government-owned Bharat Sanchar Nigam Limited (BSNL) is the country's fourth-largest cell phone provider, and in many remote rural areas BSNL is the only option. Cell phones can be used almost anywhere in the country, although they will incur roaming charges for both incoming and outgoing calls when you're out of state. Receiving text messages generally won't incur roaming charges. Keep in mind that in some states, including Jammu and Kashmir and Assam, prepaid cell phones from out of state don't work.

People living in big cities tend to choose either Airtel or Vodafone as their cell phone provider, usually basing the decision on the service used by the other people they frequently call. Note that cell phone number portability is not currently available in India, so if you change providers, you also have to change your phone number. To get a cell number, you have to go to a branch office of the provider of your choice or to an authorized dealer. Take along two photographs and proof of your address (such as a rental agreement) as well as a photo ID, such as your passport. You will get a SIM card right away, although you may have to wait a few hours for the activation to be processed. In most cases, your new connection will be working within 24 hours. Indian cell phone companies don't offer free or discounted phones to customers signing up for certain plans—instead, you have to buy a phone separately or use one you already have. If you are using a phone

You'll have plenty of options for communicating in India.

you already own, make sure it's unlocked first. This can usually be done by calling the cell phone provider in your home country and asking them to do it by proxy. Alternately, you can take your phone into most cell phone repair shops in India and have it covertly unlocked for a few hundred rupees.

Prepaid Versus Postpaid

When signing up for your first Indian cell phone, you will be given the option of prepaid (or pay-as-you-go) and postpaid connections. Each option has benefits and drawbacks. Prepaid connections are better for people who spend only a limited amount of time in India or who plan to leave for long stretches and then come back, and thus don't want to be tied into a monthly contract. However, prepaid connections have much higher costs for phone calls and text messaging than postpaid connections do, so if you are a frequent phone user, a postpaid connection will save you a lot of money. It can also be quite a pain when you run out of credit in the middle of the night or during a storm and don't want to go out looking for a place to add to your balance.

Prepaid connections have two components: talk time and validity. When you go to add to your balance (known as recharging in India), you will want to specify whether you want balance, validity, or both. Validity refers to the amount of time you want your number to be valid, and it can be bought in various denominations, with a minimum of at least a month. Note that validity starts from the day you purchase it, so if you have two weeks left on your phone and you pay for another month, the additional month won't be added to extend your validity to six weeks; instead, you will only get one month, so it's a good idea to wait until a day or so before your validity expires before purchasing more. Some providers also offer a lifetime validity option, although people with lifetime validity generally pay more per call than those with limited validity.

Both talk time and validity can be purchased from most cell phone shops and small grocery stores. Shops selling recharges usually have signs bearing the logo of the company whose recharges they sell hanging from the shop's awning. You can buy scratch-off recharge coupons for smaller denominations that can be saved and used later if need be. For larger amounts, simply tell the shopkeeper how much credit you want to add to your phone, and he will text your details to the phone company. If the transaction is successful, you immediately receive a text message confirming the details of your recharge. You then pay the shopkeeper directly.

In most cases, you will be charged VAT at just over 12 percent for your purchase, which is deducted from the total amount of your recharge. For example, if you recharge for ₹100, you will end up with just under ₹87 in credit. Cellular providers sometimes offer special "full talk-time" deals in which taxes are paid by the company. These specials are usually only available at higher recharge denominations, generally above ₹500.

Overseas Phones

Cell phones from other countries will work in India, provided that they are tri-band models and that your service provider has an international roaming plan. However, this is a very expensive option and only makes sense if you need to have a number in your home country that people can use to contact you without having to pay international dialing charges. Some expats find it useful to invest in a dual-SIM phone, a cell phone with slots for two SIM cards. This allows them to switch back and forth from their Indian line to their home country line using the same device.

LANDLINES

Although the popularity of cell phones has caused landline usage in India to significantly decrease over the past decade, it's still quite normal to have a landline at home, and most Internet packages include, or require, a landline connection. BSNL is the largest provider of landlines, and as a state-owned entity it has traditionally had a monopoly in the industry. However, Internet service providers such as Airtel have been responsible for a large proportion of new landlines in recent years, likely as part of Internet bundles.

VOIP

Using Voice over Internet Protocol (VoIP) is an excellent way to call home without spending any money. The technology uses the Internet to transmit sound and video streams. A main player in the VoIP trend is Skype, free downloadable software that can be used like a computer-to-computer videophone, provided that the users on both ends have a webcam and microphone. Skype users can also buy subscriptions and pay-as-you-go credit online, which can be used for calling both fixed and cell phone lines anywhere in the world. You can even use Skype to call U.S. 800 numbers for free; other calls to the United States cost around 2–3 cents per minute.

Internet Access

India's largest Internet service providers (ISPs) are BSNL, Airtel, and to a lesser extent, Reliance and Tata Indicom. Setting up your own broadband connection in India is similar to setting up a cell phone, and if you already have a landline connection established in your home, the process is fairly straightforward. You have to provide photo ID and proof of residence and either buy or rent a DSL modem and, if you want Wi-Fi, a router. After you submit all the necessary paperwork, a representative from your ISP comes to your house and installs your connection, usually within a couple of days (although BSNL is reputed to take longer). Unfortunately, the ISP representative may not appear on time, and you may have to spend a few days waiting around at home before the person actually shows up.

If you have a laptop and want to be able to access the Internet from anywhere, you may prefer to use a wireless connection device such as a USB modem or a data card instead of a traditional broadband connection. These cards allow you to access the Internet via the cellular network anywhere that your provider offers service. Such devices are especially useful for people who travel a lot, as Wi-Fi hot spots are still relatively rare in India. If you choose this option, you have to purchase the data card or USB modem (around ₹3,000), although providers occasionally run promotions that include free data cards for new users. Reliance, Airtel, and Tata Indicom are the main providers.

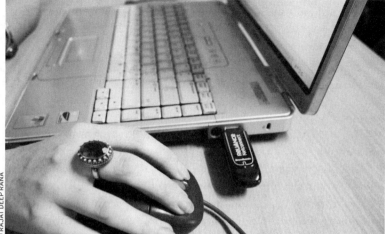

© RAJAT DEEP RANA

USB Modems are popular for Internet on the go.

OUTSIDE THE HOME
Internet Cafés

If you don't have a data card or USB modem, you can still get online fairly easily in most large cities and tourist areas. Even smaller rural towns often have an Internet café or two, although these are generally fairly crude setups, usually consisting of nothing more than a couple of very old computers and a dialup connection that will make you feel like you've traveled back to 1996. You will have much better luck in larger cities and areas frequented by travelers, where it's easy to find broadband-equipped Internet cafés with new systems and perks such as scanners, webcams, and color printing facilities. Interestingly, many of the upscale neighborhoods favored by expats still have fairly rudimentary Internet cafés when compared to more rundown areas popular with the budget traveler set. This is likely due to a lack of demand—most people in expat neighborhoods have Internet at home, so the demand for Internet cafés is not as high.

Wi-Fi Hot Spots

The concept of Wi-Fi hot spots in India is still fairly new, although it's picking up quite quickly in urban areas. Most coffee shops don't offer Wi-Fi, but those that do usually provide it as a free service for their customers. In most cases, the staff will ask you to write your name, address, and the details of your photo ID in a logbook before they give you the Wi-Fi password. Internet cafés and Wi-Fi providers are legally required to record this data as part

DAILY LIFE

of heightened information security regulations that were put in place across India after the November 26, 2008, terrorist attacks in Mumbai.

Postal Services

INDIA POST

At first glance, India's national postal service, known as India Post, seems like yet another bureaucratic government-run agency. However, when it comes to actually using it, you will likely find that it's surprisingly efficient and reliable. To be fair, a visit to an Indian post office can be a bit harrowing: You may have to deal with long lines and languid postal workers who seem to take interminable *chai* breaks, all in a sweltering unair-conditioned environment. However, once you get to the counter, your letters and parcels will be dealt with quickly and professionally, and they will almost always end up reaching their final destination—eventually.

If you are only posting a letter, you normally have to take it to the counter to have it weighed. The cashier will then sell you stamps, which may or may not have adhesive. Little pots of paste for sticking on stamps can usually be found at counters flanking the walls of most post offices, although you may have to use a piece of scrap paper or your finger to apply the paste, as they don't usually have brushes. You then have to take your letter to a row of postboxes and deposit it in the proper slot, depending on its destination. There are normally at least three slots: one for local intracity post, one for international destinations, and a third for "outstation" (out of town) domestic locations. Letters weighing less than 20 grams cost ₹5 to send within India and ₹20 to send abroad.

If you need to send a parcel overseas, the cheapest way is to do so by ship, although it can take up to three months to reach North America or Europe. This option costs ₹40

© MARGOT BIGG

an India Post mailbox

for the first 100 grams and ₹30 for each additional 100 grams to anywhere in the world. Air mail, known as International Speed Post, is naturally much quicker, but you will have to pay a hefty premium for the service. Shipments to North America using this option cost ₹425 for the first 250 grams and ₹100 per additional 250 grams. International Speed Post shipments to Europe cost ₹675 for the first 250 grams and ₹75 per additional 250 grams. A happy medium can be found in the Surface Air Lifted (SAL) option, which combines air mail and sea shipping. As of 2010, SAL costs ₹310 for the first 250 grams and ₹65 for each additional 250 grams to North America (₹35 for each additional 250 grams to Europe).

India's national postal system

DAILY LIFE

PRIVATE COURIER SERVICES

Private courier services are very common in India and are commonly used to send sensitive documents such as checks and contracts. There are plenty of private couriers in large cities, some that operate only within a certain geographical area and others that can send documents across India and abroad

---

THAT'S A WRAP

If you have to send large parcels overseas, you may be required to wrap everything up in white fabric, sew it shut, and then seal the seams with red wax. You then write the recipient's address directly on the fabric using a black marker. This keeps your package protected from possible tampering, and most major post offices near tourist hot spots have tailors set up nearby who specialize in parcel packing; they can pack your parcel for just a few rupees. Just remember that not all post offices have parcel packers nearby, and not all tailors deal with such work. It's often easiest either to send your packages from post offices in touristy parts of town or simply buy a red candle and stitch your parcels up yourself.

(sometimes in conjunction with other companies). One of the most reliable is DHL's Blue Dart Express, although it's also one of the more expensive. For local services, you may find the rates of a smaller company more advantageous. In Mumbai, Mirakle Couriers is a good intracity option with a social welfare side: They hire deaf people who may not otherwise be able to find decent jobs to sort and deliver parcels.

For parcels and overseas shipments, the best private options are the international big three: UPS, FedEx, and DHL. These companies all provide international-standard levels of service and a variety of shipping and insurance options. However, they charge dearly for their services, so if you are not in a hurry and not sending valuable items, you may prefer to stick to India Post.

Media

NEWSPAPERS

India is home to the world's second-largest newspaper market, with hundreds of daily titles in English, Hindi, and regional languages. The most popular English-language national dailies are *Times of India, Hindustan Times, The Hindu, The Deccan Chronicle, The Deccan Herald, The Telegraph, DNA, Asian Age,* and *The Indian Express.* Dailies usually cost a meager ₹3 or so and generate much of their revenue from advertising.

MAGAZINES

India's magazine industry is enormous, and there are more English-language titles issued every month than most people would have time to read. There are local versions of many American and European titles, most of which are a mix of local and international content. Locally published international titles include *Rolling Stone, Cosmopolitan, GQ, Elle, Vogue, Marie Claire, Maxim, Condé Nast Traveler,* and *People.* There are also plenty of homegrown titles, including news magazines such as *India Today, Outlook,* and *Tehelka.* Magazines intended for worldwide distribution, such as *Newsweek* and *The Economist,* are also available at most newsstands.

BOOKS

Major publishers such as HarperCollins and Penguin have operations in India and publish both local and international titles for the South Asian market. Locally published books are much more affordable in India than they are in other English-speaking countries, ranging ₹100–295 for trade paperbacks and

© MARGOT BIGG

There are Indian editions of many of the world's leading magazines.

₹395–595 for hardcover editions. Books published overseas are normally sold for the published price converted into rupees. There are plenty of bookstores stocking English-language titles in all Indian cities, although the best deals and selection are usually online. Popular sites include http://bookvook.com, which also stocks foreign magazines, and http://flipkart.com.

TV

If you like television, you will have plenty of options in India. There are over 400 channels, of which more than 50 are in English. Prior to India's 1991 economic liberalization, which opened the market to foreign television channels, television in India was dominated by the state-owned Doordarshan channel. These days you will find everything from music channels, including MTV and VH1, to the BBC and CNN. Discovery, The National Geographic Channel, Cartoon Network, ESPN, and HBO also broadcast in India.

If you want to take advantage of

© MARGOT BIGG

Satellite television in India is accessible and affordable.

India's extensive cable offerings, you have to set up Direct to Home (DTH) satellite cable. Major providers include Tata Sky, Big TV, and Airtel Digital. You have to buy a starter kit consisting of a set-top box and a small satellite dish—these usually run around ₹1,500, although the prices are quickly dropping. Monthly rates run from around ₹200 for basic packages to around ₹400 for large packages (around 150 channels). Payment is made via recharge coupons, which can be purchased online or through an authorized dealer.

RADIO

India has scores of FM radio stations, many of which are broadcast in Hindi and regional languages. Although radio serves as a news source for many people in remote areas, its biggest function is for entertainment purposes, especially for music. Bollywood music dominates the airwaves, but most small- and medium-sized cities also have channels devoted to English-language songs of the Top 40 variety. India's national radio station, All India Radio (AIR), has local-language broadcasts across the country and operates a national news service in Hindi and English.

TRAVEL AND TRANSPORTATION

Whether you are staying in your city or traveling out of town, getting around in India is always an adventure. There are so many different types of transportation available that you may not know where to start. If you are going long distances, you may want to save some time and simply fly on one of the country's many air carriers. You may prefer the train, which allows you to catch a glimpse of Indian rural life as you speed through the countryside. Depending on where you are traveling, you may even find a long-distance bus more convenient.

You will also need to find your way around the city, and as most Indian metropolises are sprawling, polluted, and overheated, you probably won't want to attempt getting around on foot or by bicycle. Instead, you have to decide whether a car is right for you or whether you prefer to get around by taxi or autorickshaw. Some cities have metros and city trains of variable quality, and

© MARGOT BIGG

TRANSPORTATION

while they all have buses, this is not the most comfortable way of getting around town. However and wherever you decide to travel, you'll surely get to see something fascinating and new. Make sure to grab a window seat.

By Air

Not long ago, India was known in the travel industry for having horrible airports with few facilities and more cockroaches than passengers. In those days, you were lucky if you could get a microwaved samosa and a cup of sugary instant coffee while you waited between flights. The toilets were mainly of the squat variety, and the chairs looked like they had been upholstered in the 1970s and never cleaned. Fortunately for India's frequent fliers, a lot has changed in the last half-decade. Airports in hubs such as Hyderabad and Delhi have undergone facelifts, transforming them from ugly to bedazzling. With their shiny new interiors, great shopping and dining options, and well-organized departure lounges, India's new airports are on par with, if not better than, their counterparts in more developed countries.

Delhi, Mumbai, Bengaluru, and Chennai are well-connected to the rest of the world, and most major international carriers operate flights to at least a couple of India's metropolises. India also has three major international airlines of its own: Air India (the national carrier), Kingfisher (often called the Virgin Atlantic of India), and Jet Airways. These three airlines operate worldwide, and all three are set to join international alliances in the near future.

Up until recently, air travel in India was quite expensive, and it made much more sense to take the train for travel within the same region. However, over the past few years, many low-cost airlines have sprung up that serve not only the major hubs but also smaller cities. This has made airplane travel easier than ever before, and remote locations are more accessible to people with little time and limited budgets.

Popular budget airlines include SpiceJet, IndiGo, and GoAir as well as Southern India's Paramount Airways. Major air carriers also have budget services, namely Kingfisher Red, Jet Lite, and Air India Express. Budget flights between major cities are generally much better value than flights from larger hubs to smaller destinations, regardless of the distance. A flight from Mumbai to Bengaluru or Delhi shouldn't cost more than ₹4,000 each way. Domestic tickets can be booked through agents or directly with the airlines, although the best deals are often found on flight-booking websites like www.ClearTrip.com, www.MakeMyTrip.com, and www.Yatra.com.

INDIA'S FOREIGN PILOTS

Imagine being on a flight thousands of feet above the ground, sipping on a *nimbu paani* and gazing out the window at a thick mass of clouds, when a voice comes on the loudspeaker to welcome you on board. The voice is from the cockpit and is speaking in informal, fluent English without a hint of Victoriana; instead, it has a distinctive Texas twang. If you were on a United flight to New York, this would come as no surprise, but you are on a SpiceJet flight from Kolkata to Mumbai.

In the mid- to late 2000s, hundreds of pilots from overseas were recruited to work in India, where a shortage of experienced domestic pilots prompted some of the newer airlines to begin recruiting outside the country. Pilots need a certain number of flight hours as copilots before they are legally allowed to pilot commercial aircraft, and there simply weren't enough qualified pilots in India to meet the new demand created by the many new airlines. In 2009, however the Indian government gave airlines a mid-2010 deadline to phase out their foreign pilots, which they later extended for another year. Many people fear that this crackdown will lower the hiring standards of domestic airlines.

It's also not unheard of to travel by helicopter in India, and while this is generally a means of transportation reserved from the rich and famous, choppers are often used as quicker alternatives to road transportation in areas where infrastructure isn't great. Helicopters are often used to ferry pilgrims to difficult-to-reach sacred spots in the hills and for transporting people from cities with airports to smaller localities that would otherwise have to be approached by road.

By Train

An exciting and interesting way to see India is by train. Trains give you access to parts of the country that you might never otherwise experience as an urban expat: the villages and rural expanses. There's nothing homogeneous about India—language, culture, and landscape change every few miles—and there's no better way to observe this phenomenon than through the window of a train. The only downside to train travel is that understanding the offerings and booking a ticket accordingly can be a challenge for the uninitiated.

TYPES OF TRAINS

There are numerous different types of trains in India, from commuter trains that link large cities with nearby villages to long-distance trains meant for travelers. The most comfortable trains are the Rajdhani Express and the Shatabdi Express. Rajdhani trains link major cities, are good for overnight travel, and move faster and with fewer stops than regular trains. Meals are also included. Shatabdi trains are similar to Rajdhanis except they are for shorter distances (the entire route is usually less than 6–7 hours). Meals, tea, water, and morning newspapers are included in the ticket price for this type of train.

Indian trains normally have two types of toilet facilities, signposted as "Indian WC" (for the squat-style latrines) and "Western WC" (for toilets with seats). Neither are kept very clean, and it's a good idea to bring hand sanitizer and toilet paper for your journey, as these are not always available.

TRAIN CLASSES

Once you have figured out what type of train you want to take, you have to determine which class is best for you. The cheapest is called Second Seating (2C) and is usually quite full. Seating in this unair-conditioned section is not always assigned, and it's not worth it unless you are traveling a very short distance. If you want to lie down during your trip, you have four options, three of which have air-conditioning and one that doesn't. At the lower end, Sleeper Class (SC) is an unair-conditioned compartment with sections containing two rows of three berths each (a bottom one, a middle one, and a top one), plus two side berths (one upper, one lower). During the day, the middle berth can be folded against the wall to act as a backrest for the bottom berth, and all three passengers from each section sit on the bottom berth. If you are in the

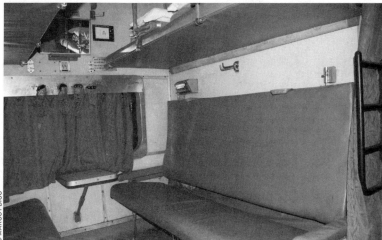

© MARGOT BIGG

a "2AC" class carriage in an Indian train

bottom berth and are a late sleeper, you may find that people end up perching on your berth once the sun rises, so you may prefer to request an upper berth instead. You have to bring your own bedding for this class.

If you prefer air-conditioning, you are better off reserving a seat in Third (3AC), Second (2AC), or First Class (1AC). The 3AC class is similar to Sleeper Class in layout, although it's air-conditioned and tends to be a bit cleaner. The next class up, 2AC, has four berths in each section instead of six, and comes with reading lights and curtains. In 1AC, you have a closed booth containing either two or four berths that are wider than in the other classes. Bedding is provided free of charge in all three of these classes.

If you are traveling by Shatabdi and other local trains, you are normally able to choose between Chair Car (CC) or First Class (1A, sometimes called Executive Chair Class). Most foreign travelers find that CC is adequate for them, but those wanting a little more legroom may prefer the larger, plusher seats in 1A. Some trains in this category also have an unair-conditioned 2C class with assigned seating.

RESERVING TRAIN TICKETS AND WAITING LISTS

First-time train travelers in India may prefer to book their tickets through an agent who can help them navigate the many classes and types of tickets available. Others prefer to book online at the government's Indian Railway Catering and Tourism Corporation (IRCTC) website (www.irctc.co.in). If there are no seats available on a train you want to take, you still have the option of buying a waiting-list ticket, which comes in two varieties: Reservation

© MARGOT BIGG

inside the train station in Haridwar

Against Confirmation (RAC) and bona fide Waitlist (WL) tickets. If you have an RAC ticket, you will be allowed to board the train, and the conductor will usually be able to help you find an empty seat or berth. Those with WL tickets are not allowed to board unless enough people have canceled their voyage. All tickets, waiting-listed or otherwise, come with a Personal Name Record (PNR) number. To find out the status of your reservation, you can enter your PNR at one of the computerized kiosks at most stations or online at www.indianrail.gov.in.

Tickets for Indian trains often sell out months in advance, so it's a good idea to book as far ahead as you can. For last-minute travel, you can sometimes save yourself the worry and hassle of being on a waiting list and instead take advantage of one of the many quotas that Indian Railways has to offer. The most popular is the Tatkal quota, which allows passengers to buy last-minute tickets up to two days before a train's departure for an additional charge (10 percent or 30 percent of the ticket price, depending on the class of seat you reserve). A few trains have special coaches for women traveling alone, and tickets for these seats can be bought using the Ladies Quota. Foreigners with tourist visas can buy last-minute Foreign Tourist Quota Tickets, which are available from the International Tourist Bureau located in some major railway stations, although residents of India (those on employment visas) do not qualify for this quota.

DAILY LIFE

By Bus

CITY BUSES

Very few expatriates choose to use city buses, as most are crowded, rustic, and rarely on schedule. If you do take the bus, note that women and elderly people will be given priority seating, and if you are a woman traveling alone, it's a good idea to stay as close to the driver as possible because harassment and groping are common. You buy your ticket on the bus from a bus employee (not from the driver) who will either make his way up and down the aisle or sit somewhere near the back door. When you need to get off the bus, make your way to the nearest door and try to get the attention of the driver by yelling out or waving your hand.

LONG-DISTANCE BUS TRAVEL

India is well-connected by bus, and you may find yourself using this means of transportation for short trips. Many popular resort towns in the Himalayan foothills are inaccessible by train, and you may find that taking a long-distance coach is an easier and more affordable option than renting a taxi.

When traveling between major destinations, you have the choice between local buses and private coaches. Local buses are slower and don't have air-conditioning or assigned seats. These buses pick up passengers along the way and can get very crowded at times. They're also the cheapest way of getting around and a good way to experience firsthand how the majority of Indians get around. The more comfortable option is what is called a Volvo, or private air-conditioned bus. Despite the name, they are not necessarily manufactured by Volvo. These buses usually have assigned seats (two on each side of the aisle) and only stop every few hours so that passengers can get a cup of tea or use the restroom. For long-distance travel, you can also take a bus equipped with sleeper or semisleeper seating arrangements. Semisleeper buses have rows of seats that recline really far back so that you can attempt a good night's sleep during your voyage (although you may feel like you are on the lap of the person behind you). Sleeper buses have full-on sleeping berths, usually for single or double use, and can be quite comfortable. Both types of bus may or may not be air-conditioned.

By Car

If you plan to spend more than a few months in India, you may find it worthwhile to get a car. If you've been sent over by your company, it will normally arrange this for you and foot the bill. Otherwise, you will have to organize a car for yourself.

You can rent or lease a car, although leasing often requires the intervention of your company, which may not want to put the contract in their name. Most foreigners find it easier to buy a car outright. In India, cars retain their value better than they do in the West. While buying a new car will still run you a lot more than a secondhand model, it won't loose as large a chunk of its value when you drive it off the lot as in the West.

If you buy a used car, it's better either to buy it from a dealership that offers some sort of guarantee or from someone in your general network, perhaps an expat who is leaving or a friend of a friend. India's roads cause a lot of wear and tear on cars, much of which is not visible, so it's important that there is at least some level of accountability with the person you are buying from lest you end up with a lemon. You can also check on expat websites and bulletin boards at international schools.

Once you have decided to buy a car, you must officially register your vehicle or transfer the ownership into your name. If you buy your car from a dealership, it will usually take care of this for you—otherwise, you can hire an agent to take care of the necessary registration formalities on your behalf. If you want to register the car yourself, you have to approach the nearest zonal office of the Transport Department. For new cars, you are required to submit proof of address, evidence that you've taken out car insurance, forms filled out by the car's manufacturer attesting to its suitability for the road, proof of sale, proof that you've paid duty on the car, and registration fees. To transfer ownership of a vehicle, you need proof of your address and insurance, a certificate that the car meets prescribed emissions standards, and the original registration certificate. You and the previous owner also need to fill out and sign an application for transfer of the ownership deed. Make sure that you always carry the *original* copies of your registration and insurance with you, as the police often stop cars at random to verify that you have your documents in order.

Most foreigners, and a lot of Indians, hire a driver instead of driving themselves. If you want to rent a car on a short-term basis, say for a trip out of town, you will find that hiring a taxi with a driver is much cheaper than hiring a self-drive vehicle. Apparently this is because without a driver, car rental companies won't necessarily find out if you get in an accident or otherwise damage their car, so it's better for them to fork over the monthly ₹5,000–8,000 it costs to employ a driver.

DRIVING YOURSELF

If you decide to drive yourself, you need to learn the unstated rules of the road in India. It's a good idea to have a local friend or an expat with a lot of experience navigating India's streets come with you when you first try driving in your city to help you get the hang of it. You'll be sharing the road with trucks, pedestrians, cyclists, motorcycles, rickshaws, trucks, bullock carts, and the occasional camel or elephant, and it's important to understand a few key principles before you get behind the wheel. In most cities, lanes are rarely respected. If you can line up five cars side-to-side on a street, why would you bother sticking to only three allocated lanes? The larger and faster your vehicle is, the higher your status on the right-of-way hierarchy. Cars pass motorcycles, motorcycles pass bicycles, bicycles pass pedestrians. However, the lumbering goods trucks, while large, are not very fast and usually let you pass, even though your vehicle is smaller. If you feel more comfortable driving slowly, keep to the left. As people drive on the left in India, this is considered the slow lane. This will help keep you out of the way of the faster, more aggressively driven vehicles. If you want to pass another vehicle, you have to make your presence known. The easiest way to do this during the day is by sounding your horn. In India, horns are not used as warnings the way they are in many countries; instead they are used to indicate one's presence or express frustration, aggression, and even boredom. People even honk their horns in traffic jams and similar situations where honking does absolutely nothing to solve the problem. At first, this constant din can be a bit intimidating, not to mention harsh on the ears, but you'll soon get desensitized to it. At night you use your "dipper," or high beams, to indicate your presence. Simply position your vehicle to the right of the vehicle you want to pass and flash them quickly once or twice. The vehicle in front of you will normally move over to the left to allow you to pass.

Driver's Licenses

If you plan to drive in India, it's a good idea to obtain an International Driving Permit (IDP) in your home country prior to traveling. These are easily obtained from an automobile association, such as AAA in the United States, the CAA in Canada, or the AA in Britain. You are able to drive in India legally for up to one year with such a permit. If you want to get an Indian driver's license, you have to apply to your local Regional Transport Office (RTO) and will possibly be asked to get a learner's permit first, which can later be converted into a proper license. An easier way to do it is to go through a driving school. They can give you lessons on navigating the madness of the Indian roads and can usually process your driver's license on your behalf for a fee.

HIRING A DRIVER

You may prefer to spare yourself the driving and instead hire a driver. In most cases, your driver will live off-site and come to your house daily (by bus or motorcycle) to work. It's common for drivers to work six days a week, and their work hours can range 10–14 hours per day. It's common for people to hire drivers for daytime and then drive themselves at night, although such a situation is not ideal for everyone. Single women, especially younger ones, should not drive alone at night, and having a trusted driver provides an extra level of security.

TAXIS

Short-term expats and those who don't need to travel long distances regularly may prefer to stick to taxis. In India, a taxi is anything from a metered radio cab (or "dial-a-cab" as they are generically referred to) to an unmetered vehicle that looks more or less like any other regular car except that it has a

DAILY LIFE

© RUI MARTIN

In some cities, price charts are used to convert fares from outdated meters.

yellow license plate. In some cities, including Mumbai and Kolkata, there are black cabs, unair-conditioned vehicles that can be hailed on the street and use a meter.

Traveling in the City

If you are traveling within your city, you will have plenty of taxi options. If you just need to be dropped somewhere, you can call a metered radio cab. Companies such as Meru Cabs and Easy Cabs operate in most major cities and can usually get a taxi to you within half an hour of your call. However, during peak times, such as on weekend evenings and during the morning commute hours, these services sometimes run out of cabs, so it's best to book well ahead. Another possibility is to call your local "taxi stand." A taxi stand is not quite the same as one you would find in the West; it is rather a private taxi service with its own fleet of vehicles. Taxi stands usually provide either metered black cabs, unmetered air-conditioned cars, or both. If you only need to be dropped somewhere and your local stand doesn't have metered cabs, you have to negotiate a price. If you need a taxi for a longer term, you can rent them by the day or the half-day. Taxi stands usually offer set-rate packages of four hours/40 km or eight hours/80 km. Any additional hours or kilometers that you use will be added to the bill, as will any night charges. Make sure to check whether the fare you are being quoted includes use of the air-conditioning. Also note that the odometer will start when the taxi leaves the stand, not your house, so it's best to get your taxi from a nearby location.

Long-Distance Travel

If you want to go on a road trip in India, you won't need a car of your own. Instead, you can simply rent a private taxi from your local taxi stand and take off. Depending on how many passengers you have with you and what kind of terrain you will be traversing, you may be fine with a small car or you may prefer something more substantial. The cheapest cars available are usually dinky little Tata Indicas, which will get you from point A to point B just fine but aren't as roomy or comfortable as larger models. Larger groups will want to stretch their legs out in a Qualis or other large vehicle. If you plan to go to the mountains, you may want to request something akin to a jeep (such as a Gypsy or a Scorpio), but bear in mind that not all large vehicles are equipped with four-wheel drive.

Taxi stands and travel agents will quote you a rate for your out-of-town travel, which will be based on the distance traveled and the number of nights out of town. You will be charged a per-kilometer rate plus a daily fee to offset additional costs the driver may incur while on the trip. You will not be expected to pay for your driver's food or accommodations, although it's a nice gesture to foot the bill if you stop for tea or food along the way. If you are staying at an upscale hotel, there is usually some sort of dormitory-style setup for drivers, but if you are staying in a budget guesthouse, your driver may end up sleeping in the car. You will not have to pay extra for petrol or any taxes charged at the borders of new states, as these will be covered by your per-kilometer rate. You will be responsible for toll charges and parking fees, however. Make sure you clarify all of this with your travel agent or taxi stand before agreeing on the arrangements.

Other Modes of Transportation

BY MOTORCYCLE

Many foreigners, especially in smaller cities and in places like Goa, get around by motorcycle or motor scooter. You have to follow more or less the same procedures for getting your bike registered and insured that you do for a car. You also need a motorcycle license, also obtainable from the RTO. In most cities, drivers are required to wear helmets, unless they wear turbans, although passengers are not. It's a good idea for everyone to wear a helmet as India's roads can be dangerous and motorcyclists are pretty low on the motor-vehicle food chain.

WHY NOT CYCLE?

© MARGOT BIGG

Bicycles are a good way to get around outside of major cities.

If you live in a small town without a lot of traffic, you will find that cycling is a great way to get around, especially on cooler days. However, if you've come to India for work, you will probably end up in a large city, where maddening traffic and thick pollution make cycling an unreasonable form of transportation for all but the avid enthusiast.

Plenty of people ride bicycles in India, although in most cases they ride them not for sport or leisure but because bicycles are an economical form of transportation that require little maintenance and small initial investment. That's not to say that people don't cycle for fun; it's just not as common as in many other countries. Most expats who cycle in India were already very passionate about their hobby before moving here.

If you are interested in getting around this way, it's a good idea to invest in a filtration mask that will reduce the amount of pollution you inhale while cycling. Buy it and any other special gear you might need in your home country, as the availability of cycling accessories is somewhat limited in India. Also, bear in mind that bicycles are very low on the road hierarchy, and you will probably find yourself yielding a lot to larger vehicles. While a few cities have bike lanes, motorcyclists and autorickshaws often use the lanes as shortcuts, and you will have to yield to them too.

BY RICKSHAW
Autorickshaws

In many cities, autorickshaws (sometimes abbreviated as "autos" or "ricks") are the most convenient and affordable way of getting around town. These three-wheeled vehicles look a bit like a golf cart, although if you took one apart, you would find that it is more similar to an encased motorcycle. In many cities, autorickshaws run on compressed natural gas (CNG), which makes them cheaper to operate and less polluting then diesel- or gasoline-fueled vehicles.

In most cities, autorickshaws run on meters, although autorickshaw drivers, known as "autowallahs," often prefer to quote a set fee, often an exorbitant one. If you know your way around, it's best to try your hardest to go by the meter. In cities such as Mumbai, Bengaluru, and Hyderabad, this usually isn't a problem. In Delhi it's more difficult, although recent hikes in the rates have made most autowallahs more cooperative. In Chennai, meters aren't even part of the package. If you travel between 11 P.M. and about 6 A.M., you are expected to pay a night charge of 25 percent of the metered fare.

Prepaid autorickshaw stands are available at major tourist points and trains stations in most cities. These booths are generally run by a government authority (usually the local police) and have fixed rates depending on the approximate number of kilometers you will be traveling. Simply state your destination at the booth and take a receipt—in most cases you pay upfront and then give the receipt to your driver in lieu of the fare, although in some cities you buy the receipt for a rupee or two and then give the fare printed on it directly to

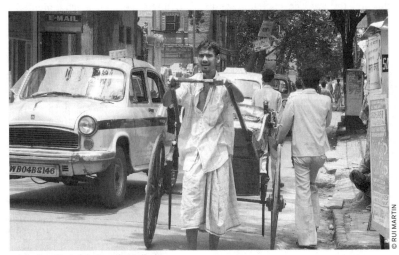

a hand-pulled rickshaw in Kolkata

© MARGOT BIGG

Cycle rickshaws are an inexpensive and eco-friendly way of getting around.

the driver. In the absence of such booths, you have to flag an auto by simply sticking your hand out and giving a little wrist flick (like you would if you were hailing a taxi) or yelling "auto" as loud as you can.

In some cities you can also find shared autos, sometimes called *vikrams,* a larger cousin of the standard autorickshaw that are usually designed to accommodate about eight passengers (but in reality can pack in quite a few more). These autos usually follow set routes with set fares depending on the distance traveled, and while you can usually get a good deal with this kind of transportation, you might find it a cramped and sweaty way of meeting your neighbors.

Bicycle Rickshaws

One of the greenest and most economical ways of getting around your local area is by bicycle rickshaw, which is basically a cart attached to the front part of a bicycle frame with one wheel in the front and two in the back. They usually have shade covers that are either fixed or collapsible. It's a good idea to hold on to the cover's frame, as it's not unheard of for inattentive passengers to go flying off on sharp turns. Fares should be negotiated before you climb aboard. Remember that the people who pedal these vehicles are among the poorest people you will interact with, and the work they do is grueling, especially on hot days, and low-paid; be generous.

PRIME LIVING LOCATIONS

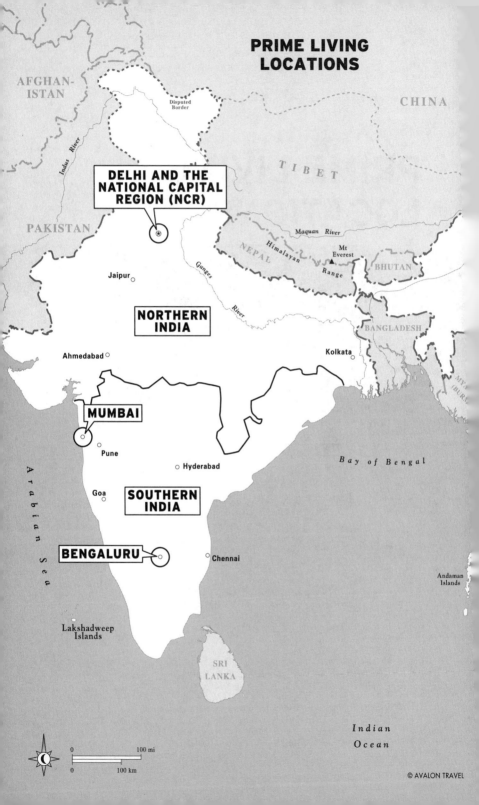

PRIME LIVING LOCATIONS

AFGHAN-ISTAN

CHINA

Disputed Border

Indus River

PAKISTAN

DELHI AND THE NATIONAL CAPITAL REGION (NCR)

T I B E T

Maquan River

NEPAL

Himalayan

Mt Everest

BHUTAN

Range

Jaipur

Ganges

River

NORTHERN INDIA

BANGLADESH

Ahmedabad

Kolkata

MYA (BUR)

MUMBAI

Pune

SOUTHERN INDIA

Hyderabad

Bay of Bengal

Goa

A r a b i a n   S e a

BENGALURU

Chennai

Andaman Islands

Lakshadweep Islands

SRI LANKA

I n d i a n

O c e a n

0 ___ 100 mi

0 ___ 100 km

© AVALON TRAVEL

OVERVIEW

Where you end up living in India depends on a number of factors, including your personal interests and your line of work. However, in most cases, you won't have the chance to decide where in India you'll be living: your employer will do that for you. If you do get to decide where to live, there are a number of factors you'll want to consider. The following section is designed to give you insight into India's prime destinations for foreigners. Although there are plenty of foreigners settling in India's many backpacker towns, the areas covered in this section are those with many employment and educational opportunities for foreigners, with long-term residents in mind.

Delhi, Mumbai, and Bengaluru, India's three most significant hubs for business and industry, are covered first. Areas with smaller expat populations are also covered and divided into two sections in this book: Northern and Southern India, the most common way that the country is divided. Ahmedabad, Jaipur, and Kolkata are in the north, and Chennai, Goa, Hyderabad, and Pune are in the south. Note that there is much debate in India over whether

WHAT'S IN A NAME?

Many Indian place names are simply variations of local-language names that were misinterpreted by colonial settlers. Across India, cities, states, and streets are shedding their colonial-era monikers, changing their official names back to the local language. Here are a few examples:

Old	New
Bangalore	Bengaluru
Benares	Varanasi
Bombay	Mumbai
Calcutta	Kolkata
Cochin	Kochi
Madras	Chennai
Pondicherry	Puducherry
Poona	Pune
Uttaranchal	Uttarakhand

Maharashtra and Goa are part of the north or the south, as they share many cultural and linguistic elements with the north but are geographically in the south. We've opted to go with the geographical definition, so they appear with the coverage of Southern India.

If your city of choice is not covered, don't despair: You'll still be able to glean a lot of relevant cultural information by flipping to the section on the part of the country you want to live in. Moreover, you may find yourself visiting one of the cities listed in this section to visit your consulate, buy international groceries, or network with other expats in your region.

Delhi and the National Capital Region (NCR)

Delhi is the nation's capital and hub for the central government and new media. It's a sprawling city, the largest of its size in the country and second only to Mumbai in terms of population. Add the suburbs and satellite cities of the NCR, namely Gurgaon and Noida along with Faridabad and Ghaziabad, and you have one seemingly endless metropolis stretching across two states and a union territory. Although the city now known as Delhi has served as India's capital on and off for centuries, the NCR cities of Gurgaon and Noida have shorter histories. Gurgaon was just a village surrounded by farmland until

© MARGOT BIGG

Most of Delhi's residents live in houses that have been divided into apartments.

developers began buying up land in the 1990s and transforming it into the hub for multinational corporations that it is today. Noida's development began a bit earlier, in the late 1970s, and today it's home to many of the region's call centers and office parks.

Many residents of Delhi and the cities of the NCR have roots elsewhere. During partition, large numbers of Hindu and Sikh Punjabis from what is now Pakistan moved to the city, and entire neighborhoods were set aside to resettle them. More recently, Gurgaon's many corporations have attracted new graduates from across the country who come for better job opportunities than they would have back home. Delhi also has large communities of people from neighboring countries, including Afghans, Burmese, and Nepalese. There is also a large Tibetan community, although most young Tibetans in Delhi were born in India, home to Tibet's government in exile. There are also plenty of expats in Delhi working in everything from embassies to small NGOs.

Mumbai

The home of the Hindi film industry and India's financial capital, India's most populated city is fast and fun. The long, thin stretch of land that makes up Mumbai is flanked with coastline to the west, so you are never far from a bit of sea breeze respite if life in the congested city begins to feel stifling. In many ways, Mumbai is like the Los Angeles of India, with its year-round sunshine, designer boutiques, movie star mansions, and hordes of sunglass-sporting socialites. It's also comparable to Manhattan, not only because it's the home of

© MARGOT BIGG

Mumbai is one of India's most sophisticated cities.

India's stock market but also because of the crowds, the fast-paced lifestyle, and the no-nonsense attitude of its residents. It's also one of the most expensive places to live in India, but what it lacks in affordable housing it makes up for in glamour. Although Mumbai is a fast-moving place, it has a very casual side, and you will find that people don't dress as conservatively or as formally here as they do in other Indian cities. Like Delhi, Mumbai has residents from across India, although high housing costs make it difficult for a lot of people to move here. There are also plenty of expats in Mumbai working in everything from finance to media, and the city's cosmopolitan vibe makes it a good city to have an international lifestyle while still experiencing a new culture.

Bengaluru

India's third-largest city by population, the high-tech metropolis of Bengaluru is often referred to as the Silicon Valley of the East. The city formerly known as Bangalore is home to many of India's top IT companies, including Wipro and Infosys. The city is a hub for industries such as biotechnology and telecommunications. Many government undertakings are also based in Bengaluru, especially those dealing with heavy electronics and aeronautical engineering. While people from all over India move to Bengaluru to work, life here is equally about play. The city has great nightlife, with events going on every night of the week. It's also the pub capital of India, although most bars and clubs only stay open until 11 P.M., so if you are looking for late-night entertainment, you may be better off sticking to one of the many coffee shops scattered around the city, some of which stay open 24 hours. While the combination of IT companies and a rich nightlife definitely lend an air of youthfulness to Bengaluru, it's also a nice place for families. It's one of India's most noticeably green cities, and there are plenty of sprawling parks throughout the city, not to mention trees everywhere. The result is that the air in Bengaluru is easier to breathe than in many other Indian cities despite the plague of very bad traffic.

Queen Victoria Statue in Cubbon Park, Bengaluru

© MARGOT BIGG

Northern India

Northern India stretches across Himalayan India and the "Hindi Belt" that covers the northern plains, and by some definitions (including the one used in this book) encompasses the nonpeninsular top of the subcontinent. This climatically diverse part of the country has everything from snowcapped peaks to sparse deserts, plus a number of important cities for expats. The Gujarati capital of Ahmedabad, arguably India's most up-and-coming destination for expats, is a relatively clean and comfortable city and an increasingly popular place for people working in everything from oil to software development. Although expat numbers are still lower here than in some of India's larger cities, a growing number of Gujarat natives have returned from long stints overseas to make Ahmedabad their home, bringing with them a demand for foreign products and world-class services and infrastructure.

Jaipur, Rajasthan's capital and a hub for handicrafts, is ideal for people wanting to deal in art or handicraft manufacture, and is also popular with Hindi language students. Despite being the capital of India's largest state, Jaipur is relatively compact and easy to get around. Moreover, the city is a major hot spot on India's tourist map, so there's no shortage of Western comforts.

Despite the city's size, Kolkata's expat community is relatively small.

To the east, Kolkata, the former capital of British India, lacks the intimacy and relative serenity that smaller cities can offer, although it's lively and cosmopolitan in its own right. It's the veritable hub for Bengali culture, which is saying a lot considering that the Bengalis are known nationwide for their keen interest in the arts and letters. Like most of India's major cities, Kolkata has a growing IT sector. It is also home to India's second-largest stock market, the Calcutta Stock Exchange.

WHERE SHOULD I LIVE?

Your experience of India will be quite different depending on what side of the Deccan Plateau you end up living on. If you have the choice of where to live in India, the north versus south debate will come into play. If you want to learn Hindi, Northern India, especially Delhi or Jaipur, is the place to go. Although people in many southern states use Hindi regularly, local languages are also used, so you won't get the same exposure to Hindi that you would in the north.

If you are interested in dance or Carnatic music, Southern India has more options, especially Chennai. Retirees may prefer the tranquil atmosphere in Goa, as do people with small children who don't need to work (although keep in mind that the schools there aren't great).

If you want to start a handicraft or export business, a base in Jaipur would be the best option (although Goa is also popular for this).

If you want to start a software company, India is your oyster, as most major cities have at lease some kind of IT sector. The biggest IT hubs are still in Bengaluru, Hyderabad, Pune, and Gurgaon.

If you work in finance or the entertainment industry, or if you want to be in a cosmopolitan and fast-paced city, Mumbai is the place for you.

Southern India

India's tropical half, the peninsula of Southern India often feels like a different country from the north and in many ways, the two parts of the country feel like polar opposites. When Northern Indians drink tea, southerners drink coffee. Northern Indian languages emerged from Sanskrit, and Southern Indian languages belong to the Dravidian family. The food, architecture, climate, and customs are all different, but the beauty of India is that these differences can only make a country that practices unity in diversity even stronger. One thing that most Indian cities share is a strong orientation toward the IT industry. This is most noticeable in the twin-cities of Hyderabad and Secunderabad, a former suzerainty that is as known for its IT industry as for its *biryani* and pearls. Although Hyderabad is situated in Andhra Pradesh, people here speak Hindi-Urdu along with the local Telugu language and English.

This isn't the case farther south in Chennai, where Tamil and English are used almost exclusively. This tropical coastal city once known as Madras is home to India's automotive industry, and it is a major hub for health care, manufacturing, and—you guessed it—IT. On the opposite coast, the tiny state of Goa borders the Arabian Sea. Although there's not much industry here, the state's laid-back lifestyle and excellent beaches have made it a popular destination for foreign tourists and expats for generations.

Just north of Goa is the state of Maharashtra, where Northern and Southern India meet and which has cultural elements common to each half of the country. Pune, the former capital of the Maratha Empire, is Maharashtra's second-largest city and is known for its many colleges and universities. This student town has an easygoing and relaxed atmosphere, and many people who move here to study end up staying, getting jobs in local companies or in the Pune offices of IT giants such as Microsoft.

an example of South Indian temple sculpture

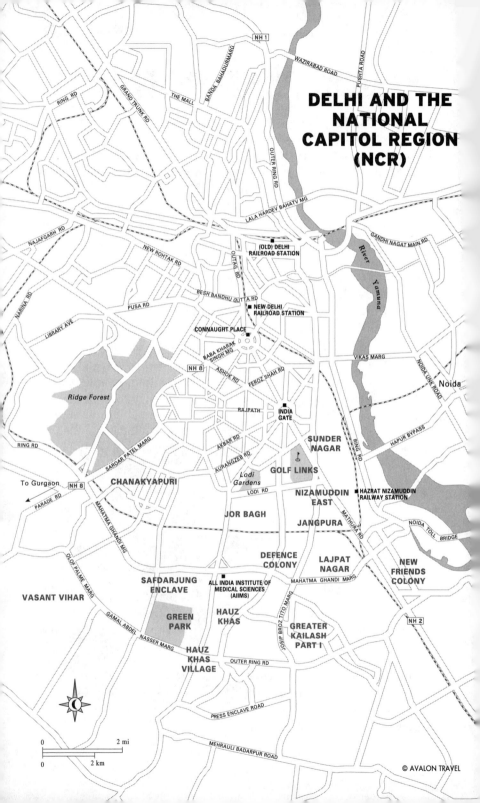

DELHI AND THE NATIONAL CAPITAL REGION (NCR)

Delhi is the seat of India's federal government. The land on which modern Delhi stands has been inhabited for well over two millennia and has been home to seven different cities, each built by a different ruler in a different era. Delhi was also the capital of India under the rule of the Delhi Sultanate and during much of the Lodi and Mughal eras, and it remained the center of power until it became part of British India in 1857. In 1912 the capital was shifted back to Delhi.

Delhi sits at the heart of the National Capital Region (NCR), an agglomeration that includes Delhi, Noida, Gurgaon, and a number of smaller cities and villages in the neighboring states of Haryana, Uttar Pradesh, and Rajasthan. When most people talk about the NCR, however, they are really only referring to the urban central areas of Delhi, Noida, and Gurgaon, as well as Faridabad and Ghaziabad on the outskirts.

People who have come to India as tourists are often shocked to hear that Delhi and environs are a great place for expats to live. The Delhi of tourists is one of smog, touts, and Mughal monuments that begin to look the same after you have visited too many of them. Sure, it's known by tourists as a great spot to shop as well as one of the better places in the country to go clubbing, but most visitors to India see Delhi as a transit point, a place to get in and get out as quickly as possible.

Living in Delhi and the NCR is an entirely different story. Sure, you have to put up with a lot of pollution, touting, eardrum-piercing car horns, and nasty traffic. Nevertheless, it's easy to get around and has great shopping options and international-quality restaurants.

The Lay of the Land

Delhi sits on the west bank of the River Yamuna, which is now heavily polluted despite being sacred in Hindu culture. West of the city is the forested Delhi Ridge, an extension of the Aravalli mountain range, said to be the oldest in the world. While the Yamuna makes Delhi's soil good for agriculture, the Ridge Forest helps keep the city relatively breathable, although heavy pollution and lots of dust make Delhi a harder place then most to get a lungful of fresh air.

Delhi is divided into many smaller neighborhoods and villages, and it is encircled by two major thoroughfares: Ring Road and Outer Ring Road, which feature overpasses at major intersections that allow vehicles to avoid stopping at every traffic light. If you are driving to Gurgaon, you have two main options. You can either follow MG Road (which actually stands for Mehrauli–Gurgaon Road, not Mahatma Gandhi Road) or take the toll-supported Delhi–Gurgaon Expressway, a stretch of National Highway 8 (NH-8) that connects Delhi with Mumbai. There are a few bridges that cross over the Yamuna into Noida, although the most convenient way for most people heading to the central Sector 18 part of town is the toll-supported Delhi Noida Direct (DND) Flyway, which most people erroneously call the DND Flyover or just the DND.

CLIMATE

Delhi's climate is arid and extreme. Summers (April–June) are very hot, with temperatures often exceeding 110°F. Monsoons in July and August can make it a bit muggier, and the humidity can linger as late as mid-October. Winters

© MARGOT BIGG

strolling in Delhi

can get bone-chillingly cold when temperatures can drop to near freezing in December and January. While many people from Western countries are used to subfreezing temperatures, remember that Delhi houses rarely have central heating, and that most homes are built to keep residents cool, with marble flooring and limited access to sunlight. The inside of your house may be colder than outside, and you may find yourself sleeping under layers of thick blankets. The most pleasant months are the mid-October–November and mid-Febraury–March shoulder seasons.

LANGUAGE

Delhi's population is diverse, and you'll likely hear languages and dialects from across the country spoken regularly. There are three main languages used in day-to-day interactions: Hindi, Urdu, Punjabi, and English. Because Delhi has a large Punjabi population, the Hindi spoken here has a lot of Punjabi elements. In Gurgaon, you will likely hear a lot of Haryanvi, a dialect of Hindi spoken by the Jat people of the region. English is widely understood and spoken with native fluency by the educated classes. Household help and taxi or autorickshaw drivers may not know much English, but they will understand words like *left* and *right* as well as numbers.

CULTURE

As a diverse city, Delhi doesn't have one specific culture. There are people from across the country living here, and most people maintain their own

CAPITAL LETTERS

From CP to the SDA, people in the NCR love to use acronyms, which newcomers to the city can find quite confusing. Here are a few common acronyms that will help you start speaking like a Delhiite in no time:

- **AIIMS:** Pronounced "aims," and sometimes referred to by Hindi-speakers simply as "Medical," the All India Institute of Medical Sciences is an important transit point and landmark on South Delhi's inner ring road.

- **BRT:** Bus Rapid Transit. "The BRT" also refers to the stretch of road running from Dr. Ambedkar Nagar to Delhi Gate that has lanes sectioned off for bus use only.

- **CP:** Connaught Place, a central Delhi commercial area.

- **DDA:** Delhi Development Authority, responsible for much of Delhi's city planning and public building. A lot of land in the capital is officially under DDA control but has been illegally settled. Any land belonging to the authority is called DDA land rather than public land.

- **DLF:** DLF Ltd., originally Delhi Land and Finance, a large property developer and the first to develop Gurgaon. Parts of Gurgaon are named after the developer (DLF I, DLF II, etc.). For this reason, DLF is also used as a synonym for Gurgaon, especially by people who grew up in Delhi.

- **EOK:** East of Kailash, a south Delhi neighborhood.

- **NCR:** The National Capital Region, which includes Delhi and parts of the surrounding states of Haryana, Uttar Pradesh, and Rajasthan.

- **NFC:** New Friends Colony, a south Delhi neighborhood.

- **SDA:** Safdarjung Development Area, a south Delhi neighborhood.

cultural traditions. Nevertheless, there are a few things that are perceived as quintessentially Delhi. The first is a love of food. Delhi is known for its classic snacks, known as *chaat,* as well as popular Mughlai and Punjabi dishes. Food preferences here are seasonal: in summer, people relish cooling yogurt-based varieties of *chaat* along with sweet dishes such as *kulfi* (similar to ice cream), *chuuski* (shaved ice), and many varieties of mangoes. In winter, *parantha* (stuffed flat bread) becomes the favorite dish, and many Delhiites head to a place called Paranthe Waali Gully in Old Delhi's Chandni Chowk neighborhood to feast on miniature deep-fried versions of the popular bread. The quintessential winter dessert is *halwa,* made from carrots or mung beans and served piping hot.

Shopping is another major pastime in Delhi, and with a huge selection of markets and malls, you'll never run out of new shopping spots to discover. The city is also home to a thriving arts scene, with countless galleries, dance performances, book launches, and theater productions.

People in the rest of India view Delhiites as loud, aggressive, pushy, and ostentatious. There's no denying that many Delhiites do like to flaunt their wealth and that life here can be edgier than in other parts of the country. However, if you think about it, most major cities get stereotyped in a similar way. New Yorkers are often described as rude and aloof, but if you go to New York you can meet some of the warmest and politest people on the planet. In the same way, people may tell you that Delhi is a rough city, but once you arrive you'll probably find just the opposite.

the Lotus Temple, Delhi's famous Bahá'í House of Worship

Where to Live

If you are moving to the NCR, you'll probably end up in either Delhi, Gurgaon, or Noida.

DELHI

Although there are no official statistics on the number of expats living in each of India's major cities, most estimate that Delhi has a larger non-Indian population than anywhere in the country. While you can find foreign residents in almost every neighborhood in town, there are a few that are especially popular with the overseas crowd. Delhi is a huge city, but most expats live in the relatively newer parts of town, mostly in south and central Delhi. A few people live in north Delhi—mainly students at Delhi University's North Campus—and in West Delhi, although neither of these areas is popular with expats or have expat communities.

South Delhi

Most of Delhi's expats live in one of the many upscale neighborhoods in South Delhi, where a good number of the city's best restaurants and shops are located. Although the South Delhi administrative district only covers the southeastern quadrant of the city, the area most people refer to as South Delhi spans from Vasant Vihar in the west across to the River Yamuna in the east. Unlike many other Indian cities, Delhi's expat homes are quite spread out. Moreover, most Delhi neighborhoods and colonies are clearly demarcated, cut off from one another by major roads and overpasses, and generally don't merge into one another. South Delhi's most popular neighborhoods for expats are Lajpat Nagar, Greater Kailash Part I, Defence Colony, New Friends Colony, Green Park, Hauz Khas, Safdarjung Enclave, and Vasant Vihar. Of these, Lajpat Nagar has the cheapest housing options, and Vasant Vihar rents are among the highest.

LAJPAT NAGAR

Lajpat Nagar is popular with younger expats as well as Indian students, especially the south part of the neighborhood, Part IV and Amar Colony, where you can get a two-bedroom unfurnished apartment for as little as ₹10,000 per month. Tack on another 10–20 percent if you want to live in the slightly quieter, more upscale parts of Lajpat Nagar (Parts II and III), north of the ring road. Although the area is quite congested, it's conveniently located in the center of commercial South Delhi.

GREATER KAILASH PART I

To the south of Lajpat Nagar sits Greater Kailash Part I (GK 1), another top spot for expats. This leafy neighborhood has a very reliable electricity supply, and while there were water shortage problems in the past, these more or less seem to have been resolved in recent years. It's also home to a couple of upscale markets, named for the blocks they are located in (M-Block Market and N-Block Market). Rents here are considerably more than in Lajpat Nagar, and you'd be hard-pressed to find an unfurnished three-bedroom apartment here for less than ₹30,000 per month. However, in the adjoining Kailash Colony neighborhood, you may be able to find something about 20 percent cheaper.

DEFENCE COLONY

Defence Colony, known locally as "Def Col," is another top spot for expats, especially in recent years. Locals often remark that every other face they see in the neighborhood market is foreign, and the large community of expats here has drawn in even more foreigners, simultaneously driving up prices. Def Col is in the northern part of South Delhi, making it a convenient spot to live if you work in the center but still want to be close to the action in the south. While rents in the area used to be a little bit cheaper than in GK, rents in the two areas are pretty much on par at about ₹30,000 per month for an unfurnished three-bedroom apartment.

NEW FRIENDS COLONY

On the easternmost end of South Delhi, New Friends Colony is quickly becoming a small expat hub. It's a convenient place to live if your office is in Okhla, Noida, or even Nehru Place, and its market is known for good restaurants and bars. It's a little far away from the center of Delhi, but you can get very nice apartments here for much less than in other similar South Delhi localities. An unfurnished four-bedroom could run you as little as ₹25,000 per month.

HAUZ KHAS, GREEN PARK, AND SAFDARJUNG ENCLAVE

If you want to be closer to the western or central regions of South Delhi (especially useful if you plan to live in Delhi and commute to Gurgaon), the neighborhoods to look into are Hauz Khas, Green Park, and Safdarjung Enclave. Hauz Khas proper is a mix of upscale areas and more affordable, albeit shabbier, apartments. A fully furnished one-bedroom here could cost you upward of ₹18,000 per month. The nearby enclave of Hauz Khas Village has become very

© MARGOT BIGG

bohemian Hauz Khas Village

popular with expats in the last couple of years. The area, which actually does resemble a village, has been gentrified considerably recently, first by fashion designers and later by art curators. It's now home to scores of little boutiques and galleries as well as a few cafés and restaurants. In 2007 you could get a two-bedroom unfurnished apartment here for ₹8,000–9,000 per month. These days, a comparable apartment goes for about ₹14,000.

One of the major reasons you might want to live in Hauz Khas is that it's very close to Deer Park, a beautiful green space filled with deer, peacocks, and crumbling Mughal-era monuments. It is a great

Green Park is a popular neighborhood for expats.

© MARGOT BIGG

place to jog or picnic, and there are even drum circles every other Saturday. Other areas that border the park include Green Park and Safdarjung Enclave, each of which has its own charms. Green Park has been popular with expats for many years and has an excellent fruit and vegetable market, plus one of the best-stocked news agents in the south part of the city. The market also has a good selection of eateries and cafés. However, it's one of the more expensive parts of the area, with unfurnished two-bedrooms starting around ₹25,000. Expect to pay nearly double that for something furnished. For a more afford-able park-side alternative, try Safdarjung Enclave. This neighborhood has a good mix of accommodations options, including a few studios, a rarity in Delhi. It also has a few apartment complexes. Expect to pay around ₹10,000 per month for an unfurnished one-bedroom.

VASANT VIHAR

Vasant Vihar has been one of southern Delhi's most popular expat neighbor-hoods for years due to its proximity to both the diplomatic enclave of Chanaky-apuri and to Gurgaon. It also has many very luxurious apartments, making it popular with expats with large housing budgets. A three-bedroom furnished apartment could easily set you back ₹120,000 per month, especially if you go through a relocation agency specializing in working with expatriates.

Central Delhi

If you work in Central or West Delhi, you may prefer to live somewhere north of Lodi Road, the unofficial border between the central and south segments of

Gyarah Murti statue, depicting Gandhi's famous Dandi march, in Central Delhi

the city. Jor Bagh, Golf Links, and Sunder Nagar are excellent living locations in this part of town, although some are more accessible than others. Jangpura and parts of nearby Nizamuddin West are in the central-south buffer zone and offer more variety in housing options than the neighborhoods to the north.

CHANAKYAPURI

Embassy staff often choose to live in the diplomatic neighborhood of Chanaky-apuri, where most of the larger embassies are situated. However, if you come to India as a diplomat, you will most likely be provided housing in your country's embassy compound. Most other housing options in the neighborhood are reserved for employees of the Indian government, although furnished apartments occasionally go on the rental market. Landlords in this area often expect foreigners to move in, and this is reflected in the rental rates. A three-bedroom, 1,600-square-foot furnished apartment in this area could easily cost upward of ₹200,000 per month.

JANGPURA

Jangpura is very popular with expats and has a huge community of journalists (expat and otherwise). It is known for its many trees, and one of the benefits to living here is that it stays a few degrees cooler in summer than many other nearby neighborhoods. The sections of this neighborhood known as Jang-pura Extension tend to be the least expensive, and good deals can be found in the south part of the area near the *phatak* (railroad crossing) that divides Jangpura and Lajpat Nagar. In this part of the neighborhood, you can get a two-bedroom with a large living room for around ₹12,000 per month. On the northern end of the neighborhood, however, especially in the northwest quadrant, you can end up paying upward of ₹40,000 per month for a three-bedroom. The rental prices in the more upscale parts of Jangpura are comparable to those in Nizamuddin West, a fashionable colony to the northeast of Jangpura. While this neighborhood is quiet, calm, and relatively clean, it's also near a train station, so it can get noisy in some places.

SUNDER NAGAR, JOR BAGH, AND GOLF LINKS

Farther north, the neighborhoods of Sunder Nagar, Jor Bagh, and Golf Links are good places to move if you want a large, exclusive space for your family. Sunder Nagar, near the zoo, is full of beautiful majestic houses, and if you rent a ground-floor property, your apartment will probably come with a small garden. You have to have money to move here, though, as rents are rarely under ₹100,000 per month. Jor Bagh rents are similar, and while the area isn't quite as pretty as Sunder Nagar, it's a little closer to the embassies in Chanakyapuri (and actually houses a few diplomatic mission offices of its own). If you really want exclusivity, try to find a place in Golf Links. Rents here are as high as in Jor Bagh and Sunder Nagar. This area is populated mostly by old Delhi families, although you may find some have made sections of their family homes available for rent.

GURGAON

Delhi's major satellite city, Gurgaon is known for office parks, shopping malls, and dust. Until recently, the now very developed city in the state of Haryana was nothing more than stretches of farmland. Then DLF, a property developer, stepped in and began a building trend that has turned Gurgaon into the city it is today. If you work here, you may want to save yourself a potentially long commute and find a house here.

Although expats can be found all over town, you may find that you can get a three-bedroom in a modern housing "society," or tenement, for as low as ₹12,000 per month. Expect to pay a little more if your building comes with a pool and a fitness center. There are many benefits to living in a housing society, namely that your society will probably have an on-site power generator and round-the-clock security. However, these perks may also incur extra charges paid to the society's welfare association, so check with your landlord to see who is expected to pay for what before you sign your lease.

If you want the privacy of a stand-alone apartment on a residential street, you may prefer to move to an area such as Sushant Lok or South City. These areas have a lot of medium-sized stand-alone houses, as well as large houses divided into apartments. A single unfurnished apartment in one of these areas costs around ₹15,000 per month. If you want a whole house, expect to pay around ₹30,000 per month for a four-bedroom with servants quarters and a small driveway.

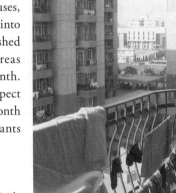

NOIDA

The only real reason to live in Noida is if you work here. The city was originally called the New Okhla In-

Housing societies are common in Gurgaon.

dustrial Development Authority but now only goes by its acronym. Noida is often described as drab and soulless, and while it has good roads, hospitals, schools, and shopping malls, it also faces regular water shortages and electricity outages. Therefore, if you do move here, you are probably better off finding a place in an apartment complex, where infrastructure issues such as water and backup electricity will be taken care of for you.

Until recently, Noida's rents were notoriously cheap, although prices have gone up significantly in the last few years, especially in prime areas such as the central Sector 18, home to the most popular malls, cinemas, and nightlife venues. If you move to Noida, try to be in or near this sector, as this is where you will have the most dining and entertainment options. You can get a two-bedroom furnished apartment within a few miles of Sector 18 for ₹16,000–18,000 per month.

You'll likely want to avoid moving to an area known as Greater Noida, unless you work here, as it is a sparsely developed area and is actually more than 10 miles from Noida. If you do move here, you will need your own car. Furnished apartments in the area start at around ₹22,000 per month for a three-bedroom.

Daily Life

EXPAT SOCIAL SCENE

Delhi has a lot going on for expats, and most expats turn to the Internet to find out what's happening. The largest community resource is Yuni-Net, a simple Yahoo mailing list that expats use to look for roommates, sell furniture and appliances, and post general questions about life in Delhi. The group is moderated, which keeps spam at bay, but unfortunately the moderators also have a reputation for misusing the group for their own financial benefit, charging landlords money to advertise housing on the list. Some members felt this practice was corrupt and decided to start an unmoderated spin-off group called DelhiNet, also on Yahoo Groups, where apartment listings can be posted for free. Yuni-Net is more popular, but if you are looking for a place to live, it's recommended that you join both groups.

Dillinet, a social network supported by the Ning platform, is a good place to meet new people who are genuinely interested in learning more about Delhi and helping others do the same. Dillinet hosts regular coffee, dining, and educational events in Delhi and Gurgaon and is increasingly becoming the primary online site for the NCR's younger international crowd. Delhi Network is one of the NCR's older social clubs and attracts a slightly older crowd. While they do have an online presence, their activities are much more frequently conducted in person. They hold coffee-and-pastry meet-ups every Tuesday morning in South Delhi's Hyatt Hotel, and meetings for members are held the third Tuesday of the month. They also have a small office in the hotel that also has a book exchange. Although the club is open to everyone, you'll notice that most, if not all, people at the weekly meetings are women. Gurgaon has its own club, Gurgaon Connection, which hosts regular events for its members and their families. The British and Australian High Commissions and the U.S. Embassy also have organizations for their citizens.

HEALTH CARE

Delhi is home to a number of world-class medical facilities that offer services at a fraction of what they would cost in the West. One of the best in Delhi is arguably Max Super Specialty Hospital in Saket. They also have a clinic in Panscheel Park. The East West Medical Centre in GK is a small clinic with attentive doctors and a lot of foreign patients. They also have a few hospital rooms where they can treat general issues that don't require a lot of special equipment, such as food-borne illnesses. Hospitals associated with the Apollo

DELHI *CHAAT*

Street food is big in India, and a street-side cart is a great place to pick up an Indian snack dish, collectively known as *chaat*. While *chaat* is famous all over India, it has been refined to an art in Delhi, and entire chains of restaurants specializing in *chaat* have opened up, providing a cleaner way to enjoy street food. Not sure what to try first? Here are a few favorites:

- *aloo tikki:* spiced, potato-based cutlets, drenched in tamarind and coriander chutney and served piping hot

- *chole bhature:* spicy chickpea curry *(chole)* served with deep-fried puffed pancakes *(bhature);* a popular breakfast item that has its roots in Punjab but is sold across Delhi in great quantities.

- *panipuri* (also known as *gol gappa*): thin, hollow balls filled with chopped potatoes and cold, spicy water

- *papri chaat:* deep-fried wafers similar to thick chips covered with sweetened yogurt and tangy chutney

- *raj kachori:* a large, crisp puff with a filling similar to *papri chaat*

and Fortis chains also have good reputations, especially the Escorts Heart Institute and Research Centre. The All India Institute of Medical Sciences (AIIMS) is among the best in the country, although it is a government hospital and some report it to be a bit chaotic.

In Gurgaon the standard hospital for foreigners has been Paras Hospital on MG Road, a small, well-established clinic offering personal care. More recently, Max Hospital opened a branch in Sushant Lok. Artemis hospital is another new player in Gurgaon that's popular with expats. If you are in Noida, your best bet is Max Hospital in Sector 19 or Apollo Hospital in Sector 26.

EDUCATION

Delhi has a number of international schools of varying quality. The top two for English-speaking children are the very expensive American Embassy School and the British School, both of which offer the IB curriculum and admit children from preschool to grade 12. The École Française (French School) and the Deutsch Schule (German School) are also popular with non-Anglophones. Pathways World School near Gurgaon is a good, slightly more affordable, IB option, and they are currently building a day school in Noida. Popular preschools with foreigners include Aadyant and Magic Years, both in Vasant Vihar. The British and American embassies also have preschools for the children of staff.

ENTERTAINMENT

Cinema is huge in India, and you will find no shortage of cinemas in Delhi and the NCR. If you plan to go to an opening-night screening, or pretty much any weekend showing, you should buy tickets ahead of time as they sell out fast. Popular cinemas include those run by the PVR chain and Noida's Wave Cinema, a deluxe multiplex with a Platinum Lounge featuring blankets and reclining chairs.

Delhi also has a music scene, although the popularity of venues ebbs and flows quite regularly. Rock fans will like Cafe Morrison

© RUI MARTIN

taking a break in central Delhi

and Hard Rock Cafe. The Love Hotel, in the Japanese restaurant Ai, holds a lot of electronic music events. Classical Hindustani music concerts are regularly held at central Delhi's various cultural centers and auditoriums, especially the India Habitat Centre, the India International Centre, and Kamani Auditorium. Overseas cultural organizations, such as the French Alliance Française, the German Goethe-Institut, and Spain's Instituto Cervantes also hold cultural events on a regular basis. Epicentre is Gurgaon's main cultural center, and it hosts regular performances and exhibits.

SHOPPING

Biased as it may sound, Delhi is the best place in India to shop. This is the city where you can buy everything from designer handbags to kitschy knickknacks. You can spend hours getting lost in bazaars that appear to have been plucked from the Middle Ages or while away your time at upscale air-conditioned shopping malls.

South Delhi

Not long ago, people who wanted to buy brand-name clothes from European and American chains headed straight to the shops of Ring Road's South Extension. While this is still a good place to buy blue jeans and little black dresses, the newly opened malls in the Saket District Centre are a collection of large shopping malls aimed at Delhi's well-heeled. However, if you don't mind bargaining, crowds, and heat, you can save a lot of money by shopping at Sarojini Nagar Market instead. The market is like a cross between a garage sale and a factory outlet, and it is a great place to buy surplus or slightly defective garments that were manufactured in India for international brands. Bargain hard.

GK I's M-Block is a favorite shopping spot with South Delhiites and is known for its many brand-name clothing and jewelry shops. It also has a few small grocery stores that stock imported goods. N-Block Market, about half a mile away, is a bit more upscale and has a number of fancy home-furnishing stores as well as a few stores dealing in Indian women's wear, of which Cottons and the chain Fab India are the most popular with expats. Defence Colony Market has a lot of shops catering to expats and wealthy Delhiites, as well as a number of Indian and international restaurants. For everything you thought you never needed, head to Lajpat Nagar's Central Market. This is one of the larger South Delhi markets and is one of the best places to buy saris, kitchenware, and shoes at discount prices.

If you are craving food from home, you'll want to visit INA Market, a covered market specializing in international foods and "exotic" fruits and vegetables, from asparagus to mangosteen. Across the street is Dilli Haat, an open-air market featuring handicrafts from across the country. There's a ₹15 admission charge, which keeps the place from getting too hectic. There are also food stalls representing cuisine from around the country, and many a Delhiite visits Dilli Haat strictly for the food. For computers, components, and software, go to Nehru Place. This wholesale IT market is where most South Delhiites pick up computer supplies, often at much lower prices than in major showrooms.

Central Delhi

The best market in Central Delhi is arguably Khan Market, near Central Delhi's Lodi Gardens. The upscale shopping center is very popular with the diplomatic crowd, who come here for imported foods and magazines and to eat at the many fine restaurants. Central Delhi's classic shopping spot is the inner circle of the faux-Georgian Connaught Place (CP), the closest thing Delhi has to a city center. You can pick up everything from fake designer sunglasses to custom-made shoes here, but if you are buying from street vendors, remember to bargain. CP is also home to Palika Bazaar, an underground market specializing in DVDs and electronics. The Tibetan Market on Janpath, near CP's inner circle, is a good place for souvenirs and brassware. Also on Janpath, the State Handicrafts Emporium sells decent-quality crafts from across the country.

Old Delhi

For something a little different, head to Chandni Chowk, one of Delhi's oldest market areas. The markets here are a world apart from what you will find in South and Central Delhi, with fewer brand-name showrooms and many small family-run businesses. Entire streets are devoted to a single product or type of goods. One street might only have stationery stores, another will have only plumbing fixtures, and yet another only bridal jewelry. It's best not to drive here, as parking is nearly impossible and the traffic barely moves.

Gurgaon

If you like malls, Gurgaon may very well be your spiritual home. MG Road is flanked with malls on both sides featuring both Indian and international goods. The largest is currently Ambience Mall, just after the toll both off the NH-8. This mall's claim to fame is that it spans an entire kilometer, although its retail space is hardly running at full capacity. MGF Mega City Mall houses Spencer's Hypermart, an American-sized supermarket with a huge selection of imported goods and unusual vegetables. They also have their own store brands, including an organic range, a delicatessen, a bakery, and a wine shop. They even sell electronics, home appliances, and books. One-stop shopping is a rarity in India, and Spencer's is greatly appreciated by Gurgaon's expat community. Before Spencer's, expats bought their treats from Needs, in DLF Phase III, a smaller and more intimate alternative to the mall-based hypermarket. The Galleria Market is also popular with expats and has a number of small boutiques, restaurants, and coffee shops, making it a popular alternative to the malls.

Noida

Like Gurgaon, shopping life in Noida revolves around malls, including Sector 18's Centrestage Mall and Great India Place. Although chain supermarkets in Noida, such as Reliance Fresh, offer some imported foods, it's usually just easier to go to Delhi for specialty shopping.

Getting Around

When it comes to transportation in Delhi, you have plenty of choices. A few expats do drive in the city, although most prefer getting a driver, as the capital is one of the more nerve-racking Indian cities to drive in. Moreover, a lot of Delhiites drive under the influence of alcohol, and the police are often more than happy to turn a blind eye to such behavior in exchange for a few hundred rupees. Women should avoid driving alone at night, when they become easy targets for crime.

AUTORICKSHAWS

If you don't end up with a car, you can still get around using autorickshaws, shortened simply to "autos" by most Delhiites. Legally, autorickshaws are expected to use their meters (and levy an additional 25 percent "night charge" after 11 P.M.), although most will prefer to negotiate a fixed price instead. If you know a bit of Hindi and are a superstar bargainer, you can usually get most auto drivers to go by the meter, but only do this if you know the way to your destination, as they may test you en route. If the driver goes by the meter without complaint, it's a common practice to round up the final fare. Bicycle rickshaws are useful, environmentally friendly alternatives for shorter distances. Negotiate a fare ahead of time, but be generous: Pulling a cycle rickshaw is very hard work, and the people who do this job are generally very poor migrants from rural India with families to support.

South Delhi's Ring Road

PRIME LIVING LOCATIONS

© MARGOT BIGG

TAXIS

Taxis are common in Delhi, although not so common that you can flag one down on the street. Most neighborhoods have taxi stands where you can negotiate a price ahead of time or hire a metered cab. Alternately, there are plenty of dial-a-cab services in the NCR. You can also rent an air-conditioned private taxi for a day (about ₹800 for eight hours/80 km in Delhi or ₹650 for the same package in Gurgaon). You can also take buses, although the routes are not always clearly marked and bus details are often only written in Hindi. Very few expats use the Delhi buses, although those who do prefer the bright red air-conditioned buses over the more crowded green ones.

THE DELHI METRO

In the years leading up to the 2010 Commonwealth Games, Delhi's streets were torn up and traffic rerouted as the Delhi Metro was built. A combination of underground and aboveground tracks, the Metro links Delhi, Gurgaon, Noida, and the airport, and it provides an inexpensive and quick way to get around. If you want to use the Metro, you can either buy single-use tokens or a rechargeable travel card.

MUMBAI

India's wealthiest and most populous city, Mumbai is the country's financial capital and home to both the National Stock Exchange and the Bombay Stock Exchange as well as the Reserve Bank of India. Bollywood, the Hindi-language film industry, is also based here. It's a busy cosmopolitan city, and its residents, known as Mumbaikars, have a reputation of always being on the move. Although many expats come here to work in the financial services industry, you'll also encounter people working in everything from NGOs to the media.

The area now known as Mumbai was first inhabited by the Koli people, a fishing community who still live in the city today. Over the last century, it has come under the control of various Islamic sultanates as well as Portuguese and British colonialists, and has gone by many names: The Portuguese called the city Bombaim, which the British later anglicized to Bombay. Marathis called it Mumbai after the goddess Mumba Devi. In 1996 the name Mumbai was

© MARGOT BIGG

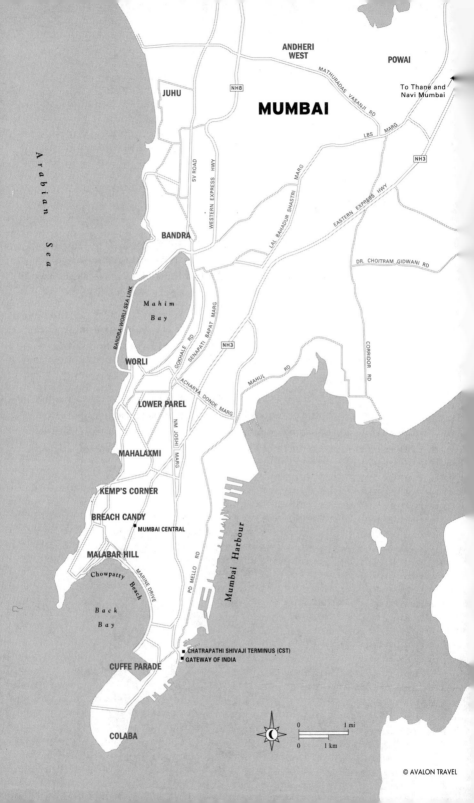

officially restored by the Shiv Sena, the right-wing Marathi nationalist party in power at the time.

Like many of India's cities, Mumbai is known as a place that people either love or hate. It's undeniably one of the most outwardly progressive cities, and women can move around more freely here than in many other cities, wearing tank tops and skirts without much hassle. There's great nightlife, restaurants, and shopping, and you are never far from the sea (although most of the beaches are not very clean). The city is also well connected to the rest of the world by air and is close enough to Goa to make weekend trips a possibility.

Despite its obvious pluses, the city is not always easy to live in. It can feel impersonal because of the large population and the fast-paced lifestyle people lead. It can also get quite hot and muggy, and monsoon floods are quite common. Moreover, the city has a very noticeable dark side, and organized crime, usually referred to as the city's "underbelly," is no secret. There have been a number of terrorist attacks in Mumbai in the recent past, and in some cases, such as in the November 26, 2008, siege of the city, foreigners were among those targeted. Because Mumbai is situated on the peninsular end of an island, traffic is also a major problem, which is only exacerbated by the city's density. The recently built Bandra Worli Sea Link, a bridge that connects Worli to Bandra, has helped reduce traffic somewhat, but commuting in the city is still nightmarish.

The Lay of the Land

Until the 17th century, Mumbai was actually seven different islands, which were joined together over a period of 150 years through land reclamation techniques. The island they now form is called Salsette Island, which the city of Mumbai shares with the city of Thane. Together Mumbai, Thane to the north, and Navi (New) Mumbai on the mainland to the east form Greater Mumbai. Salsette Island is bordered by the Arabian Sea to the west, Thane Creek to the east, and Vasai Creek to the north. Thane Creek still contains a few small islands that were not joined during the city's land reclamation. The best known is Elephanta Island, a popular tourist destination famous for its cave temples. Mumbai sits at Salsette's southernmost peninsular end. The city is also quite hilly—the highest point is Malabar Hill, which is also one of Mumbai's most exclusive neighborhoods.

CLIMATE

People often joke that Mumbai has only two seasons: the hot season and the rainy season. There are actually four seasons, but Mumbai's climate is moderate and the seasons don't always feel distinct. Winters start in late December and run through February and are a little cooler, but temperatures rarely drop below the mid-60s and can still reach the 80s on certain days. Things start to heat up in March, and humidity starts building up until summer, which peaks in May with temperatures upward of 100°F. The often severe monsoon season starts in June, peaks in July, and carries on until September, often bringing serious flooding with it. The postmonsoon season can still be quite hot and muggy, although things start to cool down quite a bit by early November.

LANGUAGE

Mumbai is home to people from all over the country, but the dominant languages here are Marathi, Hindi, and English. Like Hindi, the Marathi language has its origins in Sanskrit and uses the Devanagari script. Buses sometimes only have destinations written in Marathi or Hindi, so if you plan to take this type of public transportation, you have to learn the script or learn

GANESHA CHATURTHI

Every year during the Hindu month of Bhaadra (usually in August or September), the Hindu festival of Ganesha Chaturthi takes place in honor of Lord Ganesha, the elephant-headed god known as the remover of obstacles. Enormous idols of the god are created and housed in temporary structures, where they are visited and prayed to by the devout. After 10 days of rituals and celebrations, the idols are brought in a procession to the nearest body of water and immersed.

Although the festival is observed to varying degrees in different parts of India, the celebrations in Mumbai are the most famous. If you happen to be in town during the festivities, be sure to head to Chowpatty Beach or Juhu Beach and join in the revelry.

Ganesha, the remover of obstacles

© MARGOT BIGG

how to ask for your destination. Most foreigners prefer to pick up a few words
of Hindi rather than Marathi as it is widely understood and more useful for
travel. Marathi is virtually unused outside the state and pockets of Gujarat
and Goa. English is also well known, and you will find that the Mumbaikars
who do know English speak it well.

CULTURE

Like most major cities, Mumbai has cultural elements from around India and
the rest of the world that form the crux of cultural life. The dominant culture,
however, is still Marathi culture, which has its own traditions and festivals.
Mumbai's best-known festival is the Ganesha Chaturthi, an annual homage
to the elephant-headed god. The city also has some quintessential foods, such
as the famous *bhel puri* (puffed rice seasoned with lemon, tomatoes, onion,
and spices) and the Maharashtrian classic *pao bhaji* (tomato- and potato-based
sauce eaten with buttery buns).

Mumbai also has many art galleries and museums scattered around the city,
including the Jehangir Art Gallery and the National Gallery of Modern Art.
Every winter the Kala Ghoda Arts Festival is staged, showcasing performance,
literature, and fine arts from around the country.

Where to Live

Before you read any further, there's something really important you need to
know: Mumbai property is very expensive, and while the global financial crisis
has caused property values to decline recently, you will still pay much more for
a place here than you would anywhere else in India. Also, when looking for
a place in Mumbai, it's highly recommended that you find somewhere close
to your work and your children's school if you are a parent. Getting around
the city takes a very long time, and many Mumbaikars feel that they spend
much of their lives commuting.

Not long ago, landlords in Mumbai required a whopping 11-month security deposit, although the 2008 slowdown in the market has caused landlords
to become much more flexible, and these days you can rent a place with only
two or three months' deposit, although landlords are generally willing to drop
monthly rental prices in return for a larger deposit. Many landlords still prefer
company-sponsored leases, but they can be flexible with this rule when dealing with expats. Others refuse to rent to bachelors out of fear that the apartment will be turned into a party pad, but some single men get around this

rule by pretending to have a wife back home.

SOUTH MUMBAI

For many people, South Mumbai defines the true spirit of the city. It is the older part of town, and many of its historic buildings have that crumbling colonial charm that many people love about Mumbai. It also has some of the city's most exclusive properties, and unless you want to live in a backpacker guest-house, you will need a good salary to live here.

© MARGOT BIGG

Chhatrapati Shivaji Terminus (CST)

Colaba

Colaba is a popular tourist spot, filled with shops, touts, and plenty of hotels. There aren't loads of housing options here, but if you can find a place, expect to pay around ₹100,000 per month for a furnished two-bedroom or ₹130,000 per month for a three-bedroom. If you have a larger budget, you have the option of paying much, much more and living in complete luxury, especially if you opt for a service apartment. One such property is the Taj Wellington Mews, a deluxe service apartment complex with a pool, sports center, and every kind of service you could imagine, from imported cheese shopping to the more standard dry cleaning. You can rent a two-bedroom here for ₹800,000 per month and a three-bedroom for ₹930,000 per month.

Cuffe Parade

To the west of Colaba, Cuffe Parade is another popular spot for expats, but again, rents are quite high. The average three-bedroom is around ₹300,000 per month. This is where some of Mumbai's high-rise apartment buildings are located, but you'll be hard-pressed to find a sea-facing penthouse for rent, as most of the prime properties are occupied by Mumbai's industrialist elite.

Malabar Hill

Farther north is Malabar Hill, often described as the Bel Air of Mumbai. The hill's summit is the highest point in town, and the cost of apartments here reflects the neighborhood's elite status. A small 500-square-foot one-bedroom could easily cost ₹100,000 per month and a two-bedroom around ₹120,000 per month. However, if you rent a place in Malabar Hill, you not only get a top-notch address but also a good water supply and easy access to many green parks as well as to Mumbai's famous Chowpatty Beach.

Breach Candy

Not far from Malabar Hill is Breach Candy, which has been a prime living location for foreigners since the Raj era. Although Breach Candy only used to have large bungalows and bona fide mansions, it now has a wider variety of housing available, including many apartment buildings that come with perks such as backup electricity, elevators, and reserved parking. A two-bedroom apartment in such a building costs around ₹200,000 per month on average. The Breach Candy Club, which dates back to the days of British India, is one of the most exclusive clubs in the city and a popular meeting spot for expats. Breach Candy is well situated, with easy access to Mahalaxmi and South Mumbai, and the Breach Candy Hospital is considered one of the best in the city. The area is also close to Kemp's Corner, which has many good shopping and dining options.

CENTRAL MUMBAI

Central Mumbai is not as popular with expats as places like Bandra and South Mumbai, although there are still a lot of people who prefer to live in this area, especially if their offices are in the busy commercial area of Mahalaxmi. Expats tend to move to one of three areas: Mahalaxmi, Lower Parel, and Worli.

Worli

Worli is commercial and congested, and there aren't a whole lot of housing options compared to other parts of the city. Moreover, the Bandra Worli Sea Link makes it easier for expats working in the center of the city to live in Bandra and get

Bandra-Worli Sea Link

to work relatively quickly. However, if you do end up moving to this part of town, you'll probably end up looking at places in Mahalaxmi, Lower Parel, and Worli. Worli is economically mixed, with pockets that are bordering on slums and other areas, especially along the coast, that are luxurious and exclusive. You can get a furnished three-bedroom apartment overlooking the sea for around ₹400,000 per month, but you can also get a modest three-bedroom a ways inland for around ₹140,000 per month.

Lower Parel

Lower Parel borders Worli, and the area has witnessed quite a few modern high-rises appear in the past few years. Although there are many offices in the area, not that many expats opt to live here as it's quite a busy commercial area. An unfurnished three-bedroom in a new building with a pool costs upward of ₹120,000 per month.

Mahalaxmi

South of both Lower Parel and Worli, Mahalaxmi is another commercial area with a beautiful green racetrack and a lot of high-rise office buildings. There are some older apartments here that run around ₹75,000 per month for an unfurnished two-bedroom, ₹100,000 per month for an unfurnished three-bedroom.

NORTH MUMBAI

While South Mumbai used to be considered the heart of all the action, these days North Mumbai's many suburbs are becoming increasingly popular spots to live, especially for expats, who are drawn in by the slightly more affordable housing costs, more modern amenities, and slightly cleaner beaches.

Bandra

North Mumbai has a large international community, especially in Bandra, a trendy, leafy neighborhood that's very popular with expats of all ages. Bandra has great clubs, restaurants, and boutiques. It's also close to the Bandra-Kurla Complex (BKC), a planned development where many financial services companies and diamond traders are located. The Dhirubhai Ambani International School and the American School are also located in the BKC, and the U.S. Consulate plans to relocate to the complex.

Bandra's apartments tend to be in apartment buildings rather than in divided houses. Accommodations here are certainly not cheap, and Bandra is one of the more sought-after and consequently expensive places to live in

luxury apartment blocks in Bandra

North Mumbai. However, it's still more affordable than some of the other expat neighborhoods farther south, and its proximity to the Bandra Worli Sea Link means it is possible to live here and still drive to your office in South or Central Mumbai without spending your life in a car. You won't likely find an unfurnished two-bedroom apartment in Bandra for less than ₹60,000 per month, and you're likely to pay more like ₹80,000–90,000 for a place. A furnished three-bedroom in a decent building will run you around ₹110,000 per month on average.

Andheri West

Andheri West is a slightly more northern alternative to Bandra that is also popular with foreigners. Rents are a bit cheaper, and while it's farther from the heart of Mumbai, it's still very crowded. If you search carefully, you can get a decent unfurnished two-bedroom here for as little as ₹50,000 per month, and a three-bedroom for as little as ₹75,000.

Juhu

Between Bandra and Andheri sits suburban Juhu, popular not only with expats but also with Bollywood stars. Although Juhu is somewhat far north, it's convenient for frequent travelers who need to be near the airport. It also has a large and popular beach. You can get a furnished three-bedroom here for ₹100,000 per month, but if you want something with an ocean view you can expect to pay at least twice as much. If you have a lot of children, you might be pleased that there are also quite a lot of larger properties here, but they

PRIME LIVING LOCATIONS

come at a high price. A four-bedroom can easily cost upward of ₹220,000 per month, sea view not included.

Powai

The northeastern suburb of Powai has also witnessed an influx in expat residents in the last few years. Powai sits on the side of an artificial lake of the same name and offers plenty of high-rise apartment options, the most popular of which are located in the township of Hiranandani Gardens. The neighborhood is quite far from the center of Mumbai, so most people who move here generally do so to be near their offices. Powai is home to oil companies such as BP as well as plenty of call centers and business process outsourcing (BPO) operations. Rent is much lower than in the rest of Mumbai, with unfurnished two-bedrooms starting at about ₹60,000 per month. A furnished four-bedroom in Hiranandani Gardens currently goes for about ₹150,000 per month.

Daily Life

EXPAT SOCIAL SCENE

Mumbai has always drawn people from all over the world, and the expat social scene in the city is well established. For most expats new to Mumbai, the first step to getting involved with the expat community is by joining Bombay Expats, a Yahoo group used primarily for networking and to find housing. British expats and representatives of British companies are advised to join the British Business Group (BBG), although bear in mind that the events held by this group are focused more on business and networking than on settling in. Those in the nonprofit and social entrepreneurship sectors might want to join the Bombay HUB, a nonprofit shared workspace in Bandra.

When it comes to support groups, expatriate women have a clear advantage over men, as a few of the more active expat clubs in Mumbai are specifically for women—no doubt a remnant from the days when women usually only moved abroad as "trailing spouses." One such group is Mumbai Connexions, an expatriate women's organization that hosts coffee meetings, bridge nights, and a book club. The American Women's Club (AWC) hosts similar events, and despite its name it is open to all foreign passport holders (although only U.S. and Canadian citizens and their spouses can take over the organization's presidency). Women of all nationalities can join Indus International, a cultural association set up to provide a link between Indian and primarily American expatriate women.

© MARGOT BIGG

In many ways, Mumbai has a European feel.

Families often meet each other through the schools their children attend. On Sunday the American School of Bombay hosts a day of activities for expats, which includes Frisbee games and swimming. Expatriate mothers of babies and toddlers can also join Hopping Bunnies, a playgroup for young children and a good place to meet other expat families.

HEALTH CARE

Mumbai has plenty of high-quality hospitals to choose from, although there are a few that are reputed to be reliable and are thus especially popular with expats. Your living location will naturally determine your hospital of choice. Lilavati Hospital in Bandra is many people's first choice, and it is known across the country for its high standard of care. Also in Bandra, the Holy Family Hospital and Medical Research Centre is popular and convenient. Mumbaikars will tell you that the best hospital in Powai is Fortis Hospital in Hiranandani. If you live in South Mumbai, you may prefer to go to Breach Candy Hospital, which is clean and modern despite being over half a century old. Tata Memorial Hospital in Lower Parel is a good place to go if you live or work in the center of town.

EDUCATION

There are plenty of very good schools in Mumbai, but because of the commuting difficulties in the city, you may want to base your choice of school on its proximity to your house. If you are in Bandra, your first choice may

BOLLYWOOD

The Hindi film industry, known as Bollywood, is the largest in the world, and the heart of the industry is in Mumbai. Hindi films are flashy, melodramatic, and entertaining, and once you've seen a few, you will start to notice certain themes and influences that appear consistently. Most Bollywood movies have a hero and a heroine, and more often than not some sort of love story is woven into the plot. Many films are modeled after Indian myths and made accessible with a contemporary twist. Others appear to have been directly and unabashedly copied from recent Hollywood films or even other Bollywood films from earlier decades. Hindi movies tend to be quite a bit longer than Hollywood films and usually have an intermission.

What's most striking in most Bollywood flicks is that they usually contain a number of song and dance sequences, which are sometimes used to tell a story and advance the plot and other times seem to have been pasted into the film just to give it a bit of flair. Many of these songs, which are performed by actors and then dubbed by "playback singers," go on to become major commercial hits, often becoming more popular than the films from which they originated. This genre, known as *filmi*, often incorporates elements from other genres ranging from Qawwali to hip-hop, but it usually has some sort of Indian feel, in the vocal arrangement if nothing else. The most famous producer of *filmi* music is A. R. Rahman, the composer behind the award-winning soundtrack for *Slumdog Millionaire*.

Although Bollywood puts out more films than most people can keep track of, only a handful of actors consistently play the lead roles. The best-known actor is undoubtedly Amitabh Bachchan, known affectionately as "Big B," who made a name for himself in the 1970s and continues to light

be the American School of Bombay in the BKC, which admits students from preschool through grade 12 and offers an IB curriculum. However, fees are very high (typical of most American schools in the region), so you may not find it feasible to send your child here if your company is not footing the bill. The preschool–12 Dhirubhai Ambani International School, also in the BKC, admits many expats, and while they do offer IB preparation in high school, they follow a more Indian curriculum in lower years.

The École Mondiale World School in Juhu offers IB curriculum for all age groups, although they charge expatriates considerably higher tuition fees than Indians, which some feel is both off-putting and detracts from the international feel of the school. Even farther north, in Goregaon East, the Oberoi International School also offers IB education at the high school level, and it is convenient for people living in far-north areas such as Powai.

up the silver screen to this day. His biggest contender for the title of Bollywood's heartthrob is Shahrukh Khan, who is often likened to Big B in the media. Other big names include Salman Khan, Saif Ali Khan, Kareena Kapoor, Rani Mukerji, and Hrithik Roshan. Then there's Aishwarya Rai, a former Miss World (who is also the daughter-in-law of Big B), and Priyanka Chopra, another former Miss World and a more recent entry to the world of Bollywood.

Foreigners are often recruited to work as extras in Hindi films, and it's not uncommon to be approached in areas frequented by tourists and offered a day's work on a set. In most cases, your job will involve standing for hours on a set designed to look like a European city and simply looking foreign, although if you have rhythm, you may be asked to do a little backup dancing too. The pay is usually no more than ₹500–1,500 per day, but it can be a fun way to get an inside glimpse into Bollywood.

© MARGOT BIGG

Bollywood star Shahrukh Khan endorses Pepsi and a host of other products and services.

ENTERTAINMENT

The epicenter of India's entertainment industry, Mumbai has plenty of entertainment options to choose from. Films are naturally popular here, and all Mumbaikar expats should venture out to see a Bollywood film at least once during their stay in India. The most famous cinema in Mumbai is the art deco Metro Cinema, a historic South Mumbai movie hall that, thanks to a recent facelift, now blends old-fashioned charm with a modern cinematic experience. Theater and performance fans will want to get on the mailing list of the National Centre for Performing Arts (NCFPA), which holds regular cultural events in its five theaters and auditoriums.

For nightlife, you can either check out the bars in trendy areas such as Colaba and Bandra or head straight to where the music is. If you want to go clubbing, your best options are Zenzi Mills, Blue Frog, and Hard Rock Cafe. Both Zenzi and Blue Frog host DJs and live electronic acts regularly, and they are among the top nightlife spots for both expats and dance-loving locals. Hard Rock Cafe brings in acts from around India and abroad, including big-name artists such as Wyclef Jean. All three are located in central Mumbai.

Although Mumbai is a big city, there's still room for plenty of outdoor activities. The beaches in the city aren't very clean, and sunbathing on them is not appropriate, but sunset beach strolls are a popular evening activity. If you like sailing, you might want to join the Colaba Yacht Club or Aquasail; the latter offers sailing lessons. Children will enjoy the Esselworld amusement park and the adjoining Water Kingdom water park in North Mumbai. Esselworld also has an ice-skating rink, which can feel wonderful on sweltering summer days.

SHOPPING

Mumbai has plenty of areas to shop, but street markets are quickly being replaced with upscale malls. Some of the areas in South Mumbai that are popular with tourists are equally fun for expats, such as Crawford Market, which sells everything from spices to shoes. Then there's Colaba Causeway, where roadside stalls compete with brand-name showrooms for shoppers' attention. There are an unusually large number of vendors selling fake antique barometers and telescopes here, as well as stalls selling standard-issue tapestries and T-shirts depicting Indian deities. For cheap clothes, head to the strip of MG Road known as "Fashion Street." If you want to be guaranteed quality, or prefer air-conditioned bargain-free shopping, you may prefer restricting your shopping to the malls. Atria Millennium mall in Worli is one of the more popular in the city, and it has branches of many popular clothing chains from the West.

Kemp's Corner near Breach Candy has a lot of cute designer boutiques and is also home to Crossword Bookstore, arguably Mumbai's best bookseller. There's even a coffee shop upstairs where you can thumb through books before deciding whether or not to purchase them. Bandra also has a lot of trendy clothing shops, the majority of which seem to be targeting teenagers and young women.

Places with large expat communities, such as Bandra and Breach Candy, have plenty of shops that stock imported foodstuffs. If you're in Bandra, you'll find the largest concentration of these on the roads near Pali Market, an open-air vegetable market where the vendors sell "English" vegetables such as broccoli. Crawford Market also has a very good selection of imported goods, although you may find it too far and too hectic to visit regularly. Nature's

Basket, a grocery store specializing in organic and gourmet foods, also stocks a wide variety of foreign foods. They have chains across the city, from Cuffe Parade clear up to Powai.

Getting Around

Mumbai is known for its bad traffic, but driving is still the most comfortable option for getting around. If you don't want to buy a car, you can still get around by taxi quite easily—black cabs can be hailed on the street in most parts of the city, and they automatically use the meter. Most of these taxis have old meters set to old fares, so don't get upset when your driver pulls out a conversion chart and tells you the real fare; he's not trying to scam you. These taxis are generally old and rustic and are not equipped with air-conditioning. If you want to keep cool, you are better off paying a bit more and hiring a dial-a-cab taxi. If you live in North Mumbai, you can also take metered autorickshaws locally, but they are not allowed to go into the central or south parts of town.

COMMUTER TRAINS
Mumbai makes up for its traffic problems with the Mumbai Suburban Railway, an excellent network of commuter trains that comprises three lines: the

© MARGOT BIGG

Mumbai's ubiquitous black cabs

Western Line, the Central Line, and the Harbor Line. The network connects Mumbai with the neighboring cities of Bandra and Navi Mumbai, and if you live far away from your office, the train will probably get you there much more quickly than a car could. At the same time, the trains can get very crowded during rush hour, especially if you are headed south in the morning or north in the evening. Mumbai's often extreme heat and humidity don't make things any easier. Some people prefer to wear casuals in the train and then change into business attire when they arrive at the office.

There are a few things to bear in mind if you choose this mode of transportation. First, pay attention to the train that you are getting on. Those marked with an "F" are fast trains and only call at specific stations. Also, if you stand by the door, hold on very tightly to avoid getting pushed off or falling off the train. Every year thousands of Mumbaikars die in train-related accidents, and falling out of an overcrowded train is a common way to go. As overcrowding is a big issue, women are at high risk of getting anonymously groped. Most trains have a women's car or two, where only women and their accompanying children are allowed to board. However, if you are new to a station and the crowd is thick, you might have a hard time finding this car.

BENGALURU

Often touted as the Silicon Valley of India, Bengaluru (also spelled Benga-looru) is home to Infosys and Wipro, the second- and third-largest IT companies in the country. Countless American IT and telecom companies also have operations here, which means there is a huge expat population. It's also India's third-most populous city.

Like many Indian cities, Bengaluru recently had a name change, from Bangalore, an English take on the city's Kannada name, Bengaluru. However, the anglicized moniker is still used by most people. Popular legend has it that the name originated when a tired and hungry king came across a woman who served him boiled beans, prompting him to name the town Bendakaaluru, or City of Boiled Beans. However, historians believe that the city's name actually comes from Bengavalu, the name of a hamlet where security guards lived in the 5th century.

The land on which modern-day Bengaluru sits is believed to have been inhabited since at least the 11th century, although it wasn't until the 16th

© MARGOT BIGG

century that a city fort was built by Kempe Gowda, a vassal under the Vijayanagara Empire. The city later passed into the hands of the Mughals and subsequently the Mysore Empire before finally falling into the hands of the British at the turn of the 19th century. The British used part of the city as a military station, returning the rest to the ruler of Mysore, who used Bengaluru as his kingdom's capital during part of the 19th century. After independence, people from all over what is now Karnataka moved to the city in search of work in the then-burgeoning manufacturing sector. In the 1980s and 1990s, high-tech firms and multinational corporations began setting up operations in the city, starting with Texas Instruments in the mid-1980s, and laying the foundation for making Bengaluru the Indian software hub it is today.

Bengaluru has a lot going for it. Along with its huge IT industry, it's also home to many of India's renowned scientific organizations, not to mention the Indian Institute of Science. Bengaluru is also the capital of the state of Karnataka and is the fastest-growing metropolis in India. Moreover, with its laid-back atmosphere and relatively mild climate (by Indian standards), Bengaluru is among India's more comfortable cities for expats, and was ranked by Mercer, an international HR consultant, as the best Indian city for expats. The city is attractive to people of different age groups and lifestyles—the younger single crowd will appreciate the city's vibrant nightlife and bar scene, and families with small children will love the many parks and play areas dotting the city.

The Lay of the Land

Bengaluru sits in the center of a plateau, and most of the city is flat, although it has an elevation of around 3,000 feet. The city is encircled by the large Outer Ring Road and is crossed by National Highway (NH) 4, which links the city to Chennai to the east and Mumbai and Pune to the west. The closest Bengaluru has to a downtown is MG Road and its environs, and this is where many of the best grocery stores are situated. The strip of the NH 7 known as Hosur Road is home to many of the city's IT offices, and it links south Bengaluru to the enormous Electronics City IT Park. The recently built Elevated Tollway runs above Hosur Road, linking Bengaluru to Electronics City. This has helped to drastically reduce traffic and commute times between the IT park and the city center.

Bengaluru is a very green city, and it seems that every neighborhood has a lush park or at least a patch of grass and some trees. Because of its abundance of greenery, Bengaluru is known as India's "Garden City." The largest and best-known parks within the city limits include Lal Bagh Botanical Garden and Cubbon Park, both of which provide much-needed oxygen to the traffic-filled city. The 18th-century Lal Bagh features a large greenhouse modeled on London's Crystal Palace, a rock garden, fountains, an aquarium, a lake, and an impressive variety of plants and flowers. Cubbon Park, a short walk from MG Road, is perhaps the greenest space in the city. This sprawling park is popular with families and joggers and has a good network of bamboo-lined trails. Bengaluru also has a number of artificial lakes and tanks. One of the largest is Halasuru Lake (commonly known as Ulsoor Lake), which, though beautiful, is also very polluted. In other words, while it's a good place to stroll or go jogging, swimming is not advised.

Unlike many other cities, Bengaluru streets have names, although the system is not as straightforward as one might hope. Many neighborhoods are divided into numbered blocks (1 Block, 2 Block, etc.). Others are divided into "stages" or "phases," which are usually numbered by the order in which they were developed. The main roads will then have names (or be numbered as main roads, like "1st Main Road"), and the smaller intersecting roads will simply be referred to as numbered crossroads. For example, there's a pub in the Koramangala neighborhood called Legends of Rock. Its address is 903, 3rd Cross Road, 6th Block, 80 Feet Road, Koramengala. As there are 2nd Main Roads, 3rd Cross Roads, and 6th Blocks in many neighborhoods in the city, you'd need the entire address to figure out where to go. It sounds confusing at first, but you'll get used to it more quickly than you'd expect, and you may

the Vidhana Soudha, home of Karnataka's legislative assembly, in Bengaluru

actually find that this mathematical approach to road naming is actually more logical and specific than what you find in your home country.

CLIMATE

Because of its elevation, Bengaluru experiences a milder climate than many other Indian cities. Winter temperatures here rarely drop below the mid-50s, and summers usually don't get hotter than the low 100s. Winters are relatively dry and run December–February. Even the March–May spring–summer season is fairly dry, although occasional premonsoon showers do occur when temperatures get too high. Bengaluru remains relatively humid during much of the rest of the year, partly due to the fact that the city is touched by both the northeast winter monsoon and the southwest summer monsoon, which can drop rainfall on the city May–November.

LANGUAGE

The mother tongue of most people in Karnataka is the Dravidian language Kannada, although Hindi and, to a lesser extent, English are also widely spoken in Bengaluru. As is the case with all Indian cities, the educated classes will speak English at the level of native speakers. However, with rickshaw drivers and domestic help, some Kannada or Hindi is useful. Most signs in Bengaluru are posted in English and Kannada, although sometimes bus information is only in Kannada.

CULTURE

Bengaluru is known for being laid-back, progressive, and modern, with a good bar and nightlife scene. There's a certain sense of youthfulness to the city, bringing with it an atmosphere of innovation and creativity. However, unlike many other big international cities, Bengaluru doesn't feel rushed and aggressive. There's also a large pub culture, and although the lifestyle can be quite busy and work-oriented, many people find the time to meet with friends for a relaxing drink at the end of the day.

As the capital of Karnataka, Bengaluru is a hub for much of the state's cultural life and traditions. Karnataka is known for its performance and fine arts, especially dance. The best-known is Dollu Kunitha, a drumming and dance group performance dedicated to Lord Shiva. Another instrumental dance, where performers dance and play, is known as Kamsale, after the instrument that accompanies it. Other popular dances include Veeragase, a ritualistic dance performed by troupes during religious festivals. About 20 miles outside of Bengaluru is Nrityagram, a planned community devoted entirely to dance.

INFORMATION TECHNOLOGY IN INDIA

India is known worldwide for its strong IT sector, and most multinational software developers and hardware manufacturers have a presence in the country. Although Bengaluru is the heart of India's IT industry, many other cities have strong representation in the sector, especially Hyderabad, Pune, Chennai, Gurgaon, and even Kolkata.

The largest Indian players are Wipro and Infosys. Wipro started out as a vegetable oil manufacturer around the time of independence, expanding into the IT sector in the late 1970s. Infosys started in 1981 with an initial investment of US$250. Both Wipro and Infosys have gone from relatively humble beginnings to become multibillion-dollar companies with offices across India and abroad. Wipro and Infosys, along with hundreds of other international and Indian companies, have helped transform India into the technological hub it is today.

The city is home to Karnataka Chitrakala Parishath, an arts and culture organization aimed at preserving and promoting fine arts throughout the country. The organization has a number of galleries, as well as a publications arm and a fine arts college, and is affiliated with the Indian National Trust for Art and Cultural Heritage (INTACH). There are also plenty of smaller, independent art galleries in Bengaluru as well as a local branch of the National Gallery of Modern Art (NGMA). Many international cultural organizations also have a presence in Bengaluru, including the French Alliance Française, the German Goethe-Institut, and the British Council.

Where to Live

Bengaluru's traffic is notoriously bad, and it's a good idea to move relatively close to your office, if possible, especially if you have to commute during rush hour. Bengaluru landlords often ask for 10 months' security in advance—note that this is considered your deposit and is not the same as paying your rent up front. On the plus side, rents here are relatively lower than they are in places like Delhi and Mumbai, and decent, newer places are quite easy to find.

SOUTH BENGALURU

South Bengaluru is a popular place for the IT crowd, mostly because of its proximity to major IT Parks, most notably Electronics City. Although expats can be found in most south Bengaluru neighborhoods, the largest concentrations are in BTM Layout, JP Nagar, Koramangala, and Madiwala.

BTM Layout

BTM Layout, an abbreviation of Byrasandra, Tavarekere, and Madiwala Layout, is popular with the young and single crowd, and many people in this area live with housemates or in paying-guest (PG) accommodations. BTM Layout is somewhat busy and urban, so if you are looking for something quiet, this may not be the place for you. However, if you like the urban vibe and want to be near lots of restaurants, the area is ideal.

An unfurnished one-bedroom in BTM Layout can cost as little as ₹6,000 per month, although most of the newer developments and apartment complexes won't have one-bedrooms available. A two-bedroom usually costs in the region of ₹12,000–15,000 per month. Three-bedroom apartments average about ₹18,000 per month but can cost considerably more in a luxury complex with extra amenities such as a gym. PG accommodations (including three meals per day) cost around ₹3,000 per month for a bed in a shared room or around ₹5,000 per month for a single room.

JP Nagar

Adjacent to BTM Layout, JP Nagar has a good mix of accommodations, from apartments in divided bungalows to apartments in huge complexes. Like BTM Layout, there are a lot of young IT professionals in this area, although there are also plenty of families, and you can find calm, quiet accommodations in the area. Many of the larger apartment buildings, especially in the neighborhood's 7th Phase, also have pools, usually outdoors, but it's warm enough to swim outside most of the year. A three-bedroom in such a property will start at around ₹18,000 per month. A house may cost even less, starting at around ₹16,000 per month, although it won't likely come equipped with amenities such as backup electricity and guards that you'll get in an apartment building. A two bedroom

a statue honoring Bengaluru's biotech industry

house or a two-bedroom in a modest apartment building will cost around ₹11,000 per month.

Koramangala

Farther east, the Koramangala neighborhood remains one of the most popular places for Bengaluru's expats. It is a charming, leafy place with lots of good restaurants, shopping, and nightlife. It is also convenient to Electronics City, and a lot of major IT and engineering companies, including Wipro, Infosys, and Siemens, have offices here. However, because of its popularity as both a commercial hub and residential area, Koramangala often suffers from heavy traffic, especially during rush hour.

Koramangala has a wide range of housing options available, including houses divided into apartments and newer, more luxurious apartment buildings. Apartments in houses are usually cheaper, with two-bedrooms ranging ₹10,000–14,000 per month and three-bedrooms starting around ₹15,000 per month. An apartment in a luxury building will cost a minimum of ₹20,000 per month for a two-bedroom and about ₹25,000 for a three-bedroom. In some buildings, such as the luxurious Prestige Acropolis near Forum Mall, a three-bedroom will cost at least ₹45,000 per month. For this price, you can expect a reliable electricity supply, pool and gym access, and reserved parking. Koramangala also has a large number of service apartments, most of which can be rented on a nightly basis and include facilities such as Wi-Fi access and en suite kitchenettes, although many of these feel more like large hotel rooms than actual homes.

NORTH BENGALURU

Many of Bengaluru's younger expats prefer to live in the northern part of the city, especially those who have come to study or volunteer or who are earning "local" salaries. Many of these expats are found in the adjoining neighborhoods of Frazer Town and Benson Town. These areas are popular because they are at the same time close to the city center and relatively affordable.

Frazer Town

Frazer Town (officially Pulakeshi Nagar, but few people call it that) is a mixed residential and commercial area built by the British. Although the neighborhood is considered more affordable than many other areas in Bengaluru, it's still a charming place and combines tree-lined avenues and Raj-era architecture with the vibrancy of an Indian commercial district. Two-bedrooms in Frazer

Town usually cost ₹14,000–18,000 per month. A three-bedroom apartment starts at around ₹18,000 per month.

Benson Town

To the west of Frazer Town, Benson Town was also developed by the British and also has many old bungalows and leafy streets. It's a bit quieter and more residential than Frazer Town but still has a metropolitan feel to it. Historically, many Anglo Indians lived in the area, although now Benson Town has a large Muslim population that lives near Masjid-e-Khadra, one of Bengaluru's best-known mosques. There's also a large military population in the area. With a sizeable expat population added to the mix, Benson Town is one of Bengaluru's more diverse areas.

Rents in Benson Town are slightly higher than in Frazer Town but are still reasonable considering the neighborhood's proximity to the city center. An unfurnished two-bedroom starts at around ₹16,000 per month, and you should be able to get a furnished three-bedroom for around ₹25,000 per month.

EAST BENGALURU
Indira Nagar

One of Bengaluru's most popular neighborhoods for the expat crowd, Indira Nagar is calm, green, and well-maintained. There are a few pubs, restaurants, and cafés, as well as a few small shops, especially on the main thoroughfare between 80-Feet Road and 100-Feet Road. The Defence Colony area is the

© MARGOT BIGG

Bengaluru's leafy Indira Nagar

quietest and prettiest part of Indira Nagar, with lots of bungalows, trees, and small parks.

It is relatively easy to get to the big IT parks from Indira Nagar, and there are even a few software firms with offices in or very close to the neighborhood. Getting to the city center can be more tricky during peak traffic times (otherwise its a breeze), but many people working in the center still opt to live here for its relaxing suburban environment. Budget at least ₹20,000 per month for a two-bedroom place in Indira Nagar, but expect to pay over ₹25,000 per month if you want something in a newer building with a parking space. Three-bedrooms start at around ₹28,000 per month but can run much higher.

Whitefield

On the eastern outskirts of Bengaluru, Whitefield is an upscale planned community filled with large luxurious homes that are kept separate from the area's surrounding slums only by imposing steel gates. In the 1990s, developers began building houses and offices, including the massive International Tech Park Bangalore (ITPB). Later, luxury apartment buildings began to spring up, providing a greater selection of housing in the area. Once occupied predominantly by members of Bengaluru's Anglo-Indian community, it is now dominated by high-level tech-industry execs.

It makes sense to live in Whitefield if you work at the ITPB or if you want to live a life of luxury comfortably outside Bengaluru's city center. A three-bedroom house in a gated community can sometimes cost as little as ₹50,000 per month, although you may find it more convenient to live in an apartment building, where guard services and electricity backup are included. Two-bedroom unfurnished units in Whitefield start at around ₹15,000 per month and three-bedrooms at ₹20,000–22,000, although you can easily pay upward of ₹100,000 per month if you want something ultraluxurious.

Daily Life

EXPAT SOCIAL SCENE

Bengaluru has a large expat population, many of whom connect with each other either online or via clubs. Make sure to subscribe to the Bangalore Expats Yahoo group before you head to the city, as this is a good place to find out about events and housing, as well as just meeting other expats. The Ives Club is another popular online group, with a younger membership base and a

COFFEE SHOPS

Although Southern India has its own concoction of sugar, coffee, chicory, and milk known as "filter coffee," tea has been the hot drink of choice in most of the country since it was first introduced. There have always been old-fashioned coffeehouses in major cities, but it has only been 15 years or so that coffee-shop chains have began to spring up across the country. The first was Café Coffee Day (CCD), whose flagship outlet opened in Bengaluru in 1996. Other companies followed suit, including Barista, which started in India but is now owned by Italian coffee giant Lavazza. Britain's Costa Coffee and the U.S. chain Coffee Bean and Tea Leaf later started operations in India.

© MARGOT BIGG

Café Coffee Day

larger focus on partying and nightlife. If you are looking for shared housing, it's also a good place to post your requirements.

The Bangalore Expatriate Club (BEC) is one of the more active clubs for Bengaluru's international crowd and hosts regular events. Unlike many of India's expatriate clubs, which are aimed at nonworking spouses, the BEC club attracts large numbers of professionals, and most of their events are held outside working hours.

The Overseas Women's Club of Bangalore is another popular organization, and despite its name, it is open to both men and women as long as they are overseas passport holders or NRIs new to Bengaluru who have been out of the country for at least a decade. The club publishes a monthly newsletter and offers a slew of cultural activities, weekly coffee mornings, clubs centered around different hobbies, children's play groups, and support for expectant mothers. They also support various charities and can help you find volunteer work.

HEALTH CARE

Bengaluru has many good hospitals and clinics to choose from, and where you go will probably depend on what part of town you end up living in. Columbia Asia Hospital has a good reputation among expats, although its location north of the center in the Hebbal neighborhood makes it inconvenient for people

PRIME LIVING LOCATIONS

living in the city's southern localities. If you live farther south, you may find Fortis Hospital (formerly named Wockhardt Hospital) easier to get to, as it is just south of BTM Layout. The more central Mallya Hospital near Cubbon Park is accessible if you are working or living in the city center. Another popular choice is Manipal Hospital, southeast of Indira Nagar on Airport Road. This hospital is also reasonably easy to get to from Whitefield.

EDUCATION
There is no shortage of good international schools in Bengaluru, although many of them are some distance from the city center. The preschool–12 Indus International School offers the IB program at both the primary and secondary levels, although it is a bit of a drive from the center. The International School Bangalore offers preschool–12 education, including the IB curriculum in 11th and 12th grade, and also has a boarding school, although it's quite far out of the city unless you live in Whitefield. In northern Bengaluru, just off NH 7, the preschool–12 Canadian International School is popular with the North American crowd and offers an IB high school curriculum. The Bangalore International School, also north of the center, admits students from age 2.5 through high school and also offers the high school IB program. Many expat parents also look at Inventure Academy, southeast of the city, when choosing a school for their children. While not an international school, Bishop Cotton Boys School is considered the crème de la crème of Bengaluru's schools, although securing admission is quite difficult.

ENTERTAINMENT
Bengaluru is very much a drinking town, but oddly, by law the bars here are forced to close at midnight. Most people either start early or throw after-parties at private residences. For electronic dance music, head to Pebble near the Palace Grounds, an indoor-outdoor club and restaurant that tries to recreate a beach-like ambiance. Other popular nightspots include Amnesia, next to the pool at the Chancery Pavilion hotel, and Fuga, better known for the fact that they serve absinthe than for the quality of the music. Rock fans may prefer Pecos Pub or the more generic Hard Rock Cafe.

Bengaluru is at the heart of the Kannada-language film industry, although Hindi and English-language films are shown. Most cinemas are run by chains such as Inox and Fame. PVR also has a large cinema in Koramangala's Forum Mall. Theater performances in the three languages also abound; most are staged at the Ranga Shankara Auditorium in JP Nagar.

© MARGOT BIGG

Kannada-language film posters

SHOPPING

If you like shopping, Bengaluru will leave you satisfied with its numerous malls, markets, and shopping districts. Mall rats will like the Forum Value Mall in Whitefield and the company's more established mall, The Forum, in Koramangala. For high-end brands (think Louis Vuitton and Rolex), head to The Collection at UB City, which prides itself on being India's first luxury retail space. Your best bet for everything else is Commercial Street, where you can buy everything from saris to sandals. The shops here stay open fairly late, and it's a popular place for evening shopping. Just remember to bargain hard—Commercial Street is also popular among foreign tourists, so getting a "local price" here can prove all the more challenging.

Bengaluru has many good options for gourmet and imported foods. Food-world Gourmet on MG Road sells almost exclusively gourmet foods and has an excellent selection of domestic and imported wines and cheeses. A few shops down, Spencer's also sells a lot of imported, gourmet, and specialty food along-side Indian staples. In neighborhoods with substantial expat populations, even small general stores sell cereals and canned goods from abroad. Namdhari's Fresh is one of the best places to get fresh organic vegetables and fruit juices, and they also stock a very good selection of imported snacks and sweets. They have outlets in both Koramangala and Indira Nagar. Supermarkets under the Nilgiri's brand also keep a selection of imported goods on hand, and they have branches around the city.

PRIME LIVING LOCATIONS

Getting Around

Getting around Bengaluru would be a breeze if it weren't for all the traffic. The roads here are well maintained by Indian standards, signs are clearly posted, and people are relatively respectful of traffic lights. However, there are many one-way streets, especially as you near the center, so driving in Bengaluru can be confusing for newcomers, and most people prefer to get a driver.

If you don't plan to get a car, you still have plenty of transportation options. Public transportation is not one of them, at least for most expats, who prefer to avoid the cramped buses that ply Bengaluru's streets. The exception to this is the Bangalore Metropolitan Transport Corporation (BMTC) bus to and from the airport and a few special routes that run from city neighborhoods to the IT Parks. These buses are air-conditioned and generally well maintained. Otherwise, if you work at an IT Park, it's quite likely that your company will offer you a share-taxi or bus service (sometimes for a small fee) that will transport you and other employees living in your area to and from work.

For those who don't own cars, autorickshaws and taxis are the most common option. Taxis aren't easily hailed on the streets of Bengaluru, so it's best to call one of the many radio taxi companies, who will charge you by the meter, or a private car company, who will either charge you a fixed fare or quote you a per-kilometer rate. Autorickshaws are easy to hail on the street and will normally go by the meter, although they may ask for a small tip in addition to the metered fare if you ask them to take you a long distance.

THE METRO

At the time of writing, construction on Bengaluru's aptly named Namma Metro (Kannada for "Our Metro") is underway. The metro will be a mix of underground and aboveground stations and is expected to significantly relieve Bengaluru of some of its traffic problems. Two lines are planned so far, the north–south Green Line and the Purple Line, which will run east–west. The two lines will meet in the Majestic neighborhood near the railway station. Metro construction in Bengaluru has faced significant delays since it began back in 2006, although some parts of the system should be operational by the end of 2011.

NORTHERN INDIA

When people overseas think of India, it's often Northern India that they're imagining. Many Westerners have been exposed to Indian culture only through films and restaurants, and Northern Indian cultures seem to get exported much more than the cultures of the south. Part of this has to do with immigration—there are large Punjabi and Gujarati communities in North America and Britain, for example, and the food, entertainment, and traditions rooted in these areas are consequently more visible in the West. Moreover, if you have ever seen an Indian film, it's more likely than not to have come out of Bollywood, feature Northern Indian actors, and portray life from a northerner's point of view.

Like all of India, however, the north is so diverse that it becomes difficult to describe it in general terms. If you move to Kolkata, India's capital during much of British rule, you will be exposed to Bengali culture, which has its own rich culinary and literary traditions, not to mention political climate, that sets the state apart from the rest of the country. If you are interested in

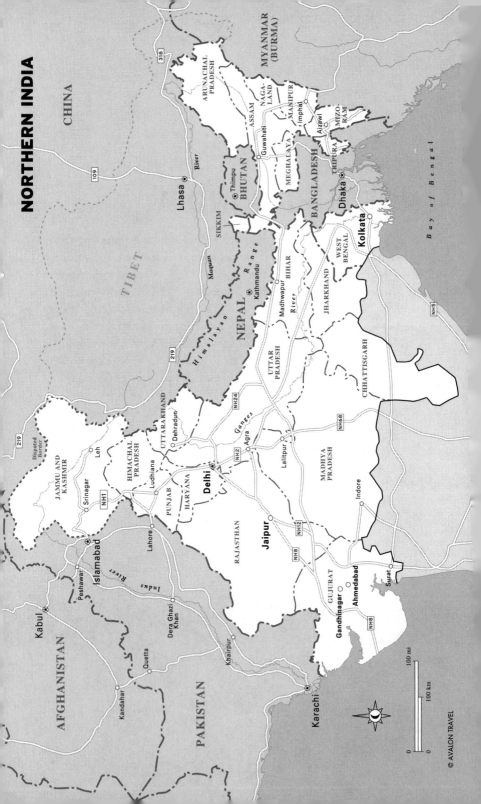

handicrafts import-export or want to study Hindi, the smallish city of Jaipur, with its royal history and easy access to Delhi, might attract you. Ahmedabad draws in people in the IT and pharmaceutical industries as well as people of Indian descent who want to connect with what Indians sweetly refer to as their "ancestral homeland."

The Lay of the Land

Some people use the term *Northern India* only to refer to India's northwestern parts, meaning Punjab and the "Hindi Belt," the area where Hindi is the common mother tongue. Geographically, the north stretches a lot farther, from Pakistan in the west to Bangladesh and the Bay of Bengal in the east. Geographically speaking, India's north also encompasses the northeastern states beyond Bangladesh that are only connected to India by a narrow strip of land (although these states are usually called the Northeast).

CLIMATE

Northern India is very large, and the climate varies greatly from region to region. In the far north, the Himalayan mountain range is icy and snowy at its peaks yet subtropical at its foothills. Much of the northern plains can be described as semiarid for part of the year and quite humid during the monsoon and postmonsoon seasons. The northern plains can get quite cold in the winter, with temperatures dropping to near freezing, and then pick up again in the summer, pushing the mercury well into the 100s in some areas. Jaipur, Rajasthan's capital, is hot and semiarid with relatively mild winters. The same goes for Ahmedabad, although it gets a bit more rain. Kolkata has what meteorologists call a tropical savanna climate, meaning that the temperatures rarely dip low enough to merit putting on a winter coat and certain times of the year are pronouncedly dry. The monsoon here is notoriously heavy and lasts for months.

LANGUAGE AND CULTURE

The languages in India's northern regions all belong to the Indo-European language group, with the exception of many of the languages of the Northeast, where the languages are closer to those found in East Asia. Hindi and its dialects are the most commonly spoken language in most of the north, and even in cities such as Ahmedabad and Kolkata, where people communicate primarily in their mother tongue, Hindi is still widely understood. Although

THE GANGES

pilgrims at the banks of the Ganges, Varanasi

The Ganges, often called the Ganga in India, is India's best-known river. It starts in the Himalayan foothills at the Gangotri Glacier in Gaumukh, Uttarakhand, flowing across India's north and through Bangladesh until it reaches the Bay of Bengal. The river is considered holy by Hindus and is believed to flow from the locks of Lord Shiva. It's also considered auspicious to scatter the ashes of the dead in the Ganges, and many elderly people come to the holy city of Varanasi to die and be cremated near the holy river.

The Ganges is also one of the world's most polluted rivers, containing so much fecal matter, human and animal remains, and toxins that it is virtually devoid of river life in many places. This extreme pollution, along with damming projects along the river, has also put a number of aquatic species in danger, including the Ganges River dolphin.

you can easily get by with Hindi, try to learn a few Gujarati words if you are moving to Ahmedabad as this will show that you are putting in some effort. The same goes for Kolkata—while learning Bengali is certainly not necessary, and may not be as useful as Hindi, it's still helpful to know a little to get by.

Northern India's cultural traditions are diverse, and it's difficult to pin down traits of its culture, especially when the term is used broadly to describe the entire north and not just the plains. Even the food varies a lot from state to state. You might notice that the architecture in the north has more Islamic elements, and the food tends to be spicier and heartier than in the south. You find a different culture in every Indian city, and this is nowhere more pronounced than in the northern regions.

Ahmedabad

The Gujarati city of Ahmedabad has come a long way since it was founded in the 15th century. Ahmedabad was historically a textile hub, although the last few decades have seen it emerge into one of western India's major centers for science, technology, and education. India's top design school, the National Institute for Design (NID), is based here, as is a branch of the Indian Institute for Technology (IIT).

Ahmedabad is split down the middle by the Sabarmati River, with the congested Old City to the east and the more upscale New City to the west. Ahmedabad is perhaps best known as the home of Mahatma Gandhi, who used it as a base for his ashrams and for much of his political activism. It is also home to many beautiful mosques and temples, the most historic of which are located in the Old City.

Many of Ahmedabad's international residents are overseas-born Gujaratis who have moved to the city to work or simply discover their familial roots.

© MARGOT BIGG

Ahmedabad's skyline

PRIME LIVING LOCATIONS

Over the past few years, the city's growing IT sector has resulted in a surge of techie expats moving to Ahmedabad and its environs. Others work in NGOs or for oil companies, or study at one of the city's many reputable institutes of higher education.

WHERE TO LIVE

Compared to many other cities in India, the cost of living in Ahmedabad is quite low. However, many expats feel that they are charged much more than locals are for comparable accommodations, especially those who balk at the idea of bargaining. Almost all of Ahmedabad's expats live west of the Sabarmati River, except the few with jobs in Gandhinagar, Ahmedabad's well-planned satellite city to the north. The most popular area is known as Satellite, although the Navangpura and Drive-In neighborhoods also have some nice residential pockets.

Satellite

If you want to be around other expats, the area known as Satellite is the place to be. Most expat s here live in apartment buildings, which usually come with guards, ample parking, and other conveniences on-site. Apartments in Satellite start at around ₹14,000 per month for an unfurnished two-bedroom and around ₹18,000 per month for a semifurnished or furnished place. A three-bedroom will cost you at least ₹23,000 per month unfurnished or ₹27,000 per month furnished, although you can expect to pay much more if you want a luxury apartment. There are very few studio and one-bedroom options in this area as most of the housing is built for somewhat affluent families. A small bungalow won't cost you much more than an apartment, although you will likely want to hire private security guards, which will cost at least another ₹12,000 per month.

SHARBAT

If you visit a Northern Indian home in the summer, you are likely to be offered an ice-cold glass of *sharbat,* or cordial, to cool you down. *Sharbat* is a sweet syrup made from flowers and herbs and is usually diluted in water. Popular varieties include *khus* (vetiver), rose, hibiscus, *phalsa* (a small, tangy fruit), and Rooh Afza (a blend of fruits, vegetables, and herbs). Many *sharbats* have medicinal properties and can help cool your system on hot days. *Sharbats* are believed to have been introduced by the Mughals, although many contain blends of herbs that make the drinks appear more closely related to ayurvedic medicine.

Many of the landlords in this area will only accept tenants on company-sponsored leases, and if they know you are an expat with a large accommodations expense account, they will try to charge as much as they reasonably can. Many will ask for two months' security (three months for fully furnished apartments) along with the first month's rent. Anything more is generally unreasonable. The easiest option is to go through a broker, who can help you deal with paperwork and negotiations. Bear in mind that brokers usually charge a fee of one month's rent for their services, so it's in their best interest to get your monthly rent as high as possible.

Gandhinagar

Gandhinagar is Gujarat's clean, green, and well-organized seat of government, just 20 miles away from Ahmedabad's city center. The city was planned by French architect Le Corbusier and is set up on a grid, so getting around is pretty straightforward. Very few expats working in Ahmedabad choose to make Gandhinagar home, simply because it's quite a commute into the city (about 45 minutes when there is no traffic). However, if you work in Gandhinagar and don't have children in one of the international schools in Ahmedabad, you may find this option more convenient. Rents here are pretty much on par with Ahmedabad's Satellite neighborhood, although houses are more popular than apartments for most people. You can also get larger properties here than in Ahmedabad, so if you need five or more bedrooms, you may prefer this option.

DAILY LIFE
Language

The local language in Ahmedabad is Gujarati, and many signs are posted only in Gujarati. Most people here speak Hindi too, and while it's helpful to learn a few phrases in at least one of these languages, you can get by on English alone, especially if you remember to speak slowly. You can find English-speaking domestic help, although expect to pay a premium for their language skills. As is the case in other major Indian cities, the educated locals will speak perfect English.

Expat Social Scene

The expat community in Ahmedabad is still quite small, although a sharp upturn in foreign investment in the area is bringing more and more foreigners to the city. Expats often connect through online resources such as Facebook or meet through mutual acquaintances. Social gatherings take place at restaurants, coffee shops, or in people's homes. As alcohol is prohibited in Gujarat, there's virtually no bar scene in the city, but if you like to drink, don't despair: Foreign nationals can obtain government-issued alcohol permits and buy booze at specially licensed liquor shops in certain hotels. If you are a short-term visitor, you can easily obtain a permit at most alcohol outlets. If you are a resident of Gujarat, you have to go through the painfully bureaucratic process of obtaining a permit from the Prohibition and Excise Department in the Old City. Once you have an alcohol permit, you are allowed to purchase a restricted amount of alcohol (which depends on how much is allotted to you on your permit), although you must consume it in a hotel room or in a private residence.

If you want to learn more about the culture and history of Ahmedabad, you have plenty of options. The Ahmedabad Municipal Corporation runs regular guided tours of the old city, and if you visit on a Sunday morning, you'll get a chance to see the Old City's weekly market being set up. Culture buffs will want to keep abreast of the many evening performances held at the Natrani Auditorium near Ashram Road.

Health Care

Ahmedabad has many hospitals, although the quality can vary. Shalby Hospital is popular among expats, and its main campus is just a few miles south of the Satellite neighborhood. Sterling Hospital in the Drive-In neighborhood also has a good reputation. Both have pediatric wards.

Education

The Mahatma Gandhi International School is located in Mithakali Gam in the center of the New City and admits students in all grades. It follows the Cambridge system for primary schools and an IB curriculum for middle and high school. The SGVP International School on the northwest outskirts of Ahmedabad may be a more convenient option if you are based in Gandhinagar. The school has K–12 education and provides preparation for the Cambridge examinations for older students. SGVP also has a boarding school.

Food and Shopping

Gujarati food is well known across India, although it's definitely an acquired taste. Many local dishes are less spicy than in other parts of the country, but you'll find that the Gujarati take on staple Indian dishes, such as dal or vegetable curry, will have a distinctly sweet flavor. Even if you are a big fan of the Indian food that you've tried overseas or in other parts of the country, you may find Gujarat's sugary dishes take some time to get used to—many

© MARGOT BIGG

Ahmedabad's Art Book Center has an amazing selection of rare art books.

PRIME LIVING LOCATIONS

foreigners and Indians from other parts of the state prefer to avoid Gujarati food at all costs. Also, if you are fond of red meat, you may need to adjust your diet. Most Gujaratis are vegetarian, and while there's no shortage of fresh vegetables, you may have to go to specialty shops to buy things such as chicken and fish; note that beef is illegal in Gujarat. Icy Pik on Drive-In Road is a popular place to buy frozen meat, and they also offer a good selection of imported goods, including cereals and pasta sauces. If you're feeling homesick, there's no shortage of malls in Ahmedabad, most of which are chock-full of the showrooms of Western brands like Levi's and Benetton. Himalaya Mall and Devarc Mall also have movie theaters that regularly run Hollywood hits, although be warned that English-language films rarely play in Ahmedabad's cinemas for more than about a week.

GETTING AROUND

Most expats in Ahmedabad go the car-and-driver route, although the traffic here is calmer than in many other cities, making self-drive a possible option for confident drivers. The city has grown a lot over the past few years, so rush-hour traffic can be a bit harrowing. Many companies offer their expatriate staff chauffeur-driven cars as part of their relocation package, but if yours doesn't, you can rent a small car with a driver for around ₹18,000 per month. Alternately, there's no shortage of autorickshaws, which run by the meter (averaging around 40 cents per mile). Ahmedabad has a well-developed bus system, although the crowds and heat make this an unpopular option with expats.

Jaipur

As a major stop in the "golden triangle" of Northern Indian tourist hot spots along with Agra and Delhi, Rajasthan's capital has a constant stream of foreign visitors. Moving here is a little different. The expat community is not as sizeable as in larger cities, but there are still plenty of people who move here to work in NGOs, set up their own businesses, or study Hindi. Many expat-run enterprises involve gems and jewelry, block printing and apparel design, and interior design and furnishings. It's an easier place to get around than many other cities, and you'll find that because of its status as a tourism hot spot, even the rickshaw *wallahs* seem to be fluent in English. However, knowing some Hindi never hurts, especially when it comes to bargaining.

WHERE TO LIVE

Jaipur's expat community is small, and while there aren't any specific neighborhoods where foreign residents flock en masse, there are a few upscale areas that tend to attract the international crowd. Landlords generally ask for one month's deposit.

C-Scheme

A mix of leafy, quiet neighborhoods and busy commercial streets, C-Scheme is not far from the Pink City and has plenty of things to do, including a few large shopping malls and a number of gyms, cafés, and restaurants. There are also a number of newer and refurbished properties in this area. A three-bedroom in this category will run you ₹18,000–25,000 per month. A two-bedroom in C-Scheme rents for an average of ₹14,000 per month, although this can vary depending on the quality of the apartment.

University Area

Slightly farther out, the adjoining neighborhoods of Bapu Nagar, Tilak Nagar, and Raja Park also have quite a few expat residents and are popular with students due to their proximity to Rajasthan University. Apartments in this area are a bit cheaper than in C-Scheme, and you should be able to find an unfurnished one-bedroom for around ₹10,000 per month. A comparable three-bedroom shouldn't cost more than ₹20,000 per month.

DAILY LIFE
Expat Social Scene
As Jaipur's expat community is smallish, there's not much in the way of so-cial clubs for expats. Instead, people meet up at places like Cafe Kooba in C-Scheme and TaBlu at the Clarks Hotel. Younger expats can get in touch with AIESEC, an international internship program for university students that also organizes a lot of community events.

Although Jaipur doesn't have a huge expat social scene, you'll still find that there's plenty to do. The city is filled with historical sites and museums, and it's also a good base for exploring other parts of Rajasthan. Jaipur also hosts quite a few annual festivals, including a very popular elephant festival and an international literature festival.

Health Care
Fortis Healthcare has one of their signature "multi super specialty" hospitals in South Jaipur's Malviya Nagar neighborhood. The hospital has a good reputa-tion for its cleanliness and the professionalism of its staff, although there have been reports of overcharging foreigners. Bapu Nagar's Santokba Durlabjhi Memorial Hospital has treated many expats and foreign visitors over the years and maintains high standards and more reasonable prices.

Education
Step-by-Step High School is currently Jaipur's only IB school. The name is misleading; the school admits students in preschool through grade 12, but they only offer the IB curriculum at the high school level. If you have daughters, you could consider the Maharani Gayatri Devi Girls' Public School (MGD), one of the best schools for girls in India. If you have boys and are considering boarding school, Mayo College in Ajmer (a 3–4-hour drive away) is one of the best schools in the country.

Shopping
Shopping in Jaipur's touristy and historic Pink City can be simultaneously delightful and harrowing. There's far too much to choose from, a lot of touts, and shopkeepers sound like auctioneers when they bargain. How-ever, with a little persistence you can get good deals on everything from silk bedspreads to silver jewelry. If you prefer fixed prices or are looking for brands from back home, you might be better off in one of the many new shopping malls—Crystal Court in City Palms has a mix of Indian

and international stores. For imported foodstuffs, try Shopper's Paradise in C-Scheme.

GETTING AROUND

Jaipur is a planned city and is easy to get around, but because it's very touristy, you will have to bargain hard. For short distances, there are bicycle rickshaws aplenty, but if you are leaving your neighborhood, you'll need an autorickshaw—although Jaipur is somewhat small by international standards, it's still fairly spread out. Very few expats use the bus, but some people buy a car or motor scooter. Driving in Jaipur is not too hectic by Indian standards, although the traffic circles can get a bit congested and confusing.

Kolkata

The city formerly known as Calcutta was developed by the East India Company from the 17th century, and it became the capital of India once the British government took over, loosing its status to Delhi only in 1912. During partition, the bulk of the cultural-linguistic region of Bengal was divided into East Pakistan (later Bangladesh) and West Bengal, and many Muslim Kolkatans migrated east, while Hindus from what is now Bangladesh moved into the city.

For many years Kolkata has been the cultural, intellectual, and commercial

© RUI MARTIN

Much of Kolkata's architecture dates back to the Raj era.

© RUI MARTIN

golfing in a Kolkata park

capital of India's east. Kolkatans have strong intellectual, artistic, and literary traditions, and the city is known nationwide for its vibrant cultural life. Despite being India's third-most populous city, Kolkata still has a relatively small expatriate community, and like many Indian cities, it draws a good number of its foreign employees in the IT sector and trade.

WHERE TO LIVE

Be prepared to pay a deposit equivalent to at least three months' rent when you move into your Kolkata home. Some landlords ask for a deposit equal to six months or even up to a year's worth of rent, so don't be afraid to negotiate if you feel uncomfortable paying so much up front.

Alipore

South Kolkata's historic Alipore is home of many of the city's expats. The wealthy neighborhood was once popular with high-ranking British colonialists, and many of the large bungalows and houses in the area date back to the Raj era. As this is one of the most in-demand places to live in Kolkata, rental apartments come at a premium. A furnished three-bedroom can easily cost upward of ₹40,000–50,000 per month, and a four-bedroom stand-alone villa with a garden can easily cost over ₹200,000 per month. There are also apartments in the area. Just south of Alipore, the planned neighborhood of New Alipore has a larger selection of apartments with reasonable rents. Expect to pay ₹6,000–8,000 per month for a one-bedroom in this area. A two-bedroom will run at least ₹12,000 per month. A three-bedroom averages ₹20,000–25,000 per month but can cost considerably more if furnished.

PRIME LIVING LOCATIONS

Mother Teresa was one of Kolkata's most famous residents.

Ballygunge

Also in South Kolkata, the upmarket Ballygunge neighborhood is home to Kolkata's old families as well as a large share of the city's expats. The area has plenty of tree-lined streets and independent villas as well as a smattering of apartments, but if you want to live here, remember that you will be paying for your address as much as for the quality of your housing. Two-bedrooms here start at around ₹20,000 per month, and three-bedrooms don't generally drop much lower than ₹30,000 per month.

Salt Lake

Also known as Bidhan Nagar, the east Kolkata township of Salt Lake City, named for having been built on saltwater marshlands, is West Bengal's very own take on an IT city. Companies such as Wipro and IBM operate out of Salt Lake's Sector V, and expats working in Salt Lake often prefer to shorten their commutes by living nearby. Living in Salt Lake has many advantages—it's clean, well planned, and easy to get around. However, it can take well over half an hour to drive into central Kolkata on a good day, so it's really only worth moving here if your office is nearby. Housing costs in this part of town vary dramatically, with two-bedroom apartments starting as low as ₹9,000 per month. A comfortable three-bedroom will cost you at least ₹14,000 per month but can cost up to double that for something ultraluxurious. If you want a stand-alone house, potentially with a small garden, budget at least ₹25,000 per month for a three-bedroom.

DAILY LIFE
Language
The mother tongue of most Kolkatans is Bengali (also known as Bangla), an Indo-Aryan language that evolved from Sanskrit. Many of India's most renowned writers and poets, including Rabindranath Tagore, composed much of their work in the language. Bengali has its own script that shares some similarities with Devanagari and is used alongside English in much of the city's signage. You'll find that most Bengalis also know Hindi to some extent, and the educated classes will know English fluently. Although Bengali shares a linguistic history with Hindi, the two are not mutually comprehensible, so while learning Hindi will surely help you get around, it won't help you understand the Bengali conversations around you very well.

Expat Social Scene
Kolkata's expat community is quite small compared to other Indian cities of its size. There are expats from all over the world, although a large number hail from English-speaking countries. There's also a sizeable Chinese population, and while they are not exactly expats—many have lived in India for generations—they add an international feel. The Kolkata International Women's Club is a good source of information on expat life in the city, and attending their monthly meetings and special social events is a good way to meet other expats. The Indian Council for Cultural Relations (ICCR) Rabindranath Tagore Centre also hosts regular cultural events that are popular with Bengalis and expats alike.

Health Care
If you are based in or around Alipore, your closest well-known hospital or clinic is Woodlands Hospital and Medical Research Centre. AMRI Hospital on Gariahat Road has a good reputation for emergency care. They also have a branch in Salt Lake City. Apollo has a hospital just outside of Salt Lake City, and Bhagirathi Neotia Woman and Child Care Centre is known for births and neonatal care.

Education
Kolkata has many excellent schools, including St. Xavier's Collegiate School, one of the most reputable (not to mention selective) boys schools in the country.

PRIME LIVING LOCATIONS

Most expatriates choose to send their children to either the American School Kolkata or the Calcutta International School, each of which has its plusses and minuses. The American School is affiliated with the American Embassy School in Delhi and offers an international curriculum and small class sizes. However, they currently only have an elementary school program, and the tuition fees are too high for many expat families or their companies to afford. The Calcutta International School is more affordable and admits students in grades preschool–12, although the school's curriculum is based on Indian educational methods and may be harder for overseas children to adapt to.

Shopping

Kolkata has very good shopping and is especially known for leather goods (much of which are produced by the Chinese community) and Indian instruments. Many of the expat neighborhoods have small shops selling imported goods, although the easiest way to get your international food fix is to head to one of the many branches of Spencer's, a supermarket chain with shops comparable in size and selection to what you would find in the West. Alternately, you can brave the enormous New Market, where you can buy everything from rubber sandals to freshly baked bread.

GETTING AROUND

There are plenty of ways to get around Kolkata. If you get a car, you might want to hire a driver too, as Kolkata traffic can be a bit maddening. Otherwise, you can take taxis, rickshaws, the metro, or the tram. You'll only find autorickshaws and bicycle rickshaws in the suburbs, although hand-pulled rickshaws are available in the city center (these are unusual in the rest of India). The idea of sitting on a cart while an often barefoot man runs down the street pulling you can be a bit disturbing, and while you may choose not to use this type of transportation, be prepared to see it.

Taxis are a more common way of getting around the city and can easily be hailed on the street. If you aren't familiar with where you are going, you may find it easier to negotiate a price ahead of time, although most drivers will happily go by the meter. As in many Indian cities, the meters in Kolkata are out of date, so drivers carry conversion charts to calculate the correct fare.

Kolkata has a very good public transportation system, and while you may want to avoid using the cramped buses, the metro is a more comfortable and efficient way of getting around. Individual fares depend on the zone you travel to, or you can buy a monthly pass if you want to use the system regularly.

SOUTHERN INDIA

Most of the expats in India who don't move to Delhi end up somewhere in Southern India. While Northern India still dominates the country culturally and linguistically, the south has become India's high-tech powerhouse, with Bengaluru and Hyderabad firmly established as international IT cities. Southern India has been home to foreigners for centuries; some of the first international traders set up shop here. Former colonies such as Portuguese Goa, Dutch Cochin in Kerala, and the Gallic Puducherry in Tamil Nadu still retain markedly European architecture and cultural elements. These days, most foreigners end up either in Mumbai and Bengaluru or one of four other key areas: Chennai, Goa, Hyderabad, and Pune. Chennai, the capital of Tamil Nadu, attracts foreigners working for automobile companies and students of Southern Indian arts and music. Goa doesn't have much industry, but people from around the world flock here to set up small businesses in the idyllic beach-lined state. With their many software companies, Hyderabad and its twin city, Secunderabad, are almost like a mini version of Bengaluru, and they attract

SOUTHERN
INDIA

PAKISTAN

HARYANA

NH1

DELHI

NEPAL

Maquan
219
River

Mt
Everest
Kathmandu

Bikaner

NH2

UTTAR
PRADESH

Ganges

Jaisalmer

Jaipur

Agra

RAJASTHAN

NH8

Kota

NH16

Gwalior

NH25

Jhansi

Kanpur

NH28

BIHAR

River

Varanasi

NH2

JHARKHAND

WEST
BENGAL

NH14

Udaipur

NH12A

NH7

GUJURAT

NH3

MADHYA
PRADESH

CHHATTISGARH

Kolkata

Ahmedabad

Indore

Nagpur

NH6

Raipur

NH215

NH8

NH3

MAHARASHTRA

NH7

ORISSA

NH201

NH5

Paradip

Mumbai

Pune

NH222

NH16

Arabian Sea

NH4

Sholapur

NH9

Secunderabad

Hyderabad

Vishakapatnam

KARNATAKA

ANDHRA
PRADESH

NH9

Vijayawada

GOA

Marmagoa

Guntakal

NH5

NH17

NH4

Mangaluru

NH7

Bengaluru

NH4

Chennai

NH45

TAMIL
NADU

LAKSHADWEEP

NH47

Gutuvayoo

Tiruchirapalli

0   100 mi

0   100 km

Madurai

KERALA

NH7

NH47

Tuticorin

Kanniyakumari

SRI
LANKA

Indian Ocean

© AVALON TRAVEL

plenty of techies along with a growing number of NGO workers. Pune also has a thriving IT sector, and while many professionals in the Maharashtrian city work in this industry, the city's many colleges and universities also attract a steady stream of overseas students.

Despite the long history of interaction between Southern India and the West, most of the exposure non-Indians get to Indian culture has distinctly Northern Indian roots. The food in North American and European Indian restaurants tends to be of the northern tandoori variety rather than the rice and coconut curries of the south. The dance and music styles most often showcased overseas are from the north, and the widely exported Bollywood movies, with their Hindi-speaking, fair-skinned superstars, are unabashedly Northern India–centric. When you move to India, many notions you had about the country will fly out the window, even more so if you move to one of the southern states.

The Lay of the Land

The landmass of peninsular Southern India starts at the Deccan Plateau, the source of many of its rivers, and forms a triangle shape at the town of Kanyakumari at its southernmost tip. From here, you can watch the moon rise and the sun set simultaneously over two oceans. To the northwest is the state of Maharashtra, where the popular college town of Pune is located. Farther south along the coast is Goa, India's tiniest state and a popular place for tourists and independent expats alike. To the east is Andhra Pradesh and its capital city of Hyderabad, a former principality that's now known for its tech industry. The southeast corner of the country is occupied by Tamil Nadu and its capital, Chennai, home to much of India's automotive industry.

CLIMATE

Southern India is India's rainiest half, with monsoon showers starting in June and sometimes carrying on well into the winter months. Unlike the northern part of the country, where weather patterns are influenced by activity in the Himalayas, the south has a relatively stable climate year-round. Summers here can get quite hot, and you can go for weeks without seeing the temperature drop below 100°F, even at night. Winters can provide some respite, when temperatures drop to the upper 70s, although humidity levels remain high, especially near the coast.

LANGUAGE AND CULTURE

The languages of Southern India vary widely, from the Indo-Aryan Marathi spoken in Maharashtra to the Dravidian Tamil spoken in Tamil Nadu. Telugu is spoken in Andhra Pradesh, although many people in this traditionally Muslim city speak Urdu. The language of Goa is Konkani, an Indo-European language that is rooted in Sanskrit but also retains elements of Portuguese left over from colonial rule. Many Goans also know Portuguese and Marathi along with English and Hindi.

© MARGOT BIGG

Dravidian temple architecture

Although there is no uniform Southern Indian culture, there are certain elements associated with the south. Meals tend to be rice-based rather than wheat-based, and in many states food is served on a banana leaf and eaten with the hands. Carnatic music and related dance forms emerged in the south and are distinct from their Northern Indian equivalents. Temple architecture in the south is remarkably different, and temple roofs in Dravidian parts of Southern India are adorned with sculptures of deities and sometimes painted in vivid colors.

Chennai

The coastal city of Chennai, formerly known as Madras, is a sprawling agglomeration of smaller townships that together make up India's fourth-largest city. Chennai is a lot younger than many of India's other urban hubs, and much of it was developed by the British during colonial times. The architecture is a mix of traditional Dravidian (mostly seen in temples) and the Indo-Saracenic mix of Indian and European architectural elements pioneered by the British.

Chennai is a hub for manufacturing, and its automobile industry draws expats from all over the world, especially Japan, Korea, and Germany. The city also draws in professional dancers from around the world who come to study Bharatanatyam dance at the renowned Kalakshetra Foundation. If you

SOUTH INDIAN CUISINE

The culinary delights of Southern India are quite different from what you may be used to seeing in Indian restaurants in your home country. Southern India's favorite dishes are vegetarian and served either for breakfast or as snacks. They are usually accompanied with *sambar,* a lentil-based stew, and coconut chutney. Here are a few of the most popular:

- **dosa:** Similar to an eggless crepe, it is the quintessential Southern Indian dish. *Dosas* are made from a batter of finely ground rice and dal and come in many varieties. The best-known is the masala *dosa,* stuffed with spiced potatoes and curry leaves. The *rava dosa* is made with semolina and has a holey appearance. The paper *dosa* is an extra-thin version and can be stretched out into a family-size dish.

- **idli:** These round, spongy cakes are made by fermenting a mixture of ground rice and husked lentils and then steaming the batter in a metal mold. Alone they are nearly flavorless, and most people prefer to eat them with *sambar,* yogurt, or chutney.

- **pongal:** This rice-based dish is popular for breakfast and is usually mildly seasoned with pepper and yellow lentils. The annual harvest festival in Tamil Nadu is also called Pongal, when a sweet variant of the dish is served.

- **uttapam:** Savory flat breads sometimes dubbed "South Indian pizza," they are made from a batter similar to *dosa* with a variety of vegetables cooked into the dough. They are a lot thicker than *dosas* and resemble a savory pancake.

- **vada:** A doughnut-shaped snack food popular in the south that many people like to have with their afternoon cup of coffee. Although the deep-fried *vada* come in plenty of varieties, the most common are made with gram flour. They are served with the same condiments as *idlis.*

move to Chennai to work for a multinational corporation or a software company, you may find yourself working in one of two places: Tidel Park, one of India's largest IT business parks, or the Old Mahabalipuram Road (OMR), officially known as Rajiv Gandhi Salai.

WHERE TO LIVE

Most expats live either on the coast or in the more central neighborhood of Nungambakkam. Many of the neighborhoods along coastal Chennai merge into each other and thus have been grouped together in this section. Landlords will expect a deposit equivalent to three months' rent, or a little more for a furnished apartment. Keep in mind that Chennai has a notoriously bad water supply, so try to find a place with a water reserve in place, or buy a few large trash cans with lids and fill them with water just in case your taps run dry.

Coastal Chennai

The East Coast Road, which is usually shortened to ECR, is a long high-way that runs along the Bay of Bengal starting at Thiruvanmiyur. The many small townships along this road and just north of it have become quite popular with expats, although if you want a place on the beach side of the road, expect to pay a premium. Although expat households can be found in many of the coastal neighborhoods, the highest concentration is in Besant Nagar, Thiruvanmiyur, and Adyar. The leafy neighborhood of Mylapore is a bit farther north along the coast and has quite a few service apartments for short-term expats. All of these areas have a wide range of accommodations, with apartments running ₹18,000–22,000 per month for a two-bedroom.

Many expats prefer Besant Nagar over other coastal neighborhoods, partly due to its proximity to Elliot's Beach, a relatively clean stretch of golden sand that's popular for evening strolls and is home to a number of decent restaurants and coffee shops. Keep in mind that it's better to have your own vehicle if you opt to live in this area, as the availability and quality of public transportation here is not very good. If you work in Tidel Park in Thiruvanmiyur or along the OMR, however, your company may have a shuttle bus available. If you are looking for a property in this area, it's recommended that you try to find something north of Uthandi; the electricity supply south of here is reputed to be sketchy.

PRIME LIVING LOCATIONS

© MARGOT BIGG

Elliot's Beach, Chennai

AUROVILLE: UNIVERSAL CITY IN THE MAKING

Just north of the French colonial town of Puducherry is Auroville, a self-described "universal city in the making" and home to people from all over the world. The township was formed in 1968 under the auspices of the Sri Aurobindo Society, a Puducherry-based spiritual group, as something like a stateless state where people from all over the world could live in harmony. Today it is home to over 2,000 people of 45 different nationalities, many of whom were actually born and raised in the township. Auroville has schools, a health clinic, restaurants, and shops. Residents support themselves through activities ranging from cosmetics manufacturing to cheese production.

The pinnacle of Auroville is the Matrimandir, a large golden sphere reminiscent of the Spaceship Earth building at the Epcot theme park in Florida. The Matrimandir houses a large crystal ball on which the sun's rays are beamed throughout the day. The hall is used for

© MARGOT BIGG

Auroville's Matrimandir

meditation by practitioners of Integral yoga, the spiritual tradition of Auroville's residents. Visitors come by the busload to visit the Matrimandir every day, although you have to apply in advance for permission to enter the building.

PRIME LIVING LOCATIONS

Nungambakkam

As one of the oldest parts of Chennai, the central neighborhood of Nungambakkam has been a prime location for expats since before independence, when it was home to many high-ranking civil servants. These days it is an upscale enclave for well-off locals and expats alike, and there are enough shopping and dining options that you really don't need to venture out except to go to work. The neighborhood is also home to a number of cultural centers, including the Alliance Française on College Road as well as the German Goethe-Institut, and it is only a few miles to the British Council. This area is very convenient to both Tidel Park and the OMR, plus it's well served by public transportation. A two-bedroom no-frills apartment in this area could cost you as little as ₹15,000 per month, but you could easily pay up to twice that if you want something luxurious.

DAILY LIFE
Language
The main language in Chennai is Tamil, and while signs are often posted in the language's curlicue script, they are usually accompanied with an English equivalent. It's useful to pick up a few words in Tamil for bargaining with rickshaw drivers, although most shopkeepers will know enough English to be able to communicate with you. People in Tamil Nadu do not speak Hindi unless they studied it as a foreign language in school or picked it up through Bollywood films. Some Tamils vehemently resist Hindi for political reasons, namely its de jure status as India's national language despite being only a regional language with no historical ties to the south.

Expat Social Scene
As it's a hub for auto manufacturing, Chennai has large populations of expats from Japan, Korea, and Germany, and nationals of those countries often have their own set of social groups and activities. Commonwealth citizens and other people from the English-speaking world may find solace in the British Business Social Club (BBSC), which is open to all. The Hash Harriers, the worldwide "drinking group with a running problem," has a Chennai chapter with lots of expat involvement. The Overseas Women's Club of Madras (OWC), which has been running since 1972, is very active and hosts luncheons, family activities, and charitable events. If you are the outgoing type, you can also head to the Leather Bar at the Park Hotel, where you are sure to find a few expat faces on most nights.

Health Care
Like all of India's major cities, Chennai has excellent medical facilities available, for a price. The Apollo Hospital, just east of Nungambakkam, has some of the best facilities in the city, and most expats opt for treatment here. They also have a 24-hour pharmacy.

Education
Most American expats who can afford it put their children in the American International School, which offers the IB curriculum, and parents will find this a good place to meet other expat families. There's a long waiting list, so

many of the families tend to be long-term expats. British expats may prefer the British International School, which follows a traditional British model. Other popular alternatives include the Gateway International School, which offers British and U.S. curricula, and Vael's Billabong High International School.

Shopping

Shopping in Chennai can be quite a delight, and the city is known for its textiles, especially silk saris. The best area for trendy boutiques and international brands is Khader Nawaz Khan Road, although if you prefer the cool environs of a shopping mall, you might want to check out the upmarket City Center Mall. The gargantuan Spencer's Plaza is also popular, although you may find its size and crowds overwhelming. One of the best places to buy imported foods is the large Amma Naana department store in Teynampet, which has foods from all over the world and a large variety of fresh fruits and vegetables. The Southern Indian supermarket chain Nilgiri's has outlets dotted around the city, most of which stock some imported dry goods as well as excellent cheeses sourced from Auroville, an international spiritual community a few hours south of Chennai.

GETTING AROUND

Transportation in Chennai is notoriously frustrating, and the autorickshaw drivers here are known nationwide as some of the cheekiest extractors of money. If you live and work near a train station, you may find the train to be your best option, although railcars can get pretty crowded during rush hour. The women's car, for women and children traveling without a male companion, can sometimes be more comfortable. Most expats living along the ECR have their own cars and drivers. Given Chennai's hot and muggy climate, this air-conditioned option might be best if you don't want to show up to work every day drenched in sweat.

Goa

India's smallest state, Goa has long been a favorite with expats interested in making India their home. The Portuguese were the first foreigners to arrive here in the 16th century. Although Goa officially became part of India in 1961, the Portuguese influence remains in everything from Old Goa's architecture to the local cuisine. In the early 1970s, hippies from France, Germany, Britain, and the United States moved to Goa in droves, lending a bohemian atmosphere to the state that remains to this day. While most have since returned to the rat race in their home countries, a few still live in Goa, where they run restaurants, guesthouses, and clothing shops. Other expats live here half of the year (normally the October–March tourist season), either eking out a living selling apparel or teaching yoga or just relaxing under the sun. While you are unlikely to find a job in this little piece of paradise, you may find it an ideal spot to start your own business, especially if you have a background in tourism or import-export. Intrepid foreigners have cashed in on the state's large number of foreign and Indian tourists, starting up ventures ranging from importing olives to paragliding. There's even a European man who supports his Goan lifestyle by setting up a telescope on the beach and charging a few rupees to passersby in return for a glimpse of the moon.

WHERE TO LIVE

As Goa is a state rather than a city, housing options here are quite spread out. Most expats choose to live at or near the beach, and the farther inland you go, the cheaper housing becomes.

North Goa

The traditional hippie hub, North Goa is a popular and convenient place for foreigners who want cheap accommodations and access to great nightlife, continental food, and other tourists. Popular spots for the dreadlocked crowd include Arambol, to the far north, and Anjuna, a little farther south. In the last five years, the tiny beach town of Morjim has boomed from a few huts into an expanse of seaside shack-style bars and restaurants, catering mostly to the influx of Russian tourists that Goa has recently experienced. While the guesthouses in North Goa are cheap enough that you can rent a room long-term (often for as little as ₹5,000 per month) you may prefer to rent a house if you plan to stay for more than a couple of months. Most landlords in the area are fine with short-term leases covering the tourist season, although they often make up their losses in the off-season by charging more than the market

© MARGOT BIGG

Goa's beaches are a big draw for many expats.

rate. A three-bedroom furnished house complete with all major appliances except air-conditioning and a spacious lawn runs ₹15,000–20,000 per month. A smaller shack with one or two rooms will cost about half that much. If you want luxury accommodations, you could easily be charged hundreds of thousands of rupees per month, especially if you are looking for a mansion with a swimming pool and servants. However, luxury homes are generally rented out by the night or the week rather than by the season.

South Goa

Although not as established for expats as the north, South Goa is quickly becoming a popular alternative for people who want to get away from the party atmosphere farther north. Although the southern part of the state is traditionally more affluent, housing prices across the state are more or less on par, although you may find that landlords aren't as used to dealing with foreign renters as they are up north, and fewer furnished houses are available. Although Palolem is quite a popular beach destination, it also caters mainly to tourists, which drives up prices and noise levels. A nearby alternative is Patnem, just to the south, which is both quieter and more affordable.

DAILY LIFE
Expat Social Scene

You'll have no problem meeting other foreigners in Goa simply because there are so many. There are a lot of travelers and expats from Russia, many of whom stick to their own, often because of the language barrier. Goa also has an established Israeli population, and there are a number of synagogues near the tourist hubs alongside the many Hindu temples and Catholic churches that dot the region.

Much of Goa's expat scene revolves around dance parties and smoking hash, so if that is your thing, you may have found a slice of heaven. Don't despair if you are the sober type; there's plenty of swimming, sunbathing, and relaxing to be had in Goa. If you don't mind crowds, you'll definitely want to pay a visit to one of Anjuna's two major markets, held on Wednesday during the day and on Saturday nights. Expect to find everything from the pashmina shawls that are hawked virtually everywhere in India to hot pink ninja boots designed by foreigners.

Shopping and Health Care

Although imported foods are readily available in shops throughout the state, Oxford Stores in Anjuna is a great place to do your shopping, and you'll be able to find everything here from miso flown in from Japan to locally produced pepper cheese that tastes like it could only have been made in Europe. The selection of imported goods here is better than in India's capital.

There are plenty of hospitals in Goa, although the Margao branch of the Apollo Group of hospitals is where most foreigners go. Goa is also fast becoming a center for medical tourism, and it's likely that many more state-of-the-art hospitals will crop up in years to come.

© MARIYA ZHELEVA

shopping in Goa

Safety is a concern in Goa, and there have been a number of cases of foreigners being raped and murdered here in the past few years. Women should not go out alone after dark, and secluded beach areas should only be visited in groups, even during the day.

Education

As Goa is not a traditional destination for expat families, you won't find India's best schools here. Not surprisingly, many parents choose to homeschool, and this option is more accepted in Goa than in other parts of the country. Goa's best school is arguably the preschool–12 Sharada

Motor scooters are a popular means of transportation for Goa's expats.

© MARGOT BIGG

Mandir School in Panaji, although they do not offer an international curriculum. The European International School of Goa is another option, although it is only open during the high season. The Sunshine School in Old Goa is also popular among foreigners.

GETTING AROUND

Goa is pretty spread out, and almost everyone there seems to be on two wheels, ranging from small automatic scooters (affectionately known as scooties) to noisy Enfield low-riders, India's most popular motorcycle. You can also rent a car, and as Goa is a very easy place to drive, there's no real need to hire a driver, as long as you have a valid international driver's license. Make sure that the car you are driving comes with black license plates with yellow lettering, as these indicate that the vehicle has been registered and approved for self-drive rental. Otherwise you might find yourself pulled over for questioning quite regularly, especially if you don't look Goan. Buses regularly ply the streets from the main destinations, although you may find that you have to switch buses frequently if you are traveling long-distance. There's no shortage of taxis available, and if you are alone, you can take a motorcycle taxi much more cheaply.

PRIME LIVING LOCATIONS

Hyderabad and Secunderabad

The twin cities of Hyderabad and Secunderabad are popular expatriate hubs, and most of the cities' foreign residents work in software and social enterprise. Hyderabad is also known as the home of the Indian Institute of Management, arguably the country's top business school, so don't be surprised if you meet a few students here from elite U.S. business schools on a study-abroad program.

Although Hyderabad has recently come to be associated with the IT industry, it is equally known for its *biryanis* (a fried-rice dish), considered the best in India, and as a center for the freshwater pearl industry. It also has a thriving fine arts scene, and its plusher neighborhoods are dotted with galleries. There's also a thriving Telugu-language film industry, dubbed Tollywood, and Hyderabad is home to many of the state's local stars. Secunderabad, which more or less merges with Hyderabad, is considered by most people to be part of the same city. Unlike Hyderabad, the center of a former princely state, Secunderabad was built by the British as a military camp—Winston Churchill was even stationed here in his younger life. Although Secunderabad has merged with Hyderabad, many of the original churches and buildings remain, and the city continues to be home to a large military presence.

WHERE TO LIVE

Many of Hyderabad's IT expats work in the Hyderabad Information Technology Engineering Consultancy (HITEC) city or in Gachibowli. Most foreigners used to stick to Jubilee Hills and Banjara Hills, but over the last few years many have moved to Gachibowli, as many high-tech companies have set up operations in the area. If your office is in Secunderabad, you might find Hyderabad too far to commute from on a daily basis.

Jubilee Hills

The lush and leafy Jubilee Hills neighborhood includes much of Hyderabad's prime real estate and some of the most expensive properties in the city. It's near Film City, home to the city's film industry, and is not far from HITEC City or the many malls and shopping complexes of Banjara Hills. As this is what Indians term "a posh locality," your monthly rent could easily reach into the ₹45,000-plus range, especially if your agent believes that you have a large housing rental allowance. However, if you look around, you can probably find an unfurnished two-bedroom around ₹13,000–18,000 per month.

Banjara Hills

Banjara Hills is a little closer to the city center than Jubilee Hills, but a bit farther to HITECH city. Rental properties in this area are slightly less expensive than in Jubilee Hills. It is also a busy commercial area with lots of shopping malls and thoroughfares, so you might find it too congested for your liking, especially during rush hour. At the same time, you won't have to journey far if you want to go shopping or explore Hyderabad's bustling city center. Although there are plenty of luxury apartment complexes to choose from in this area, there are also older pockets of Banjara Hills where one-bedroom unfurnished apartments can be rented for as little as ₹8,000 per month.

Gachibowli

More and more expats have moved to Gachibowli in recent years, partly because it's where some of the major employers of foreigners, such as Microsoft and Infosys, have their offices. It's also close enough to HITEC City to make it a plausible alternative to Jubilee Hills. Gachibowli offers everything from studio apartments to sprawling houses, and rents here are comparable to those in Banjara Hills. However, it doesn't have as many malls and entertainment options as Banjara Hills or even Jubilee Hills, although this might change in the years to come as the neighborhood continues to grow.

Secunderabad

On the north side of Hussain Sagar Lake sits Hyderabad's twin city. Housing here is much cheaper than in Hyderabad—expect to pay as little as ₹6,000 per month for a two-bedroom house on the outskirts or about ₹9,000 per month in the city center. It only makes sense to live here if your office is nearby. If you have children enrolled in one of the schools in Hyderabad, you might choose to commute there instead. Depending on where you are working and what time you go to the office, your commute could be anything from half an hour to an hour or more, depending on traffic.

Hyderabad's Hussain Sagar Lake

© MARGOT BIGG

PRIME LIVING LOCATIONS

Although Secunderabad is very developed and there's no shortage of shopping or entertainment options, it doesn't have as many expats as some of Hyderabad's neighborhoods.

DAILY LIFE
Language and Health Care
The local language in Hyderabad is Telugu, although English, Hindi, and Urdu are widely spoken. Most signs are in English or in a combination of English and Telugu. Finding domestic help and drivers who speak at least some English is not usually a problem, and the easiest way to find help is through the expat grapevine. As there are a lot of foreign companies in Hyderabad, expats come in and out of the city quite frequently, so you may be able to hire someone who has worked with other foreigners in the past.

The best hospital in town is arguably Apollo Hospital in Jubilee Hills. They also have a branch in Secunderabad.

Expat Social Scene
The twin cities have a good infrastructure for expats, although sometimes people in Secunderabad feel a bit geographically isolated from all the fun. Many expats report that their social circles revolve around the industry in which they work, although that often happens whether you are at home or abroad. To meet other expats, the best way to start is to join the Twin-cities Expatriate Association of Hyderabad and Secunderabad. The club holds weekly meetings and publishes a guidebook for expats new to the area. People based in Secunderabad, however, may find that the club's meetings, held in Jubilee Hills' Walden Club, are too far away to attend.

Education
The International School of Hyderabad is the most popular school for expat children, and it offers IB education. Other IB options include the Oakridge International School and Indus International School (the latter only runs through grade 10). Sloka International School uses the Waldorf Education model, a rarity in India, and admits children preschool–grade 8. Some expats also enroll their children in Sreenidhi School, although they are not currently IB accredited.

Shopping
You may find that much of your life in Hyderabad is centered around shopping malls and large stores, simply because there are so many of these in the

© MARGOT BIGG

traffic in Hyderabad

city's expat enclaves. Although there are plenty of large local supermarkets in Hyderabad, including Reliance Fresh and Food Bazaar, they don't always stock a large selection of foreign foods. For a wide selection of imported goods, try Q-Mart in Banjara Hills. Another popular shopping spot is Pure O Natural, just down the street from Q-Mart, which is best known for its fresh organic produce.

GETTING AROUND

Although Hyderabad has a bus system, it's pretty shoddy, and very few expats rely on it. Autorickshaws ply the city, and most will automatically use their meters. If they refuse to do so, simply hail another vehicle. A few rickshaw drivers might try to take you to a jewelry store en route to your destination in the hope of getting a fat commission on any pearls or bangles you might buy. Another option is to buy your own car or motor scooter. If you are working in one of the major tech parks, your employer may offer you the option of a shuttle taxi or bus, which will ferry you and colleagues living in your area to and from work every day.

Pune

India's quintessential "college town," the Maharashtrian city of Pune is arguably one of the most comfortable cities in India to live in. It has year-round
sunshine and is at the same time smallish and cosmopolitan. Many foreigners
move to Pune to work in the IT industry or to study at one of the little city's
many colleges and universities. Pune also draws in a lot of overseas followers
of the guru Osho (formerly known as Bhagwan Rajneesh, Oregon's infamous
Rolls Royce guru, for anyone old enough to remember). You can spot devotees
by their ashram-issued maroon-colored robes. Pune was once the capital of the
Maratha Empire and is often touted as the cultural capital of the state, and
many dance and music festivals are hosted in the city every year.

WHERE TO LIVE

Prices in the housing rental market in Pune are rising rapidly as more companies open offices in the little city. A quick increase in new development, however, such as those in Viman Nagar, are helping to even things out. Deposits
on apartments here range from 2–6 months' rent.

Koregaon Park

The clean and green Koregaon Park is traditionally the most popular place
for expats, and it is also one of the more expensive parts of Pune. It's home
to quaint coffee shops and restaurants as well as the Osho ashram, so it's one
of the few places in India that is a hub for tourists and expats alike. Many
of the apartments available are in complexes, some of which come with the
benefit of backup electricity and guards. You'll be hard-pressed to find a one-
bedroom apartment here for less than ₹7,000 per month, and two-bedrooms
range ₹15,000–30,000 per month. Large bungalows with 3–4 bedrooms
occasionally go on the rental market starting at about ₹75,000 per month,
although competition for these is fierce.

Kalyani Nagar

Kalyani Nagar is a mixed residential and commercial neighborhood that is one
of Pune's more vibrant areas. It is home to many bars and restaurants as well
as shopping malls and cinemas, and it is linked to Koregaon Park by a bridge,
making commutes between the two areas fairly easy. Many large companies
also have their headquarters here. An unfurnished two-bedroom apartment
costs ₹12,000–25,000 per month, and a three-bedroom will set you back a
minimum of ₹20,000 per month.

Viman Nagar

The up-and-coming Viman Nagar is close to the airport, making it a popular place for people who have to travel a lot. Companies often rent apartments here as well, so if your employer does your house hunt for you, you may find yourself here. It's a newer development, and some of the properties can come across as a bit cookie-cutter, but this isn't always a bad thing in India, where old charm sometimes equates to falling apart. There are also quite a few offices in the area, and the Symbiosis International School and colleges are located here. Two-bedroom apartments in this area start around ₹10,000 per month, and three-bedrooms start at around ₹16,000. Houses are also available, some of which have small yards. Expect to pay ₹22,000–26,000 for an unfurnished four-bedroom.

Aundh

In western Pune, Aundh is popular with students and young tech types due to its proximity to the Hinjewadi IT Park and to many business schools and universities, such as Symbiosis and the University of Pune. This is a younger area, although not as trendy as Koregaon Park. You can rent a room in a shared apartment for as little as ₹4,500 per month, or opt for paying guest accommodations rates, which include food, at around ₹3,500 per month.

DAILY LIFE

Pune is a laid-back city with a youthful vibe, plenty of foreign faces, and infrastructure for a comfortable life. Due to its status as both an IT hub and a college town, the upscale parts of Pune remain fairly cosmopolitan, although pockets can be very traditional. The majority language here is Marathi, although seemingly everyone knows Hindi, and most people know enough English to get by.

Expat Social Scene

Expats from all over the world come to Pune to work and study. There's a large contingent of students from Iran and call-center employees from the States. Expats tend to meet each other at work or at school, although another good place to meet people is at the German Bakery, in Koregaon Park across from the Osho ashram. Pune's most beloved institution for foreigners, the German Bakery made international headlines in February 2010 when it fell victim to a terrorist attack. However, the restaurant was quickly rebuilt and brought back to life as one of the top hangouts for foreigners in Pune.

Health Care

Medical care in Pune is high-quality and widely available. Expats in Koregaon Park can seek treatment from their local Inlaks and Budhrani Hospital. Farther out, the Ruby Hall Clinic and the nearby Jehangir Hospital are among the most respected in the city.

Education

Many of Pune's expatriate children attend the Mercedes-Benz International School (MBIS), in Hinjewadi, which was set up specifically to serve Pune's international community. MBIS offers preschool–12 education, and the high school follows the IB curriculum. Boarding is also available. The Symbiosis International School in Viman Nagar offers IGCSE and IB programs and is run by the same company that runs the many Symbiosis universities across Pune. The Sharad Pawar International School offers K–12 education and an IB curriculum, although its campus is inconveniently far north of the city center.

Shopping

Shopping in Pune is decent, with plenty of malls as well as Moledina Road; MG Road also has a few large apparel shops selling both Indian and Western clothes. Cheap clothes for the college crowd can be found at Fashion Street, an open-air market behind MG Road, but you'll have to haggle. The best place to buy imported foods is Dorajbee's Supermarket on Moledina Road, which also has a decent bakery. If you are on the west side of town, you can pick up a few imported basics at the smaller Fine Foods in Aundh.

GETTING AROUND

Pune's buses are hot and crowded, so most expats rely on autorickshaws or cars to get around. Autorickshaws will usually go by the meter during the day but prefer to haggle a fixed rate at night. Pune's population has grown drastically in recent years, as has car ownership in India, so traffic is getting progressively worse. Pune is relatively small and easy to get around, so many expats, especially younger ones without families, opt to invest in a small scooter or motorcycle.

RESOURCES

Embassies and Consulates

AUSTRALIA
HIGH COMMISSION OF INDIA IN CANBERRA
3-5 Moonah Place
Yarralumla, ACT 2600
tel. 02/6273-3999
www.hcindia-au.org

CANADA
HIGH COMMISSION OF INDIA IN OTTAWA
10 Springfield Rd.
Ottawa, ON K1M 1C9
tel. 613/688-5335
www.hciottawa.ca

INDIA
AUSTRALIAN HIGH COMMISSION
1/50-G Shantipath, Chanakyapuri
Delhi 110021
tel. 011/4139-9900
www.india.embassy.gov.au

BRITISH HIGH COMMISSION
Chanakyapuri
New Delhi 110021
tel. 011/2419-2100
http://ukinindia.fco.gov.uk

CANADIAN HIGH COMMISSION
7/8 Shantipath, Chanakyapuri
New Delhi 1100210
tel. 011/4178-2000
www.canadainternational.gc.ca

U.S. CONSULATE GENERAL CHENNAI
Gemini Circle
Chennai 600006
tel. 044/2857-4000
http://chennai.usconsulate.gov

U.S. CONSULATE GENERAL HYDERABAD
1-8-323 Chiran Fort Lane
Begumpet, Secunderabad 500003
tel. 40/4033-8300
http://hyderabad.usconsulate.gov

U.S. CONSULATE GENERAL KOLKATA
5/1 Ho Chi Minh Sarani
Kolkata 700071
tel. 033/3984-2400
http://kolkata.usconsulate.gov

U.S. CONSULATE GENERAL MUMBAI
Lincoln House
78 Bhulabhai Desai Rd.
Mumbai 400026
tel. 022/2363-3611
http://mumbai.usconsulate.gov

U.S. EMBASSY
Shantipath, Chanakyapuri
Delhi 110021
tel. 011/2419-8000
http://newdelhi.usembassy.gov

UNITED KINGDOM
HIGH COMMISSION OF INDIA IN LONDON
24 Grosvenor Square
London W1A 1AE
tel. 020/7499-9000
www.hcilondon.in

UNITED STATES
CONSULATE GENERAL OF INDIA–CHICAGO
55 N. Cityfront Plaza Dr.
Chicago, IL 60611
tel. 312/595-0405
http://chicago.indianconsulate.com

CONSULATE GENERAL OF INDIA–HOUSTON
1990 Post Oak Blvd., Suite 600
Houston, TX 77056
tel. 713/626-2148
www.cgihouston.org

CONSULATE GENERAL OF INDIA–NEW YORK
3 E. 64th St.
New York, NY 10065
tel. 212/774-0600
www.indiacgny.org

CONSULATE GENERAL
OF INDIA–SAN FRANCISCO
540 Arguello Blvd.
San Francisco, CA 94118
tel. 415/668-0662
www.cgisf.org

EMBASSY OF INDIA IN
WASHINGTON, D.C.
Consular Wing
2536 Massachusetts Ave. NW
Washington, DC 20008
tel. 202/939-9888
www.indianembassy.org

Planning Your Fact-Finding Trip

TRAVEL RESOURCES
DESTINATION INDIA TRAVEL
CENTRE
78 Janpath, 1st Fl.
New Delhi 110001
tel. 011/2371-2345, 011/4375-0005,
011/4375-0008
www.indiatripmakers.com
This Delhi-based travel agency is a reliable favorite among expats and overseas visitors, and it is recommended by the Ministry of Tourism.

INCREDIBLE INDIA
www.incredibleindia.org
Official travel portal of the Indian Ministry of Tourism.

INDIA MIKE
www.indiamike.com
Online travel message boards and user reviews.

TRAVEL GURU
www.travelguru.com
Online hotel booking.

Making the Move

VISA SERVICES
Visa services in many countries have been outsourced to visa service providers. In most cases, you have to apply for your Indian visa directly with the visa service provider in your home country.

Australia
(Managed by VFS Global)
INDIA VISA APPLICATION CENTRE
P.O. Box 936
Civic Square, ACT 2608
tel. 03/9001-0189
www.vfs-in-au.net

Canada
(Managed by VFS Global)
INDIAN VISA AND CONSULAR
SERVICES CENTRE
384 Bank St., Suite 220
Ottawa, ON K2P 1Y4

tel. 613/686-3810
www.in.vfsglobal.ca

United Kingdom
(Managed by VFS Global)
INDIA VISA APPLICATION CENTRE
60-62 Wilton Rd.
Victoria, London SW1V 1DE
tel. 090/5757-0045
http://in.vfsglobal.co.uk

United States
(Managed by Travisa
Outsourcing)
INDIA VISA CENTER CHICAGO
120 S. State St., Unit 3
Chicago, IL 60602
tel. 312/332-1161
www.travisaoutsourcing.com

RESOURCES

INDIA VISA CENTER HOUSTON
4550 Post Oak Place, Suite 251
Houston, TX 77027
tel. 713/961-3500
www.travisaoutsourcing.com

INDIA VISA CENTER NEW YORK
290 5th Ave., 4th Fl.
New York, NY 10002
tel. 212/613-2223
www.travisaoutsourcing.com

**INDIA VISA CENTER
SAN FRANCISCO**
41 Sutter St., Suite 214
San Francisco, CA 94103
tel. 415/644-0149
www.travisaoutsourcing.com

**INDIA VISA CENTER
WASHINGTON, DC**
1010 Wisconsin Ave. NW, Suite 100
Washington, DC 20007
tel. 202/463-6166
www.travisaoutsourcing.com

IMMIGRATION AND FOREIGNERS REGIONAL REGISTRATION OFFICES (FRROS)

FRRO BENGALURU
Infantry Rd., Vasanth Nagar
tel. 080/226-0707

FRRO CHENNAI
Shastri Bhawan
26 Haddows Rd., Chennai
tel. 044/2345-4970

FRRO DELHI
East Block-VIII, Level-II
Sector-1, R.K. Puram
tel. 011/26711443

FRRO KOLKATA
237 Acharya Jagdish
Chandra Bose Rd.
tel. 033/2247-0549

FRRO MUMBAI
3rd Fl., Special Branch Bldg.
Badruddin Tayabji Lane (Behind St. Xavier's College)
tel. 022/2262-0446

INDIAN MINISTRIES
MINISTRY OF HEALTH AND FAMILY WELFARE
Nirman Bhavan, Maulana Azad Rd.
New Delhi 110011
tel. 011/2316-5413
http://mohfw.nic.in

MINISTRY OF HOME AFFAIRS
North Block, Central Secretariat
New Delhi 110001
tel. 011/2309-2011
www.mha.nic.in

MINISTRY OF HUMAN RESOURCE DEVELOPMENT
Shastri Bhawan, Dr. Rajendra Prasad Rd.
New Delhi 110011
tel. 011/2338-1355
www.education.nic.in

MOVERS AND SHIPPERS
AGS FOUR WINDS
www.agsfourwinds.com

PM RELOCATIONS
www.pmrelocations.com

Housing Considerations

REAL ESTATE

GLOBAL ADJUSTMENTS
www.globaladjustments.com
National company specializing in relocation support for expats.

MAGICBRICKS
www.magicbricks.com
Online real estate listings.

99ACRES
www.99acres.com
Online real estate listings.

PROPERTYWALA
www.propertywala.com
Online real estate listings.

SULEKHA
www.sulekha.com
Online real estate listings.

Language and Education

HINDI LANGUAGE PROGRAMS

AMERICAN INSTITUTE FOR INDIAN STUDIES
22, Sector-32, Institutional Area
Gurgaon 122001, Haryana
tel. 0124/238-1424
www.indiastudies.org

BHASHA BHARTI
Varanasi, Uttar Pradesh
tel. 0542/242-0447
www.bhashabharati.com

EAST WEST LANGUAGE SCHOOL (EWLI)
Nizzamudin, New Delhi
tel. 098/1888-4748
www.eastwestlanguage.com
Started by a former Landour Language School teacher and uses the same textbook and methodology.

HINDI GURU
Panscheel Park, New Delhi
tel. 011/6563-5674
www.hindiguru.org

LANDOUR LANGUAGE SCHOOL
Landour, Mussoorie, Uttarakhand
tel. 0135/263-1487
www.landourlanguageschool.com
India's oldest and most reputable language school. Offers private and group tuition in Hindi, Urdu, Punjabi, and Garhwali.

BENGALI LANGUAGE PROGRAMS

RAMAKRISHNA MISSION INSTITUTE OF CULTURE
Golpark, Kolkata
tel. 033/2464-1303
http://sriramakrishna.org

TAMIL LANGUAGE PROGRAMS

INSTITUTE OF ASIAN STUDIES, CHENNAI
Sholinganallur, Chennai
tel. 044/2450-2212
www.xlweb.com/heritage/asian/

UNIVERSITIES

BANGALORE UNIVERSITY
Jnana Bharathi
Bengaluru 560056
tel. 080/2296-1006
www.bub.ernet.in

BENARES HINDU UNIVERSITY
Varanasi 221005
tel. 0542/236-8938
www.bhu.ac.in

RESOURCES

JAMIA MILIA ISLAMIA
Mohammad Ali Johar Marg, Jamia Nagar,
Okhla
New Delhi 110025
tel. 011/2698-1717
www.jamiahamdard.edu

JAWAHARLAL NEHRU UNIVERSITY
New Mehrauli Rd.
New Delhi 110067
tel. 011/2674-2676
www.jnu.ac.in

UNIVERSITY OF CALCUTTA
Senate House, 87/1 College St.
Kolkata 700073
tel. 033/2241-0071
www.caluniv.ac.in

UNIVERSITY OF DELHI
tel. 011/2766-7011
www.du.ac.in

UNIVERSITY OF MUMBAI
MG Rd., Fort
Mumbai 400032
tel. 022/2265-2819
www.unom.ac.in

UNIVERSITY OF PUNE
Ganeshkhind
Pune 411007
tel. 020/2560-1099
www.unipune.ac.in

Health

HEALTH INFORMATION
MINISTRY OF HEALTH AND FAMILY WELFARE
Nirman Bhavan, Maulana Azad Rd.
New Delhi 110011
tel. 011/2316-5413
http://mohfw.nic.in

U.S. CENTERS FOR DISEASE CONTROL AND PREVENTION: INDIA INFORMATION
http://wwwnc.cdc.gov/travel/destinations/india.aspx

WORLD HEALTH ORGANIZATION
537 A Wing, Nirman Bhavan, Maulana Azad Rd.
New Delhi 110011
tel. 011/4759-4800
www.whoindia.org

INTERNATIONAL HEALTH INSURANCE

AETNA
www.aetna.com

PACIFIC PRIME
www.pacificprime.com

EMERGENCY PHONE NUMBERS
• National Emergency Number: 108
• Ambulance: 102
• Fire: 101
• Police: 100

Employment

JOB WEBSITES
EXCHANGE 4 MEDIA
http://exchange4media.com

MONSTER
www.monsterindia.com

NAUKRI
www.naukri.com

NAUKRI HUB
www.naukrihub.com

NGO JOBS
www.ngojobs.in

TIMES JOBS
www.timesjobs.com

Finance

BANKS
CITIBANK
www.citibank.co.in

DEUTSCHE BANK
www.deutschebank.co.in

HDFC BANK
www.hdfc.com

HSBC
www.hsbc.co.in

STATE BANK OF INDIA
www.statebankofindia.com

TAXES
ASTRAL CONSULTANTS
www.astralconsultants.com

DELOITTE
www.deloitte.com

INCOME TAX DEPARTMENT
www.incometaxindia.gov.in

PRICEWATERHOUSECOOPERS
www.pwc.com/in/en

SETH ASSOCIATES
www.sethassociates.com

Communications

TELEPHONE SERVICE PROVIDERS
AIRTEL
www.airtel.in

BSNL
www.bsnl.co.in

IDEA
www.ideacellular.com

RELIANCE
www.rcom.co.in

TATA INDICOM
www.tataindicom.com

VIRGIN MOBILE
www.virginmobile.in

VODAFONE
www.vodafone.in

RESOURCES

INTERNET SERVICE PROVIDERS

AIRTEL
www.airtel.in

BSNL
www.bsnl.co.in

RELIANCE
www.rcom.co.in

TATA INDICOM
www.tataindicom.com

TELEVISION SERVICE PROVIDERS

AIRTEL DIGITAL TV
www.airtel.in/digitaltv

RELIANCE BIG TV
www.bigtv.co.in

TATA SKY
www.tatasky.com

MEDIA

THE HINDU
www.hindu.com

HINDUSTAN TIMES
www.hindustantimes.com

INDIAN EXPRESS
www.indianexpress.com

NDTV
www.ndtv.com

TIMES OF INDIA
www.timesofindia.indiatimes.com

ZEE NEWS
www.zeenews.com

POSTAL AND COURIER SERVICES

BLAZEFLASH
www.blazeflash.com

BLUEDART
www.bluedart.com

DHL
www.dhl.co.in

FEDEX
www.fedex.com/in/

INDIA POST
www.indiapost.gov.in

MIRAKLE COURIERS
www.miraklecouriers.com

Travel and Transportation

AIRLINES

GO AIR
www.goair.in
Domestic carrier.

INDIAN AIRLINES
www.indian-airlines.nic.in
Domestic and international carrier.

INDIGO
www.goindigo.in
Domestic carrier.

JET AIRWAYS
www.jetairways.com
Domestic carrier.

KINGFISHER
www.flykingfisher.com
Domestic and international carrier.

SPICEJET
www.spicejet.com
Domestic carrier.

AIRLINE RESERVATION WEBSITES

CLEARTRIP
www.cleartrip.com

MAKEMYTRIP
www.MakeMyTrip.com

YATRA
www.yatra.com

TRAIN TRAVEL
INDIAN RAIL TICKET BOOKING SITE
www.irctc.co.in

INDIAN RAIL TRAIN ENQUIRY
www.indianrail.gov.in

Prime Living Locations

DELHI AND THE NCR

Expat Resources
DELHINET
www.groups.yahoo.com/group/DelhiNet

DELHI NETWORK
www.delhinetwork.org

DILLINET
http://dillinet.ning.com

GURGAON CONNECTION
http://gurgaonconnection.com

YUNI-NET
www.groups.yahoo.com/group/Yuni-Net

Health Care
ALL INDIA INSTITUTE OF MEDICAL STUDIES
tel. 011/2658-8500
www.aiims.edu

APOLLO HOSPITAL
Sarita Vihar
Delhi-Mathura Rd.
New Delhi 110044
tel. 011/2692-5858
www.apollohospdelhi.com

EAST WEST MEDICAL CENTRE
28 Greater Kailash I
New Delhi 110048
tel. 011/2464-1494

FORTIS ESCORTS HEART INSTITUTE
Okhla Rd.
New Delhi 110025
tel. 011/4713-5000
www.fortisescorts.in

MAX HOSPITAL (DELHI)
2 Press Enclave Rd., Saket
New Delhi 110017
tel. 011/2651-5050
www.maxhealthcare.in

MAX HOSPITAL (GURGAON)
B-Block, Sushant Lok-I
Gurgaon 122001
tel. 0124/662-3000
www.maxhealthcare.in

MAX HOSPITAL (NOIDA)
A-364, Sector 19
Noida 20130
tel. 0120/254-9999
www.maxhealthcare.in

PARAS HOSPITAL
C-1 Block, Sushant Lok, Phase-I, Sector-43
Gurgaon 122002
tel. 0124/458-5666
www.parashospitals.com

Education
AMERICAN EMBASSY SCHOOL
Chandragupta Marg, Chanakyapuri
New Delhi 110021
tel. 011/2688-8854
www.aes.ac.in

RESOURCES

BRITISH SCHOOL
San Martin Marg, Chanakyapuri
New Delhi 110021
tel. 011/2410-2183
www.british-school.org

DEUTSCH SCHULE
2 Nyaya Marg, Chanakyapuri
New Delhi 110021
tel. 011/4168-0240
www.dsnd.de

THE FRENCH SCHOOL
2 Aurangzeb Rd.
Delhi 110011
tel. 011/3042-0090
www.efdelhi.org

PATHWAYS WORLD SCHOOL
Aravali Retreat
Gurgaon 122001
tel. 0124/231-8888
www.pathways.in

MUMBAI

Expat Resources
THE AMERICAN WOMEN'S CLUB OF BOMBAY
www.awcbombay.com

BOMBAY EXPATS
http://groups.yahoo.com/group/bombayexpats

BRANNIGAN RELOCATIONS
www.branniganrelo.com

BRITISH BUSINESS GROUP
www.bbgmumbai.org

THE HUB
http://the-hub.net

MUMBAI CONNEXIONS
www.mumbaiconnexions.com

Health Care
BREACH CANDY
Bhulabhai Desai Marg, Breach Candy
Mumbai 40002
tel. 022/2366-7788
www.breachcandyhospital.org

FORTIS
Mini Seashore Rd., Sector-10, Vashi
Navi Mumbai 400703
tel. 022/3919-9222
www.fortishealthcare.com

HOLY FAMILY
St Andrew's Rd., Bandra (West)
Mumbai 400050
tel. 022/3061-0555
www.bandraholyfamilyhospital.org

LILAVATI HOSPITAL
A-791, Bandra Reclamation, Bandra (West)
Mumbai 400050
tel. 022/2675-1000
www.lilavatihospital.com

TATA MEMORIAL HOSPITAL
Dr. E. Borges Rd., Parel
Mumbai 400012
tel. 022/2416-2120
www.tatamemorialcentre.com

Education
AMERICAN SCHOOL
Bandra Kurla Complex Rd., Bandra East
Mumbai 400051
tel. 022/6772-7272
www.asbindia.org

DHIRUBHAI AMBANI INTERNATIONAL SCHOOL
Bandra Kurla Complex, Bandra (East)
Mumbai, 400098
tel. 022/4061-7000
www.da-is.org

ÉCOLE MONDIALE
Gulmohar Cross Rd., No. 9, JVPD Scheme, Juhu
Mumbai, 400049
tel. 022/2623-7265
www.ecolemondiale.org

OBEROI INTERNATIONAL SCHOOL
Western Express Hwy., Goregaon East
Mumbai, 400063
tel. 022/4236-3131
www.oberoi-is.org

BENGALURU

Expat Resources
BANGALORE EXPATRIATE CLUB
www.bangalore-expatriate-club.com

BANGALORE EXPATS
www.groups.yahoo.com/group/bangalore_expats

THE IVES CLUB
www.ives.in

THE OVERSEAS WOMEN'S CLUB OF BANGALORE
www.owcbangalore.org

Health Care
COLUMBIA ASIA HOSPITAL
Kirloskar Business Park, Bellary Rd., Hebbal
Bengaluru 560024
tel. 080/4179-1000
www.columbiaasia.com

FORTIS HOSPITAL (FORMERLY WOCKHARDT HOSPITAL)
154/9 Bannerghatta Rd., Opp. IIM-B
Bengaluru 560076
tel. 080/6621-4444
www.fortishospitals.in

MALLYA HOSPITAL
No. 2, Vittal Mallya Rd.
Bengaluru 560001
tel. 080/2227-7979
www.mallyahospital.net

MANIPAL HOSPITAL
98 HAL Airport Rd.
Bengaluru 560017
tel. 080/2502-4444
www.manipalhospital.org

Education
BANGALORE INTERNATIONAL SCHOOL
Hennur Bagalur Rd., Kothanur Post
Bengaluru 560077
tel. 080/2846-5060
www.bangaloreinternationalschool.com

BISHOP COTTONS
St. Mark's Rd.
Bengaluru 560001
tel. 080/2221-3608
www.bishopcottons.com

INDUS INTERNATIONAL SCHOOL
Billapura Cross, Sarjapur
Bengaluru 562125
tel. 080/2289-5900
www.indusschool.com

THE INTERNATIONAL SCHOOL BANGALORE
NAFL Valley, Whitefield-Sarjapur Rd.,
Near Dommasandra Circle
Bengaluru 562125
tel. 080/2263-4900
www.tisb.org

INVENTURE ACADEMY
Whitefield-Sarjapur Rd.,
Near Dommasandra Circle
Bengaluru 562125
tel. 080/782-2102
www.inventureacademy.com

AHMEDABAD

Expat Resources
AHMEDABAD RELOCATION
www.ahmedabadrelocation.com

Health Care
SHALBY HOSPITAL
Opp. Karnavati Club, S G Rd.
Ahmedabad 380015
tel. 079/4020-3000
www.shalby.org

STERLING HOSPITAL
Sterling Hospital Rd., Memnagar
Ahmedabad 380052
tel. 079/2743-7333
www.sterlinghospitals.com

Education
THE MAHATMA GANDHI INTERNATIONAL SCHOOL
tel. 079/2646-3888
www.mgis.in

RESOURCES

THE SGVP INTERNATIONAL SCHOOL
tel. 02717/24-2138
www.sgvp.org

JAIPUR

Expat Resources
AIESEC
G-59 Laxmi Complex, MI Rd.
Jaipur 302001
tel. 0141/402-0334
www.aiesecjaipur.com

Health Care
FORTIS HOSPITAL
Jawahar Lal Nehru Marg, Malviya Nagar
Jaipur 324010
tel. 0141/254-7000
www.fortishealthcare.com

MANU HOSPITAL
Saket Nagar, Shyam Nagar
Jaipur 302019
tel. 0141/229-2530
www.manuhospital.com

Education
INDIA INTERNATIONAL SCHOOL
Kshipra Path, Opposite VT Rd., Mansarovar
Jaipur 302020
tel. 0141/239-7906
www.iisjaipur.org

STEP-BY-STEP
3 Chitrakoot Scheme, Ajmer Rd.
Jaipur 302021
tel. 0141/413-2222
www.sbshigh.net

KOLKATA

Expat Resources
KOLKATA INTERNATIONAL WOMEN'S CLUB
kolkatakiwc@gmail.com

RABINDRANATH TAGORE CENTER
9A Ho Chi Minh Sarani
Kolkata 700071
tel: 033/2287-2680
www.tagorecentreiccr.org

Health
AMRI HOSPITAL
P-4&5, CIT Scheme-LXXII
Block-A, Gariahat Rd.
Kolkata 700029
tel. 033/2461-2626
www.amrihospital.com

BHAGIRATHI NEOTIA HOSPITAL
2, Rawdon St.
Kolkata 700017
tel. 033/4040-5000
www.neotiahospital.com

COLUMBIA ASIA HOSPITAL
Salt Lake IB-193, Sector-III
Kolkata 700091
tel. 033/3989-8969
www.columbiaasia.com

WOODLANDS HOSPITAL AND MEDICAL RESEARCH CENTRE
8/5 Alipore Rd., Alipore H.O.
Kolkata 700027
tel. 033/2456-7075
www.woodlandhospital.in

Education
AMERICAN SCHOOL KOLKATA
5/1, Ho Chi Minh Sarani
Kolkata 700071
tel. 033/3984-2400
http://askolkata.org

CALCUTTA INTERNATIONAL SCHOOL
724, Anandapur
Kolkata 700107
tel. 033/2443-2054
www.calcuttais.edu.in

ST. XAVIER'S COLLEGIATE SCHOOL
30 Mother Teresa Sarani
Kolkata 700020
tel. 033/2280-5197

CHENNAI

Expat Resources
BRITISH BUSINESS SOCIAL CLUB
www.bbscchennai.com

CHENNAI HASH HARRIERS
www.madrashash.com

Health Care
APOLLO HOSPITAL
21 Greams Lane
Chennai 600006
tel. 044/2829-0200
www.apollohospitals.com

Education
AMERICAN INTERNATIONAL SCHOOL
100 Feet Rd., Tharamani
Chennai 600113
tel. 044/2254-9000
www.aisch.org

THE BRITISH INTERNATIONAL SCHOOL
2/628, Sultan Ahmed St., Neelankarai
Chennai 600041
tel. 044/4213-8400
www.britishschool.in

GATEWAY INTERNATIONAL SCHOOL
ECR, Neelankarai 2/664, Ranga Reddy Garden
Chennai 600041
tel. 044/6450-0000
www.gatewayschools.in

VAEL'S BILLABONG INTERNATIONAL HIGH
480, 3rd Main Rd., Sri Kapaleeswara Nagar, ECR, Neelankarai
Chennai 600041
tel. 044/2449-2292
www.vaelsbillabonghigh.com

GOA

Health Care
APOLLO VICTOR HOSPITAL
Malbhat, Margao
Goa 403601
tel. 0832/272-5725
www.apollovictorhospital.com

Education
SHARADA MANDIR SCHOOL
Miramar Panaji
Goa 403001
tel. 0832/246-3401
www.sharadamandir.edu.in

THE SUNSHINE SCHOOL
20/1-B, Baiguinim, off NH-4A Bypass
Kadamba Rd.
Old Goa 403402
tel. 0832/329-0538
www.sunshineschoolgoa.com

HYDERABAD AND SECUNDERABAD

Expat Resources
TWIN-CITIES EXPATRIATES ASSOCIATION OF HYDERABAD AND SECUNDERABAD
www.hytea.org

Health Care
APOLLO HOSPITAL (HYDERABAD)
Jubilee Hills
Hyderabad 500033
tel. 040/2360-7777
www.apollohospitals.com

APOLLO HOSPITAL (SECUNDERABAD)
Vikrampuri Colony, Rajiv Gandhi Marg
Secunderabad 500003
tel. 040/2343-3620
www.apollohospitals.com

Education
INDUS INTERNATIONAL SCHOOL
tel. 08417/30-2100
www.indusschool.com

THE INTERNATIONAL SCHOOL OF HYDERABAD
ICRISAT-Patancheru
Hyderabad 502324
tel. 040/3071-3869
www.ishyd.org

OAKRIDGE INTERNATIONAL SCHOOL
Khajaguda, Nanakramguda Rd.
Hyderabad 500008
tel. 040/2004-2460
www.oakridgeinternational.com

RESOURCES

PUNE

Expat Resources
PUNE EXPATS CLUB
www.puneexpatclub.com

PUNE EXPATS FORUM
www.pune-expats.lefora.com

Health Care
INLAKS AND BUDHRANI HOSPITAL
7-9 Koregaon Park
Pune 411001
tel. 020/6609-9999
www.inlaksbudhranihospital.com

JEHANGIR HOSPITAL
32, Sassoon Rd.
Pune 411001
tel. 020/2605-0550
www.jehangircares.com

RUBY HALL CLINIC
40 Sassoon Rd.
Pune 411001
tel. 020/2612-3391
www.rubyhall.com

Education
MERCEDES-BENZ INTERNATIONAL SCHOOL
P-26 MIDC Phase 1, Rajiv Gandhi Infotech Park, Hinjiwadi
Pune 411057
tel. 020/2293-4420
www.mbis.org

SHARAD PAWAR INTERNATIONAL SCHOOL
Charoli Budruk, Taluka Haveli
Pune 411012
tel. 020/3061-2700
www.internationalschool.in

THE SYMBIOSIS INTERNATIONAL SCHOOL
Symbiosis Vimannagar Campus
Pune 411014
tel. 020/2663-4550
www.symbiosisinternationalschool.net

Public Holidays

NATIONAL HOLIDAYS
India's secular national holidays are recognized nationwide. Banks and government institutions are closed on these days:

January 26	Republic Day
August 15	Independence Day
October 2	Gandhi Jayanti (Mahatma Gandhi's birthday)

RELIGIOUS HOLIDAYS
India has hundreds of religious festivals and holidays rooted in the many different religions found in the country. Certain businesses and government institutions close for some or all of these holidays.

Here are a few of the most celebrated, most of which happen on different dates every year:

Christmas	December 25
Diwali	October or November
Dussehra	October
Eid al-Adha	Varies
Eid ul-Fitr	Varies
Good Friday	March or April
Guru Nanak Jayanti	November
Holi	March
Mahavir Jayanti	March or April
Rama Navami	March or April

Glossary

ashram a Hindu hermitage, often focused on yoga or meditation

autorickshaw a three-wheeled taxi built on top of a motor scooter chassis; known as a *tuk-tuk* in other parts of the world

ayah nanny

ayurveda India's traditional health system

bazaar market

Bollywood Mumbai's Hindi film industry

chai tea

chappal open-toed sandal

crore 10,000,000

cycle rickshaw a three-wheeled combination of a bicycle and a cart used to ferry passengers short distances

dal lentils

Devanagari the script used to write Hindi and some other Indian languages

dhobi person who irons and washes clothing

FIR First Information Report (police report)

FRRO Foreigners Regional Registration Office

firang foreigner

GOI Government of India

gurudwara Sikh place of worship

Jyotish Indian astrology

lakh 100,000

MHA Ministry of Home Affairs

MRP Maximum Retail Price

mandir Hindu temple

masjid mosque

NCR National Capital Region

NRI Non-Resident Indian; refers to Indians who no longer reside in India or have spent much of their lives overseas

OCI Overseas Citizen of India, the closest thing India has to dual citizenship

PAN card Personal Account Number card, similar to a U.S. Social Security card or a British National Insurance number card

PIO Person of Indian Origin, a legal status that allows residency rights to people whose spouse, parents, grandparents, or great-grandparents are from India

paan a mix of herbs and spices wrapped in a betel leaf and chewed, especially after meals

paisa 0.01 rupee

rupee India's currency, often abbreviated to Rs. or INR. Its sign, devised in July 2010, is ₹

wallah generic suffix used to imply "doer," "maker," or "seller." For example, a *paan wallah* makes and sells *paan*.

Hindi Phrasebook

Hindi translations by Abhimanyu Singh Sisodia

PRONUNCIATION GUIDE

Although Hindi is an Indo-European language that shares its early roots with English, there are many sounds that nonnative speakers find difficult to pronounce. Unlike English, Hindi is spelled phonetically when written in its official Devanagari alphabet. Some sounds don't exist in English or don't have an equivalent in the Roman alphabet. In this case, we've provided the closest possible English equivalent.

Note that a single "a" is used when transcribing Hindi into English to represent the vowel sound you hear in "sun" and "fun." The long "a," as in "father," is represented with "aa." In this guide, we've used "ay" to represent the hard "a" sound as in "pay." Hindi also has a lot of aspirated consonants, which are represented by adding an "h" to the end of a consonant. So "th" in transliterated Hindi should not be pronounced like "the" but rather like "t-ha." You'll almost need to exhale the "h" sound. Double consonants make the sound harder, so the consonant sound in "chhay" (the word for "six") is pronounced with much more stress on the "ch" than the softer word "chaar" (the word for "four").

Many English words have also made their way into Hindi. In some cases, the English word is used because there is no Hindi equivalent. Other times, a Hindi word exists but is rarely used and may sound archaic at best, incoherent at worst. In such cases, we have provided the English word, although bear in mind that to be understood, it's a good idea to Indianize your pronunciation of English words when using them in Hindi sentences.

NUMBERS

1 ek
2 do
3 teen
4 chaar
5 paanch
6 chhay
7 saath
8 aath
9 nau
10 das
50 pachaas
100 so
500 paanch so
1,000 ek hazaar
5,000 paanch hazaar
10,000 das hazaar
100,000 ek laakh
500,000 paanch laakh
1,000,000 das laakh
10,000,000 ek crore

DAYS OF THE WEEK

Sunday Ravivaar
Monday Soamvaar
Tuesday Mangalvaar
Wednesday Brihaspativaar
Thursday Budhhvaar
Friday Shukravaar
Saturday Shanivaar

TIME

today aaj
yesterday kal
tomorrow kal
the day before yesterday parso
the day after tomorrow parso
this week is haftay
last week pichhlay haftay
next week aglay haftay
this morning aaj subah
this afternoon aaj dopaher
this evening aaj shaam
tonight aaj raat
last night kal raat
one month ek mahina
six months chhay mahinay
late der (the word late is understood most of the time)
early jaldi
soon jaldi
later on baad main
now abhi
second second
minute minute
one minute ek minute
five minutes paanch minute
quarter of an hour pawnaa ghanta
half an hour aadha ghanta
that day uss din
every day har rose (people often shorten it to rose)
all day pooray din

USEFUL PHRASES

hello namaste
How are you? aap kaisay hain?
fine theek
and you? aur aap?
so-so theek thaak
thank you dhanyavaad
thank you very much bahut mehr baanee (dhanyavaad is sufficient)
You're welcome welcome; koi baat nahin (no problem)
It's nothing maamoolee baat hai
yes (correct) haan (haanjee is more formal)
no (incorrect) nahin
is hai

isn't *nahin hai*
I don't know *mujhe pata nahin*
please *kripiya*
nice to meet you *aap se milkay khushee houee*
I'm sorry *mujhe maaf keejeeyay*
goodbye/see you later *namaste/fir milaingay*
more *zyaada*
less *kam*
a little *thorda sa*
a lot *bahut zyaada*
hot (weather) *garmi*
hot (temperature) *garam*
cold (weather) *sardi; thankd*
cold (temperature) *thanda*
big *bara*
small *chhota*
better (than that) *uss say achha*
better (than this) *iss say achha*
best *sab say achha*
bad *bura*
quick, fast *tez*
slow *dheema*
easy *aasaan*
difficult *mushkil*
I don't speak Hindi well *main Hindi achhi nahin bolta* (if you are male); *main Hindi achhi nahin bolti* (if you are female)
I don't understand *Mujhhe samajhh nahin aa raha*

TERMS OF ADDRESS

you (formal) *aap*
you (familiar) *tum*
he/him *voh*
she/her *voh*
my *mera*
his/hers *uusska*
we/us *hum*
you (plural, formal) *aap*
you (plural, familiar) *tum*
they/them *woh, uun*
Mr., sir *shreemaan*
Mrs., Ms., madam *shreemati*
wife *patni*
husband *pati*
friend *dost*
son *beta*

daughter *beti*
brother *bhai*
sister *behen*
father *pita-ji; papa* (informal)
mother *maa*
grandfather (paternal) *dada*
grandfather (maternal) *nana*
grandmother (paternal) *dadi*
grandmother (maternal) *nani*
aunt *masi*
uncle (paternal, older than father) *taya; tau*
uncle (paternal, younger than father) *chacha*
uncle (maternal) *mama*

GETTING AROUND

Where is . . . ? *. . . kahaan hai?*
How far is it to . . . ? *. . . kitni door hai?*
How far is it from X to Y? *X say Y kitni door hai?*
highway *highway*
road *sardak*
north *uttar*
south *dakshin*
east *poorab*
west *pashchim*
straight ahead *seedha*
right *right* (*die* is the official word, but it's rarely used)
left *left* (*bye* is the official word, but it's rarely used)
next right/left *agla right/left*
driver *driver*
map *naksha*
toll *toll*
parking *parking*

SHOPPING

I want . . . *mujhhe...chahiye*
How much? *kitna?*
May I see? *kya main dekh sakta hoon?* (male speaker); *kya main dekh sakti hoon?* (female speaker)
this one *yeh wallah*
that one *voh wallah*
expensive *mehenga*
cheap *sasta*
Can you go cheaper? *aur sasta ho sakta hai?*

HOUSING
rent *kiraya*
apartment *kholi*
house/home *ghar*
kitchen *kitchen*
toilet *toilet*
shower *snaan* (verb), *snaan ghar* (noun)
heat *garam* (noun), *garmi* (verb)
water heater *geyser* (GEE-zer)
fan *pankha*
deposit *deposit*
landlord *landlord*
insurance *insurance*
key *chaabi*
lock *taala*

FOOD
menu *menu card*
glass *glass* (often pronounced "gilass")
fork *kaanta*
knife *chhoori*
napkin *tissue paper*
soft drink *soft drink*
coffee *coffee*
tea *chai*
sugar *cheeni*
drinking water *peeney ka paani*
bottled carbonated water *soda*
bottled uncarbonated water *mineral water*
beer *beer*
wine *wine* (*wine* is also used to refer to alcohol in general)
milk *doodh*
juice *rass*
spicey *teekha*
not spicey *teekha nahin*
eggs *anday*
apple *sayb*
orange *santra*
banana *kayla*
mango *aam*
beef *beef* (as the cow is sacred to Hindus, be careful when asking for this in certain places)

chicken *murga* (chicken is understood most of the time)
fish *machlee*
mutton *mutton*
rice *chawal*
vegetarian *shakahari*
vegetables *sabzee*
fried *tadka maar key*
breakfast *naashta*
lunch *lunch*
dinner *dinner*
the check *bill*

HEALTH
I am sick *may beemar hoon*
doctor *doctor*
hospital *hospital* (aspattaal)
pain *durrd*
fever *bukhaar*
stomach ache *payt durrd*
vomiting *ultee karna*
drugstore *chemist*
medicine *dawa*
pill, tablet *golee*
condom *condom*

AT THE BORDER
visa *visa*
residence permit *residence permit*
embassy *doothaawaas; embassy*
customs agent *custom officer*

EMERGENCIES AND SAFETY
police *police*
ambulance *ambulance*
firefighter *fire brigade*
thief *chore*
Help! *bachaao!* (literally, "Save me")
I'm lost *meh kho gaya hoon* (masculine); *meh kho gayee hoon* (feminine)
Fire! *aag!*
Can you help me, please? *Meree madad keejeeyay?*

Suggested Reading

FICTION

Bhagat, Chetan. *One Night at the Call Centre.* New York: Ballantine Books, 2007. A realistic portrayal of the lives of a few young call center employees in Gurgaon from India's most loved contemporary author.

Roy, Arundhati. *The God of Small Things.* New York: Random House, 2008. Booker Prize–winning tale of growing up in 1960s rural Kerala.

Sawhney, Hirsh (ed.). *Delhi Noir.* New York: Akashic Books, 2009. A collection of short stories set in different Delhi neighborhoods, all written in the film noir style.

Sutcliffe, William. *Are You Experienced?* New York: Penguin, 1999. A hilarious account of a young man traveling around on India's backpacker circuit.

Theroux, Paul. *The Elephanta Suite: Three Novellas.* New York: Houghton Mifflin Harcourt, 2007. Three insightful novellas, each written from the perspective of different American visitors in India.

NONFICTION

Darlymple, William. *Nine Lives: In Search of the Sacred in Modern India.* New York: Knopf, 2009. An exploration of India's spiritual side in modern times through a series of essays.

Keay, John. *India: A History.* New York: Grove Press, 2001. A comprehensive guide to India's history from ancient times to the present.

Kolonad, Gitanjali. *Culture Shock! India: A Survival Guide to Customs and Etiquette.* Tarrytown, NY: Marshall Cavendish, 2008. A comprehensive guide to intercultural communications with Indians.

Sen, Amartya. *The Argumentative Indian: Writings on Indian History, Culture and Identity.* New York: Picador, 2006. A collection of essays on contemporary Indian society from Nobel Prize–winning Indian economist Amartya Sen.

Tharoor, Shashi. *The Elephant, the Tiger, and the Cell Phone: Reflections on India—the Emerging 21st-Century Power.* New York: Arcade Publishing, 2008. Essays on change and diversity in India and what this means for the country's future.

Tully, Mark. *No Full Stops in India.* New York: Penguin, 1991. Observations on India from the BBC's former New Delhi bureau chief.

MEMOIR

Macdonald, Sarah. *Holy Cow: An Adventure.* New York: Broadway Books, 2004. An Australian expat's true-ish story about a year living in Delhi.

O'Reilly, James, and Lary Habegger (eds.). *Travelers' Tales India.* Palo Alto, CA: Travelers' Tales, 2004. A selection of short stories based in India from well-known travel writers.

Rich, Katherine Russell. *Dreaming in Hindi.* New York: Houghton Mifflin Harcourt, 2009. A New York editor moves to Udaipur, Rajasthan, for a year to learn Hindi, and provides insight not only into life in India but also into how language acquisition works.

RESOURCES

Suggested Films

- *Corporate.* Directed by Madhur Bhandarkar. Percept Picture Company, 2006. A tale of corporate rivalry set against an Indian backdrop.

- *Gandhi.* Directed by Richard Attenborough. Columbia Pictures, 1982. Academy Award–winning account of the life of Mahatma Gandhi and the Indian independence movement.

- *Lagaan.* Directed by Ashutosh Gowariker. Aamir Khan Productions, 2001. The story of a cricket game between a group of Indian villagers and a group of senior Raj officials that will determine the village's financial fate.

- *Dil Se.* Directed by Mani Ratnam. Madras Talkies, 1998. An award-winning romance that deals with terrorism, conflict, and true love. The film's sound track also helped composer A. R. Rahman rise to international fame.

- *Dilwale Dulhania Le Jayenge.* Directed by Aditya Chopra. Yash Raj Films, 1995. Known in India by the acronym DDLJ, this lighthearted comedy follows the budding romance between two young British Indians backpacking across continental Europe.

- *Monsoon Wedding.* Directed by Mira Nair. Mirabai Films, 2001. A romantic comedy set in the days leading up to an enormous Punjabi wedding.

- *My Friend Ganesha.* Directed by Rajiv S. Ruia. Kofee Break Pictures, 2007. A lighthearted children's film about a young boy who is regularly visited by a jolly animated Ganesha, the elephant-headed son of Shiva and the remover of obstacles.

- *Page 3.* Directed by Madhur Bhandarkar. Lighthouse Entertainment, 2005. A contemporary portrayal of high society journalism in Mumbai.

- *Salaam Bombay!* Directed by Mira Nair. Cinecom Pictures, 1988. A raw account of the lives of street children in 1980s Mumbai.

- *Sholay.* Directed by Ramesh Sippy. Sippy Films, 1975. The highest-grossing Indian film of all time, *Sholay* chronicles the antics of a pair of village criminals who are hired to kidnap a cold-blooded bandit.

- *Sita Sings the Blues.* Directed by Nina Paley, 2008. A beautiful animated take on the classic tale of the *Ramayana,* told from Sita's perspective. Available for free download.

Index

A

acronyms, common: 173, 212
Adyar: 278
agents: house rental 106; travel 194
agriculture: 37
Ahmedabad: 75, 261-265
air conditioning: 107-108
air pollution: 140
airports: 184, 185
air travel: 185-186
Akbar the Great: 26
Akshardham Temple: 76
Alipore: 269
All India Muslim League (AIML): 31
Amber Fort: 75
American Depository Receipts (ADRs): 170
American Institute for Indian Studies: 122
American Women's Club (AWC): 236
Amethyst Café: 76
Andheri West: 235
animals: 15-16
Anjuna: 282
Anjuna markets: 77
apartment complexes: 104
appliances: 108
Arambol: 282
arts, the: 57-60
Ashoka the Great: 24
ATMs: 165
Aundh: 291
Aurangzeb: 28
Auroville: 279
authors: 60
automobile travel: 190-194
autorickshaws: 74, 196-197, 225
Ayurveda: 135

B

Bachchan, Amitabh: 238
Bacillus Calmette-Guérin (BCG): 140
badminton: 61
Ballygunge: 270
Bandra: 234
Bangladesh: 32
Banjara Hills: 287
bank accounts, Indian: 167-168
banking: 163-168
Barbur: 26
bargaining: 166
bathrooms: 109-110, 187
beds: 107
begging: 39

Bengali schools: 122
Bengal tigers: 16
Bengaluru: 243-256; culture 247, 252-253; dining 82-83; entertainment and shopping 254-255; fact-finding trip to 72-73; geography 245-246; health care 253; map 244; neighborhoods 248-252; overview 204-205; temporary accommodations 81-82; transportation 256
Benson Town: 251
Besant Nagar: 278
Bhaadra: 230
Bhartiya Janata Party (BJP): 33
Bhasha Bharati: 122
bicycle rickshaws: 197
bidets: 110
biking: 195
birds: 16
blind people, infrastructure for: 146
boarding schools: 128
body language: 44
Bollywood: 59, 238-239
Bombay Stock Exchange (BSE): 170, 227
Bombay Stock Exchange Sensitivity Index (SENSEX): 170
books: 67, 180
Brahmins: 42
Breach Candy: 233
British Business Group (BBG): 236
British Business Social Club (BBSC): 280
British colonialism: 28-29
British East India Company (BEIC): 28-29
British Raj: 29
BSNL: 172, 175
BTM Layout (Byrasandra, Tavarekere, and Madiwala Layout): 249
Buddhism: 56
Bull Temple: 73
Bureau of Immigration: 95
burping: 45
business: cards 155; contracts 156; culture 152-155; family 48; family leave 153-154; holiday closures 158; Indian companies 148-149; international companies 148; visas 90, 94; see also employment
Business Process Outsourcing (BPO): 38
bus travel: 189-190

C

cable TV: 181-182
Calcutta Stock Exchange (CSE): 170

carrom game: 61
car travel: 190–194
caste system: 42–43
cats: 100
cell phones: 173–175
Central Board of Direct Taxes (CBDT): 169
Central Delhi: 216–218
Central Mumbai: 233
Chanakyapuri: 217
changing money: 65, 164
charity: 39
checks: 168
Chennai: 76, 276–281
Chhatrapati Shivaji Terminus (CST): 232
children: acculturating 96–97; chores for 97–98; Indian food for 97, 98; moving with 96–99; packing for 64
Chola Dynasty: 25
Chowpatty Beach: 70
Christianity: 55
cities: animals in 16, 64; autorickshaw transport 196–197; buses 189; crowds and noise 11; infrastructure 14; Northern Indian 12; taxis 193
City Market (Bengaluru): 73
civil disobedience: 30, 31
civilization, early: 22–24
classical music: 57
class system, social: 42–43
cleaning supplies: 114–115, 162
climate: general discussion 14–15; Bengaluru 247; Delhi 210; Mumbai 230; Northern India 12, 259; Southern India 13, 275; and travel time 63
clinics: 132
clothing: 45–48, 101
Coastal Chennai: 278
coffee shops: 253
Colaba: 232
Cold War: 32
colleges: *see* higher education
colonial period: 28–29, 202
communication: general discussion 171–182; about food and family 152; in English 119–121; mixed language 121–122
commuter trains: 241
complaints, filing: 146
conservative dress: 45, 47, 63
cooking tools: 112
coolers, desert: 107–108
Corbett, Jim: 19
cordial *(sharbat):* 262
corruption: 17, 146
costs: general discussion 160–163; average 160; bargaining 166; city taxis 193; domestic help 111; maximum retail 162; researching 65; *see also specific place*

Council for the Indian School Certificate Examinations (CISCE): 129
courier services, private: 179
credit cards: 167
cricket: 60
crime: 144–146
Cross-Cultural Solutions: 158
C-Scheme: 266
Cuffe Parade: 232
culture: general discussion 41–61; Bengaluru 247; business 152–155; contrasts in 10; Delhi 211; dress 45–48; ethnic groups 42; learning local 41–42; Northern India 259; Southern India 276; women's roles 50–51; *see also* religion; society
currency: 65, 159, 163
customs: immigration and 66; social 43–48

D

dance: 58
deaf, infrastructure for the: 146
debit cards: 167
Deccan Plateau: 12
DEET insect repellant: 138
Defense Colony: 214
dehydration: 142
Delhi: 209–226; accommodations 79; culture 212–213; dining 79; entertainment 222; expat social scene 220; fact-finding trip to 68–70; geography 13; map 208; neighborhoods 213–219; overview 202–203; shopping 222–224; transportation 224–225
"Delhi belly": 78, 101, 131
Delhi Metro: 67–68, 70, 225
Delhi Network: 69
Delhi Noida Direct (DND) Flyway: 210
Delhi University (DU): 124
dengue fever: 137
dentists: 134
dermatology: 133
diarrhea: 78
Dilli Haat: 70
dining: *see* food
disabilities, travelers with: 146
disease: 131, 137–139
divided houses: 104
Diwali: 46
dogs: 100
domestic airlines: 185, 186
domestic help: *see* household help
dowries: 50–51
DPT vaccine: 139
Dravidians: 42

dress: at work 154; cultural norms 45-48; for teenagers 99; packing clothes 101
drinking: cordial *(sharbat)* 262; costs 162; teenage 98
driver's licenses: 192
driving: hired drivers 110, 192; safety 143; yourself 191-192
Durga Puja: 74
Dutch traders: 28
dysentery: 138

E

East Bengaluru: 251-252
East India Company: 28-29
East West Language Institute (EWLI): 122
economy: 21-22, 37-40
education: general discussion 123-130; Ahmedabad 264; Bengaluru 254; Chennai 280; Delhi 221; Goa 285; Hyderabad 288; in English 118; Jaipur 267; Kolkata 271; Mumbai 237; Pune 292
elections: 33
electrical outages: 64
electricity: 108-109, 116
elementary schools: 126-130
Elephanta Island: 72
Elliot's Beach: 76
employment: 147-158; health insurance 135; job hunting 148-149; office etiquette 152-155; salaries 147-148, 156, 159; self- 151-152; visas 91, 158
endangered species: 16
English language: as lingua franca 118; Indian English 120-121; knowing only 119; media 171
entertainment costs: 162
environmental issues: 16
Escape Delhi: 150
ethnic groups: 42
etiquette, social: 43-48
European colonialism: 28
executive branch: 36
expat society: Ahmedabad 263; Bengaluru 252; Chennai 280; Delhi 220; Hyderabad/Secybderabad 288; Jaipur 267; Kolkata 271; Mumbai 236; Pune 291; statistics 18-19
expenses, monthly: 160-163

F

fact-finding trip: 62-85; accommodations 78; benefits 62; immigration 63, 66; packing tips 63-64, 66-67; pre-departure research 65; sample itineraries 68-78; seasonal considerations 63

family leave: 153
family life: 48-49
fashion: 45-48
female infanticide: 50-51
festivals: 158, 230
filmi music: 238
film industry, Hindi: 59, 238-239
filtration, water: 114
finance: 159-170
financial crisis, 2008: 37
First Information Report (FIR): 146
flashlights: 64
food: -borne illness 141; cooking supplies 112; costs 161; Delhi street 221; dining etiquette 44; for children 97; home versus restaurant 160; in the office 153; packing 101; safety 78; Southern India cuisine 277; *see also specific place*
footwear: 63, 101
Foreigners Regional Registration Office (FRRO): 90, 93-96
foreign-language skills: 148
Frazer Town: 250-251
French traders: 28
furniture: 102, 107

G

Gachibowli: 77, 287
games: 60-61
Gandhi, Indira: 32
Gandhi, Mohandas Karamchand (Mahatma): 30
Gandhinagar: 76, 263
Gandhi, Rajiv: 34
Gandhi, Sonia: 19
Ganesha Chaturthi: 230
Ganges River: 260
garbage service: 116-117
gas ranges: 113
Gateway of India: 70
gay people: 51-52
Gay Pride Day: 51-52
gender roles: 49-52
generators: 109
generosity: 44
geography: 12-14; *see also specific place*
geysers: 111-112
giardia: 138
Goa: 28, 77, 282-285
gods/goddesses: 53-54
Golden Temple: 33
Golf Links: 218
government: 13-14, 35-37
Government of India Act (1935): 30
Greater Kailash Part I (GK 1): 214
Green Park: 215

greetings: 51
grooming supplies: 64, 67, 101, 162
guards: 111
guesthouses: 78
guests, honoring: 43-44
Gupta Empire: 24-25
Gurgaon: 69, 218-219

H

Harappan civilization: 22
Hash Harriers: 280
Hauz Khas: 215
Hawa Mahal (Palace of Winds): 74
health: 131-146
healthcare system: 132-134; see also
    specific place
heatstroke: 142
helicopter travel: 186
hepatitis vaccinations: 139
hierarchy, office: 155
higher education: general discussion
    124-125; competition in 123, 124; in IT
    sector 34
hijras (third gender): 53
Himalaya Mountains: 12
Hindi Guru: 122
Hinduism: general discussion 53-54;
    female deities 50; Vedic period 23
history: 22-34
HITEC City: 77
HIV/AIDS: 138
holidays: 158
homosexuality: 51-52
Hope, Victor: 31
hospitality: 11, 18, 43-44
hospitals: 132; insurance 135
hotels: 78
hot water heaters: 111-112
household help: general discussion
    110-111; cost of 163; effects on children
    97; time off 158
housing: 103-117; bathrooms 109-112;
    cleaning supplies 114-115; common
    terms 105; costs 161-162; furnished
    versus unfurnished 104-105; furnish-
    ing 107-114; Internet research on 105;
    kitchens 112-114; rental agents for 106;
    secured before the move 103; tips for
    choosing 104-106; utilities 115-117
Huna people: 25
hunting: 16
Hussain Sagar: 76
Hyderabad: 76, 286-289
Hyderabad Information Technology Engi-
    neering Consultancy (HITEC): 286

I

ICICI: 135
identification cards: 169
illiteracy: 146
illness: 137-139
immigration: 18, 66; see also visas
immunizations: 63, 136, 139-140
income tax: 156, 168
independence movement: 29-31
India Gate: 68
India National Congress Party: 30, 33
Indian Institutes of Management (IIM): 124
Indian Institutes of Technology (IIT): 32,
    124, 261
Indian Ministry of Health: 91
Indian National Army: 31
Indian Railway Catering and Tourism
    Corporation (IRCTC): 188
Indian Railways offices: 145
Indian School Certificate (ISC): 129
Indian School of Business (ISB): 124
India Post: 171, 178
Indira Nagar: 251-252
Indo-Aryans: 42
Indus Valley Civilization: 22
Infosys: 248
infrastructure: communication 171; for
    travelers with disabilities 146; lack of
    sufficient 11, 14
insect repellent: 64, 138
Institute of Asian Studies: 122
insurance, medical: 134-135
International Baccalaureate (IB): 128
International Driving Permit (IDP): 192
International General Certificate of
    Secondary Education (IGCSE): 129
international schools: 127-129
international standard dialing (ISD): 173
Internet access: 176-178
Internet cafés: 177
investments: 170
IRS: 169
Islam: 54
Islamic Sultanates: 25-26
IT industry: 37, 206, 243, 248

J

Jahangir: 27
Jainism: 24, 56
Jaipur: 74, 266-268
Jangpura: 217
Jawaharlal Nehru University (JNU): 124
jeans: 45, 48
job hunting: 148-149
Jor Bagh: 218
journalist visas: 91

JP Nagar: 249
Jubilee Hills: 286
judicial branch: 36
Juhu: 235

K

Kalighat Kali Temple: 74
Kalyani Nagar: 78, 290
Kargil War: 34
Kashmir: 17, 32
Kathak: 58
Khan, Shahrukh: 239
Kharavela, King: 24
Khatakali: 58
Kipling, Rudyard: 19
kitchens: 112-114
kite-flying: 61
Kodaikanal International School: 128
Kolkata: 74, 268-272
Koramangala: 250
Koregaon Park: 78, 290
Kshatriyas: 43

L

labor laws: 156-158
Lajpat Nagar: 214
Lal Bagh Botanical Gardens: 72
landlines (telephones): 175
Landour Language School: 122
landscape: 12-13
language: general discussion 118-123;
    Bengaluru 247; body 44; Delhi 211;
    ethnic groupings 42; Hindi 118, 122;
    Hyderabad 288; Kolkata 271; Mumbai
    230; Northern India 259, 263; place
    name reclamation 202; Southern India
    276; see also English language
leases: 106
Legal Monetary Bond: 157
legislative branch: 35-36
lesbians: 51-52
libraries: 67
literature: 60
living costs: see costs
living locations, prime: Bengaluru 243-
    256; choosing 206; Delhi 209-226;
    map 200; Mumbai 227-242; Northern
    India 257-272; overview 201-207; re-
    searching 65; Southern India 273-292
Lok Sabha: 35
long-distance bus travel: 189
long-distance taxis: 194
Lower Parel: 234

M

Madras: 276
magazines: 180
Mahabalipuram: 76
Mahabharata: 60, 72
Mahajanapadas: 23
Mahal, Mumtaz: 27
Mahalaxmi: 234
mail services: 178-180
Malabar Hill: 232
malaria: 137
Mamluk dynasty: 25
Matrimandir: 279
Maurya, Chandragupta: 24
Maurya Empire: 23-24
meals: 44
media: 171, 180-182
medicine: allopathic 136; Ayurvedic 135;
    for mosquito-borne illness 137; health-
    care system 132-134; medical tourism
    92, 133; study of 91
menswear: 48
microchips (pets): 99
middle class: 40
Middle Kingdoms: 24-25
minimum wage: 156-158
Ministry of Home Affairs (MHA): 91
missionary visas: 92
Missions of Charity: 74
MMR vaccine: 139
money: exchange 65, 164;
    management 159
monsoon: 15
monthly expenses: 160-163
mosquito-borne illness: 137
motorcycles: 194
Mughal Empire: 26-28
Mumbai: 227-242; accommodations
    80-81; culture 230-231; dining 81;
    education 237-238; entertainment
    239-240; expat social scene 236;
    fact-finding trip 70-72; geography 229;
    map 228; neighborhoods 231-236;
    overview 203-204; shopping 240;
    transportation 241-242
music: 57-58
Muslim history: 25-26, 31
Mylapore: 278

N

nannies (ayahs): 110
National Capital Region (NCR): 202-203,
    209-210
National Institute of Design (NID): 76, 261
national pride: 18

National Rural Employment Guarantee Act: 40
National Stock Exchange (NSE): 170, 227
Naxalites: 17
Nehru, Jawaharlal: 32
Nepalese population: 42
networking: 149
New Friends Colony: 215
newspapers: 180
Noida: 69, 219
Non-Resident Indians (NRIs): 18
Non-Resident Ordinary Rupee (NRO) account: 167
"no-objection certificate": 91
North Bengaluru: 250-251
Northern India: 257-272; accommodations 83; Ahmedabad 261-265; climate 12, 15; dining 83; diversity 257; fact-finding trip 74-76; geography and culture 259-261; Jaipur 266-268; Kolkata 268-272; map 258; overview 205-206
North Goa: 282
North Mumbai: 234-235
Nungambakkam: 279

OP

Oddisi: 58
office etiquette: 153
Operation Blue Star: 33
Osho's ashram: 78
Overseas Citizenship of India (OCI): 18, 89, 92
Overseas Corporate Bodies (OCBs): 170
overseas phones: 175
packing tips: fact-finding trip 66-67; moving 101-102
painting: 58
paise: 163
Pakistan partition: 31
Palolem: 283
Panchayati Raj: 36
parcel packing: 179
Parsis: 56-57
Patnem: 283
patriarchal society: 49-52
pay phones: 173
permits: extending 96; re-entry 90; residential 93-96; start-up companies 151-152
Personal Account Number (PAN): 152, 169
Person of Indian Origin (PIO) cards: 18, 89, 92
pet food: 100
pets, moving with: 99-101
pharmacies: 136
phone services: 172-176

pilots, foreign: 186
place names: 202
plane travel: 185-186
plants: 15
poaching: 16
police: 17, 146
polio: 140
politics: government 35-37; political parties 17, 33
pollution: 140
polymorphous light eruption (PMLE): 142
population: ethnic groups 42; expat 18-19; urban 11, 14
Portuguese traders: 28, 282
postal services: 178-180
postgraduate research: 125
pottery: 58-59
poverty: 38-40
Powai: 236
power outages: 108-109
preschools: 130
prescriptions: 63, 64, 136
prices: see costs
prickly heat rash: 142
private schools: 129-130
prohibited items: 67
Project Tiger: 16
promiscuity: 20
property, buying: 103-104
Provident Fund (PF): 156
providers, cell phone: 173
public call offices (PCOs): 173
publishers: 180
Puduchery: 13
punctuality: 153
Pune: 78, 290-292
Punjabi suits (salwar kameez): 47

QR

quarantines (pets): 99
Quit India Movement: 31
radio: 182
Rahman, A. R.: 238
Rajasthan University: 266
Rajya Sabha: 35
Ramakrishna Mission Institute of Culture: 122
Ramayana: 60
Rao, Narasimha: 34
real estate purchases: 103-104
recreation: costs 162; researching 65; see also specific place
recycling: 116-117
Red Fort: 27-28
red tape: 11, 172
regional disputes: 32

Regional Transport Office (RTO): 192
Registrar of Companies (ROC): 151
Registration Report & Residential
    Permit: 94
religion: general discussion 53–57;
    Ganges River in 260; Hinduism 23, 50,
    53–54; Vedic era 23
rental agreements, housing: 106
reports, crime: 146
research visas: 92
Reservation Against Confirmation
    (RAC): 189
restrooms: 142
résumés: 149
retirement funds: 156
rich/poor divide: 38–40
Royal Indian Navy: 31
rupees: 163
rural living: 14

S

Safdarjung Enclave: 215
safety: 143–144
salaries: 147–148, 156, 159
salary accounts: 167
Salt Lake City: 74, 270
sanitation: 142–143
saris: 47
Satavahanas: 24
Satellite: 262
satellite TV: 182
scams: 144, 145
schools: competition for 126; elementary
    and secondary 126–130; Indian lan-
    guage 122–123; international 127–129;
    preschools 130; researching 65, 71;
    school year 126; secondary certificates
    129: see also higher education
scripture, Hindu: 23
sculpture: 58–59
seasonal weather: 14–15
secondary schools: 126–130
Secunderabad: 77, 286–289
security: 111
self-employment: 151–152
service apartments: 104
service industry: 37
sexual harassment: 143
Shah Jahan: 27–28
shipment options: 102, 179
shopping: Ahmedabad 264; Bengaluru
    255; Chennai 281; Delhi 222–224; Goa
    284; Hyderabad 288; Jaipur 267; Kol-
    kata 272; Mumbai 240
short-term housing: 104
Shudras: 43

sick leave: 157
Sikhism: 55
Sikh separatists: 33
Singh, Manmohan: 34
Skype: 176
Slumdog Millionaire: 238
society: general discussion 17–20;
    Ahmedabad 263–264; ancient 22–24;
    Bengaluru 252; business etiquette
    152–155; caste system 42–43; Chen-
    nai 280; customs 43–45; Delhi 220;
    family life 48–49; gender roles 49–52;
    Hyderabad/Secybderabad 288; Jaipur
    267; Kolkata 271; male-female interac-
    tion 51; middle class 11; Mumbai 236;
    pluralism 10; Pune 291
sons, preferential treatment of: 49, 50
South Bengaluru: 248–250
South Delhi: 213
Southern India: 273–292; accommoda-
    tions 84; Chennai 276–281; climate
    275; cuisine 277; culture 276; dining
    84–85; fact-finding trip 76–78; geog-
    raphy 13, 275; Goa 282–285; map 274;
    overview 207; Pune 290–292
South Goa: 283
South Mumbai: 232
specialists, medical: 133
spitting: 143
sports: 60–61
spouses, working: 93
Sri Aurobindo Society: 279
staring: 20
states: 13, 36
STD (standard trunk dialing): 173
Steele, Nathan: 150
stock exchanges: 170
street food: 221
strikes (bandhs): 17
student visas: 91
studies abroad: 124
Sudder Street: 74
Sunder Nagar: 218
Sunset Drive-In Cinema: 75
sunstroke: 142
Symbiosis (school): 124

T

Tagore, Rabindranath: 60
tailoring: 101
Taj Mahal: 27–28
talk time, cell phone: 174
Tamil Bharatnatyam: 58
Tamil language: 119, 123
Tax Deducted at Source (TDS): 156, 168

taxes: Indian income 156, 168; U.S. liability 169
taxis: 192-194, 225
technical skills: 148
telephone services: 172-176
television: 181
temperatures: 14-15, 63
Teresa, Mother: 19
terms: Bengaluru 243; familial address 49; household 105; Indian English 120; place names 202; street food 221
terrorism: 17-18
Thar Desert: 12
theater: 58
theft: 144
Thiruvanmiyur: 278
Tibetan population: 42
tickets, train: 188-189
tigers, Bengal: 16
Tilak, Bal Gangadhar: 29
Timur: 26
toilet paper: 110
toiletries: 64, 67, 101, 162
toilets: 109, 187
tolerance, religious: 10-11
tourism, medical: 133
tourism, volunteer: 158
tourist visas: 89-90
traffic: 131, 143, 191
trains: classes 187; commuter 241; tickets 145
train travel: 186-189
transportation: 183-197; air 185-186; bicycle 195; bus 189-190; car 190-194; motorcycle 194; train 145, 186-189, 241; map 184; pets 99-100; researching 65; taxis 67-68; see also specific place
traveler's checks: 164
Travisa Outsourcing: 63, 89
tuberculosis (TB): 140
Twin-cities Expatriate's Association: 77
typhoid: 138, 140

U
unemployment rates: 148
uninterruptible power supply (UPS): 109
union territories: 13, 36
universities: see higher education
University of Cambridge International Examinations (CIE): 128
untouchables (Dalits): 43

Upanishads: 23
urban life: see cities
U.S. Centers for Disease Control and Prevention (CDC): 132
utilities: 115-117, 161
UTI Technology Services Limited (UTITSL): 169

V
vacations: 157
vaccinations: 136, 139-140
Vaishyas: 43
Vajpayee, Atal Bihari: 34
validity, cell phone: 174
Vasant Vihar: 216
VAT: 175
Vedic period: 23
VFS: 63, 89
Viman Nagar: 291
violent crime: 17-18, 144
visas: 89-96; applications 89; changing 93; fact-finding trip 63; family members 92; types 89-92; working spouses 93
Voice over Internet Protocol (VoIP): 176
volunteering: 158
Volunteers for Peace (VFP): 158
Volvo buses: 190
voter turnout: 33

WXYZ
Waitlist (WL) tickets: 189
water: bottled 79; clean 113-114; heating 111-112; household supply 115-116; illness from 138, 141
wealth distribution: 38-40, 42-43
weather: 14-15, 63
weddings: 46, 50-51
Whitefield: 252
Wi-Fi: 176, 177
wildlife: 15-16
Wildlife Protection Act (1972): 16
Wipro: 248
wire transfers, international: 165
women: dress 45-48; safety 143; social roles 50-51
Woodstock School: 128
World War II: 31
World Wildlife Fund: 16
Worli: 233
Zoroastrianism: 56-57

Acknowledgments

So many people went into making this book a reality. Special thanks to Abhimanyu Singh Sisodia for his painstaking work on the Resources section; Mariya Zheleva and Rui Martin for their extensive photo contributions and for helping make my first year in India one of the most amazing times of my life; my friends at Designsecure in Delhi for their generous graphics and photo support; and Jasmeet Sondhi for letting me turn his house into a makeshift writer's nook.

I'm very grateful to Mohammed Shafi and everyone at Destination India Travel Centre for their wealth of information and excellent travel support; Michael Brannigan of Brannigan Relocations for sharing his vast knowledge about moving to Mumbai; David Levin and Ethan Kay for their hospitality and for giving me a first-hand experience of expat life in Mumbai; Sara Baptiste Brown for her insider's view on living in Bengaluru (and Jacek Ratajczak for introducing us); Susmita Thondapu for enthusiastically helping me understand what it's like to live in Bengaluru and Chennai; Cheb I Sabbah for his kind hospitality and wisdom in Goa; Katherine Yue for answering all of my Hyderabad questions and Adam Helsinger for his cheeky Hyderabad map; Apurva Seth for his insights on life in Pune; Reasa Selph and Laura Franczek for taking the time to tell me all about expat life in Ahmedabad; Harssh Shah for giving me the lowdown on Ahmedabad's cultural life; Laura Miller for her advice on living in Kolkata; Eric Saranovitz and Inbar Kerper-Saranovitz for their invaluable insight about moving to India with children; and Avtar Singh for being an inspiring mentor and friend—and for always reminding me that in order to be a writer, you have to actually sit down and write!

I'd also like to extend my gratitude to the entire team at Avalon Travel: my editors Elizabeth Hansen and Leah Gordon, Grace Fujimoto, Lucie Ericksen, Brice Ticen, Krissa Lagos, my copyeditor Christopher Church, and everyone else whose hard work went into creating this book.

Finally, I'd like to thank my beloved parents, Matthew and Carla Starrett-Bigg, for instilling in me the confidence to live my life to the fullest (and for putting up with my wanderlust).

www.moon.com

DESTINATIONS | ACTIVITIES | BLOGS | MAPS | BOOKS

MOON.COM is ready to help plan your next trip! Filled with fresh trip ideas and strategies, author interviews, informative travel blogs, a detailed map library, and descriptions of all the Moon guidebooks, Moon.com is all you need to get out and explore the world—or even places in your own backyard. While at Moon.com, sign up for our monthly e-newsletter for updates on new releases, travel tips, and expert advice from our on-the-go Moon authors. As always, when you travel with Moon, expect an experience that is uncommon and truly unique.

MOON IS ON FACEBOOK—BECOME A FAN!
JOIN THE MOON PHOTO GROUP ON FLICKR

MAP SYMBOLS

▭▭▭ Expressway	○ City/Town	✗ Airfield	▱ Archaeological Site
⋯⋯ Primary Road	◉ State Capital	✈ Airport	♦ Church
═══ Secondary Road			⛽ Gas Station
▫ ▫ ▫ Unpaved Road	⊛ National Capital	▲ Mountain	⬚ Mangrove
⋯⋯⋯ Ferry	★ Point of Interest	♠♠ Park	⬚ Reef
▬▬▬ Railroad	▪ Other Location	⛷ Skiing Area	⬚ Swamp

CONVERSION TABLES

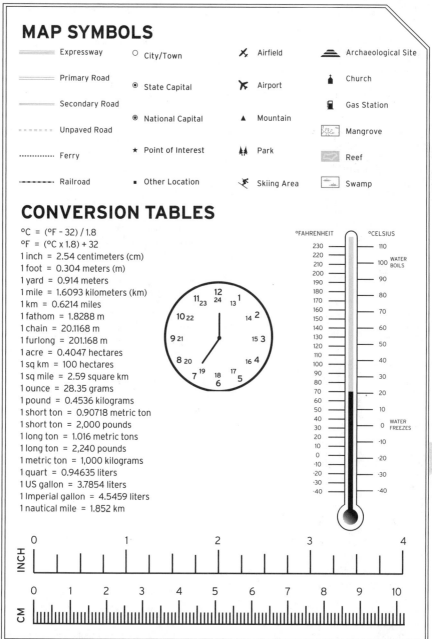

°C = (°F - 32) / 1.8
°F = (°C x 1.8) + 32
1 inch = 2.54 centimeters (cm)
1 foot = 0.304 meters (m)
1 yard = 0.914 meters
1 mile = 1.6093 kilometers (km)
1 km = 0.6214 miles
1 fathom = 1.8288 m
1 chain = 20.1168 m
1 furlong = 201.168 m
1 acre = 0.4047 hectares
1 sq km = 100 hectares
1 sq mile = 2.59 square km
1 ounce = 28.35 grams
1 pound = 0.4536 kilograms
1 short ton = 0.90718 metric ton
1 short ton = 2,000 pounds
1 long ton = 1.016 metric tons
1 long ton = 2,240 pounds
1 metric ton = 1,000 kilograms
1 quart = 0.94635 liters
1 US gallon = 3.7854 liters
1 Imperial gallon = 4.5459 liters
1 nautical mile = 1.852 km

°FAHRENHEIT °CELSIUS

WATER BOILS

WATER FREEZES

INCH 0 1 2 3 4

CM 0 1 2 3 4 5 6 7 8 9 10

**MOON LIVING ABROAD
IN INDIA**

Avalon Travel
a member of the Perseus Books Group
1700 Fourth Street
Berkeley, CA 94710, USA
www.moon.com

Editors: Elizabeth Hansen, Leah Gordon
Series Manager: Elizabeth Hansen
Copy Editor: Christopher Church
Graphics Coordinator: Lucie Ericksen
Production Coordinator: Lucie Ericksen
Cover Designer: Lucie Ericksen
Map Editor: Brice Ticen
Cartographers: Allison Rawley, Kat Bennett,
   Mike Morgenfeld
Indexer: Rachel Kuhn

ISBN-13: 978-1-59880-739-4
ISSN: 2159-5917

Printing History
1st Edition – April 2011
5 4 3 2 1

Text © 2011 by Margot Bigg.
Maps © 2011 by Avalon Travel.
All rights reserved.

KEEPING CURRENT

Although we strive to produce the most up-to-date guidebook that we possibly can, change
is unavoidable. Between the time this book goes to print and the time you read it, the
cost of goods and services may have increased, and a handful of the businesses noted
in these pages will undoubtedly move, alter their prices, or close their doors forever.
Exchange rates fluctuate – sometimes dramatically – on a daily basis. Federal and local
legal requirements and restrictions are also subject to change, so be sure to check with
the appropriate authorities before making the move. If you see anything in this book that
needs updating, clarification, or correction, please drop us a line. Send your comments via
email to feedback@moon.com, or use the address above.